THE
MEDITERRANEAN
FEUD

THE
MEDITERRANEAN
FEUD

Andrew Borowiec

PRAEGER SPECIAL STUDIES • PRAEGER SCIENTIFIC

Library of Congress Cataloging in Publication Data

Borowiec, Andrew.
   The Mediterranean feud.

   Bibliography: p.
   Includes index.
   1. Greece—Foreign relations—Turkey. 2. Turkey—
Foreign relations—Turkey. 3. Cyprus—History—Cyprus
Crisis, 1974–. 4. United States—Foreign
relations—Greece. 5. Greece—Foreign relations—
United States. 6. United States—Foreign relations—
Turkey. 7. Turkey—Foreign relations—United States.
I. Title.
DF787. T8B67 1983   327.4950561   82–16624
ISBN 0-03-061847-9

Published in 1983 by Praeger Publishers
CBS Educational and Professional Publishing
a Division of CBS Inc.
521 Fifth Avenue, New York, New York 10175, U.S.A.

© 1983 by Praeger Publishers

456789   052   98765432

Printed in the United States of America

For Juliet, as ever

CONTENTS

INTRODUCTION

In the sweltering heat of the Turkish capital of Ankara in June 1980, Joseph Luns, secretary-general of the North Atlantic Treaty Organization (NATO) addressed the spring ministerial session of the West's defensive alliance. The situation in Southwest Asia was foremost in the minds of the participants. Iran was in the throes of Islamic revolutionary turmoil. In Afghanistan, Soviet helicopter gunships were strafing mountain hideouts of the undaunted opponents of the Moscow-backed regime. Turkey itself was wracked by urban terrorism and political feuding bordering on civil war. The modernistic complex where the session took place was surrounded by helmeted troops. Roadblocks were thrown up between Esenboga airport and the heart of Ankara. On the outskirts of the capital, paramilitary units sealed off most of the grim shantytowns, traditional breeding grounds of political and sectarian extremism and violence.

The choice of Ankara for that regular spring meeting had been made long before. However, in the context of the events battering Southwest Asia, it took on a special significance. It underscored the importance NATO attached to Turkey, the southernmost guardian of its undermanned and exposed flank. It gave confidence to the country's military establishment, the best organized part of the nation and the most committed to NATO and the West.

As usual, Luns was blunt in his assessment of the situation. The Western world, he said, "must have a strategic perception that it is not confined narrowly to the region of the North Atlantic Treaty. Both Afghanistan and Iran, even though outside the geographical boundaries of NATO, are still nonetheless very much Alliance business."

The statement summarized the dilemma that had been facing NATO strategists for some time. In a way it could be considered the official birth of the theory that NATO's outer perimeter is just as important as the area covered by the treaty itself.

Barely two months later, the Turkish military seized power, suspending democratic freedoms but stopping the country's slide toward anarchy and improving its economic posture. In October of the same year, Turkey lifted some of its objections, and Greece was able to rejoin NATO's military structure after a six-year boycott caused by the Turkish military intervention in Cyprus.

Thus, at least outwardly, NATO appears to have been strengthened. Yet, the major differences between Turkey and Greece, the main defenders of the southeastern flank, remained unresolved. They centered on the ethnic feud of the divided island of Cyprus, where the Turkish army controlled the northern portion; on the conflicting claims in the Aegean sea, hugging the Turkish coastline but sprinkled with myriad Greek islands; on the fate of the Turkish minority in Thrace and the remnants of the Greek population in Turkey.

For years U.S. diplomacy grappled with the tangle of Greco–Turkish problems. On occasion there have been short-lived successes, usually averting a crisis or simply containing an escalation. Yet, with time, U.S. leverage possibilities appeared to be diminishing rather than growing.

In mid-1982 the situation was further clouded by the strongly nationalistic stance taken by Greece's socialist government under its premier, Andreas Papandreou. The process of the reintegration of the Greek armed forces into NATO was, once again, in jeopardy. Despite some progress on minor points in the intercommunal dialogue on Cyprus, there were no signs of a significant breakthrough. The Aegean remained an explosive area, with troop concentrations in its idyllic scenery. Ankara was accusing Athens of persecution of the Turks in Thrace, and Greece replied with similar accusations about its minority in Istanbul.

At the same time, NATO's outer perimeter had grown to include the Persian Gulf area, made even more vulnerable by the Iran–Iraq war. Although officially the Rapid Deployment Force (RDF) off the Persian Gulf was a U.S. operation, there was little doubt that NATO was involved—or certainly would be in the event of intervention in the Persian Gulf oilfields.

In this framework, Turkey with its infrastructure of U.S. bases was increasingly needed as a possible springboard or transit area for the Persian Gulf. Of considerable importance was nonaligned Cyprus, where the United Kingdom maintained two well-equipped and stocked sovereign base areas. No one underestimated the value of Greece, the historic link between southern Europe and the Middle

East, with its four major U.S. installations and a NATO early-warning system.

However, as long as the two main protagonists—Greece and Turkey—were unable to solve their disputes, the defenses of the southeastern flank could only be partially effective. NATO certainly would be hampered in the event of large-scale hostilities or a Persian Gulf contingency.

The purpose of this study is to analyze the extent of the crisis, its impact on Western defenses, and the dilemma of the United States which has found itself in the cross fire between Greece and Turkey. The study attempts to trace the roots of the conflict and explain the attitudes and problems of the countries involved. It points out the damage done to Western security and tries to suggest ways in which some points of friction could be eliminated, possibly paving the way toward more tangible political gestures.

The idea for the study was born in 1977, when the sectarian strife in Turkey gained intensity and the Turkish armed forces were being increasingly crippled by the punitive U.S. arms embargo. Offers of financial subsidies have been made by official and semiofficial representatives of the countries which are the subject of the study. For obvious reasons, they had to be declined. I applied for grants to a number of U.S. foundations. Several described the study as "extremely worthwhile" but were unable to provide funds. One felt that the Greco–Turkish problem had been solved by the lifting of the U.S. arms embargo against Turkey in 1978.

In the end, I decided to write the study without any financial help, using the extensive experience of some 15 years of reporting on the area, intimate knowledge of the countries involved, and personal acquaintance with some of the main actors on the East Mediterranean stage. The gathering of some of the material was traumatic, particularly "commuting" across the Cyprus barricades to hear the impassioned and often equally convincing views and claims of both sides. I have developed friendships in Turkey, Cyprus, and Greece; some of them are likely to be strained by the publication of this study. A typical illustration of the highly emotional feelings was a statement made to me by Turkish Cypriot leader Rauf Denktash: "If you're not with us, you're against us." With minor exceptions, it can be said that such an attitude prevails in the whole area.

The objective of this work is not so much to dwell on the mistakes of the past, the various vicissitudes and ephemeral triumphs. They are now part of history, obscured by a series of often meaningless treaties and agreements, buried under tons of paper yellow with age and forgotten in the torrent of more immediate events.

Obviously, history is an essential part of the Mediterranean feud, and a number of historical references had to be made to explain the issues to the reader, particularly in tracing the reasons for Greco-Turkish animosity as well as the Cypriot tangle. The political ups and downs of modern Greece had to be mentioned as well as those of Cyprus and Turkey. For this reason a number of historical studies were of help as well as official documents, monographs, and journals dealing with the most recent period. Much of the study, however, is based on my interviews and day-to-day analytical coverage of the East Mediterranean. The intention is to give a direct, immediate meaning to the tensions and complications of the present and the uncertainties of the future.

The author would like to thank all of those who, over the years, have given time and expertise to help him understand the problem. They include ambassadors and cabinet ministers, members of opposition groups, writers, journalists, and, above all, simple people. It is the average citizen in Greece, Cyprus, and Turkey who usually bears the brunt of political mistakes and passions, often fueled artificially. The people in Cypriot refugee camps, in the squalid Turkish shantytowns, and in Greek island villages perhaps best convey the meaning of the Mediterranean feud.

Note

1. Official text of a speech given by NATO Secretary-General Joseph Luns in Ankara, June 25, 1980.

THE
MEDITERRANEAN
FEUD

Chapter 1

THE EXPOSED FLANK

The greatest challenge that faces the alliance today is in the south.
General Bernard Rogers,
Supreme Allied Commander in Europe,
February 22, 1981

The late 1970s were marked by two dangerous developments for the West: the coming of age of the USSR as a major maritime power and the virtually simultaneous erosion of the strength of the North Atlantic Treaty Organization (NATO) in the Mediterranean. The two were not connected but appeared equally ominous. There was little the West could do about Soviet defense spending and naval expansion. What was perhaps even more alarming was the fact that the West was almost as helpless in the face of the Greco–Turkish feud, which continued to cripple the southeastern flank of the alliance into the 1980s.

The traditional antagonism of the two defenders of NATO's exposed flank was accentuated by the Turkish military intervention in Cyprus in 1974. It led to Greek withdrawal from the military structure of the alliance, which lasted six years. It caused a punitive U.S. arms embargo against Turkey, which further weakened the West's defensive posture, leaving deep psychological scars in Turkey long after its lifting in 1978. It was a period of fumbling by Western strategists, punctuated by mostly unheeded warnings of dangers threatening the southern defenses.

1

In 1981 the defense of the flank suffered even more with the withdrawal of some warships of the U.S. Sixth Fleet to the areas of the Indian Ocean adjacent to the explosive Persian Gulf. The gulf itself was on fire, with the Iran–Iraq war gaining in intensity in the spring of 1982. The fundamentalist Shiite revolution of Iran was knocking harder on the doors of virtually defenseless gulf countries, a repository of close to one-fourth of the world's known oil reserves.

Early in 1982 strategists already talked of the post-Khomeini era in Iran. The ailing 81-year-old ayatollah, who installed his revolution on the ruins of the shah's Peacock Empire, was increasingly leaving most political decisions to his potential successors. There were few clear indications in the West of the direction post-Khomeini Iran would follow. The country could easily be plunged into more conflict, pitting the young military establishment against the fanatics of the revolutionary guard and the bearded mullahs, armed with assault rifles and the Koran. While the West had no apparent strategy for Iran, the USSR intensified its infiltration in the form of massive arrivals of experts. Some 20 Soviet army divisions were poised along the Soviet border on both sides of the Caspian Sea.

The south of NATO's outer perimeter was largely the Arab world—volatile, wracked by internal feuds, and frustrated by U.S. support for Israel. In pro-Soviet Syria, President Hafez-al-Assad pursued a relentless campaign against Muslim Brotherhood terrorists. Lebanon was more or less a fictitious state at the mercy of its neighbors. Egypt continued its dialogue with Israel amid growing uncertainty.

U.S. strategy in the area appeared to depend on four pillars, all risky for different reasons: Pakistan in the east, Turkey as the point where Asia and Europe meet, Israel, and Egypt. The United States—and consequently NATO—had the use of a number of friendly ports and staging areas but lacked men and equipment to carry out far-flung operations and defend the vulnerable southern area of Europe.

The socialist victory in Greece in October 1981 once again raised the specter of possible Greek withdrawal from NATO's military wing. In the best of circumstances, it spelled involved negotiations, demands difficult to satisfy, and growing complications. The strong nationalistic line, with neutralist overtones, adopted by Greek Premier Andreas Papandreou enhanced the value of Turkey to the alliance. But Turkey was a controversial partner, with the ruling military National Security Council conducting a "purification campaign" amid considerable Western European criticism and clamor for a return to democratic rule. The Turkish armed forces were large, but their equipment was hopelessly outdated. This was the ally to whom NATO assigned the defense of the 370-mile border with the USSR and the vital straits between the Mediterranean Sea and the Black Sea. On the successful performance of this task (in the event of hostilities) depended much of Western strategy in the central and western Mediterranean, including the continuing flow of Middle Eastern oil to Western Europe.

Complicating Turkey's task was Ankara's preoccupation with Greece and the Aegean Sea. In the early 1980s, 47 percent of the Turkish army was deployed either in European Turkey facing Greece or in the Aegean. This included 60 percent of the nation's vintage tanks.

All this was obvious to U.S. and Western European policy makers. It was not the appreciation of the situation that was lacking but the means, leverage possibilities, and cohesion of the alliance. As far back as May 1978, in testimony before the Senate Committee on Foreign Relations, Warren Christopher, deputy secretary of state, said:

> The Eastern Mediterranean is the junction point of several critical areas—western Europe, the Soviet Union, the Balkans, and the Middle East. The strategic significance of this area is clear. A strong and effective NATO alliance posture throughout the southern flank is essential to protect our interests and those of our NATO partners. Unfortunately, over the last several years the effectiveness of this flank has been eroded in a manner that is of grave concern to this administration and to our allies.[1]

The Reagan administration inherited all the problems of the southern flank—and more. The outer perimeter appeared to have grown, with its built-in instability and threat. Yet, despite a barrage of warnings, there were few indications that Western public opinion understood the magnitude of the problem. There was little "Mediterranean consciousness" in Europe, even less in the United States.

Describing the situation of the southern flank to news correspondents in February 1981, a NATO spokesman in Naples said, "The southern region faces many uncertainties. In our Mediterranean neighbors we find political instability, social turmoil and the potential for rapid change in political orientation. This leads us to the conclusion that the most likely threat of a Soviet initiative short of general war is here, in the southern region."[2]

The area where Greek and Turkish passions clashed—the subject of this study—is part of a larger theater of operations, stretching from the straits of Gibraltar in the west to the wind-swept mountains of eastern Turkey. Already in the late 1960s the Mediterranean had stopped being the exclusive preserve of the West and the U.S. Sixth Fleet. Soviet warships have become an inseparable part of the Mediterranean scenery. According to U.S. Admiral William Crowe, commander-in-chief of allied forces in Southern Europe, "the Soviets, in the short space of two decades, have created a sophisticated and powerful 'blue water' fleet."[3] As the Soviet naval capability grew, that of the West appeared to diminish. This was particularly felt in the Mediterranean.

The Mediterranean is a comparatively small sea, covering only 969,000 square miles. The 17 nations along its coast represent 325 million people. On an average day, some 1,000 merchant vessels are in its waters, including 300 to 400 tankers carrying an estimated 20 to 25 million barrels of crude oil. It is a beautiful sea and its scenery is frequently breathtaking, particularly under the cloudless blue sky of the six-month-long summer. Poets have written of its charms. Tino Rossi and Benjamino Gigli brought audiences to tears singing about it. For years tourists have flocked to its shores.

The Mediterranean is also a highly polluted sea. Some scientists regard it as a death trap, with cholera, typhoid, dysentery, polio, and gastroenteritis lurking in its azure waters. Factories belch chemicals into it, and coastal cities spill millions of tons of waste, ultimately killing fish, plants, and marine life. Every year tankers leave an estimated three million tons of tar on its lovely beaches and coves.

In the 1970s and 1980s, U.S. strategic plans in the Mediterranean consisted mainly of creating a valid NATO shield, maintaining the Sixth Fleet as a credible deterrent against the Soviet naval presence and military threat, and securing the flow of oil from the Middle East to Western Europe and, to a lesser extent, the United States. Given the diversity of the 17 Mediterranean nations, the caldron of the Arab world, and the animosity between Greece and Turkey, it was not an easy strategy to carry out.

NATO planners regard the Mediterranean as being of the utmost importance to the USSR for a variety of compelling political and military reasons. The sea has been a traditional Russian expansion route since the eighteenth century, when Catherine the Great first became aware of the Levant. Conversely, the Mediterranean is the West's gateway to the Black Sea and to the powerful concentration of Soviet industrial and agricultural potential. The Soviet Black Sea coastline provides access to the Ukranian wheat-belt and the industrial complexes responsible for the production of 40 percent of Soviet steel, 34 percent of its coal, and 50 percent of its pig iron. The USSR sees the Mediterranean as the historic Western attack route, as demonstrated in the Crimean War in the nineteenth century. Finally, in Soviet eyes, since World War II the Mediterranean has been "one of the main staging areas of Western military power targeted against the Soviet Union."[4] Of capital importance to the USSR is the fact that the Bosporus and the Dardanelles straits are controlled by a NATO power, Turkey. It is a serious weakness in Soviet global strategy, and it can be assumed that in the event of major hostilities in the area, one of the first Soviet moves would be an effort to seize the straits. In simple terms, the straits could either bottleneck the Soviet Black Sea fleet or, if captured, open the doors to a flow of Soviet warships and materiel westward. The Black Sea harbors one-third of Soviet naval facilities and one-fourth of its warships.

The straits—a 16-mile waterway which separates Europe from Asia—are vital to the USSR in other ways. About one-half of Soviet merchant shipping passes through them, including many spy ships. The Bosporus and Dardanelles are, unquestionably, the Soviet maritime window on the Arab world, Southern Europe, and Africa.

In the early 1980s NATO commanders did not believe in the possibility of a surprise Soviet attack on the straits, mainly because of the permanent electronic watch over the Black Sea by U.S. monitoring stations in Turkey. Still, defense of the area was of considerable concern, mainly because of the obsolete equipment used by the Turkish troops assigned to the task. Compounding the problem was the growth of the Soviet Black Sea fleet, which by the end of 1981 was believed to consist of about 180 warships. This force included two Kiev-class aircraft carriers, two helicopter carriers, 11 cruisers, 29 destroyers, 27 frigates, 24 submarines (some of the ultramodern Whisky class), and a number of smaller ships, such as guided missile patrol boats and torpedo boats.*

According to NATO Secretary-General Joseph Luns,

> the steady increase of Soviet naval power . . . has been remarkable and has brought considerable change in the makeup and tasks of the Soviet navy. Its traditional task was to protect the maritime approaches to the USSR and to provide close support for ground forces. Now is has three new missions: to contribute to potential world-wide offensive and defensive strategies; to conduct naval

---

*These figures are based on Western reports and can only be regarded as approximate, particularly in view of the steady expansion of the Soviet navy. It is estimated that every year the Soviet navy has been acquiring about 20 new warships of various categories.

operations in every ocean; and to support Soviet policy and promote Soviet interests world-wide. Even though still limited, the Soviet navy as now constituted provides the USSR with incomparable opportunities for action and influence, particularly in the Third World, and its power has implications for the security of vital Western sea lanes of communication.[5]

In the Mediterranean itself, NATO officials cite the use of the Soviet navy in support of foreign policy goals during the Lebanese missile crisis in May 1981, as well as during the joint Soviet–Syrian maneuvers in July 1981. There was a concentration of Soviet warships off the coast of Libya in December 1981 in what appeared to be a joint exercise, but little information has filtered through.

The southern littoral of the Mediterranean is extremely important to the USSR. A quick look at a map shows its political fragmentation and military alignment: pro–Soviet Syra, which could serve as the route to the Arab heartland; chaos-torn Lebanon; pro-U.S. Israel; Egypt, dependent on the United States but seeking better ties with the Arab world; strongly anti-U.S. Libya, with its vast arsenal of Soviet weapons; Tunisia, leaning toward the United States; quasi-radical, Soviet-equipped Algeria; and finally pro-Western Morocco.

When the Syrians deployed their surface-to-air missiles in Lebanon in the Spring of 1981, a Soviet naval task force cruised close to the Syrian and Lebanese coastlines in a demonstration against mounting U.S. pressure. Following the Israeli raid on Iraq's nuclear reactor in June 1981, the Soviet navy conducted a series of exercises meant to underscore the Soviet presence of Moscow's backing of the Arab cause. These exercises were culminated with a mock assault on the Syrian coastline north of Latakia, with the objective of "capturing" that strategic port, defended by the Syrian Seventh Armored Division. An unspecified number of Soviet troops actually went shore and were "repulsed" by the Syrian defenders. A total of 53 Soviet and 20 Syrian warships took part in the maneuvers, which were the first joint exercises between Soviet and Arab forces.

Its purpose appeared to have been entirely political. There is no evidence that Syrian and Soviet forces actually came into contact, aside from the joint military supervisory teams observing the maneuvers.* This politicomilitary operation followed a statement by Israeli

---

*They included Marshal Sergei Sokolov, first deputy Soviet defense minister, General Mustafa Tlass, Syrian defense minister.

Premier Menachem Begin describing Syria as being "in the forefront of Soviet activity in the Middle East." U.S. intelligence experts did not need convincing; for some time they had regarded Syria as part of the Soviet "triangle of steel" in the Middle East, which included Libya and South Yemen, the latter at the tip of the Arabian peninsula.

The Soviet navy has been patroling the Mediterranean Sea since 1964. In 1967, the Fifth Squadron of the Black Sea Fleet was permanently assigned to the Mediterranean theater. Its strength is roughly 55 ships, including tankers and other supply vessels. However, on a number of occasions, such as periods of international tension or maneuvers, as many as 100 Soviet naval ships have been observed in the Mediterranean. A typical Soviet naval combat deployment at any given time includes a helicopter or aircraft carrier, two cruisers, four destroyers, and a dozen submarines.

One of the major difficulties facing the Soviet navy in the Mediterranean is the lack of permanent naval bases. Soviet warships have called in on such Syrian ports as Latakia, Baniyas, and Tartus as well as in Libya. However, neither the Syrians nor the Libyans wanted to grant a permanent naval facility to their Soviet backers. In 1982 the Soviet navy had two repair facilities in the Mediterranean, on the Greek Island of Siros and in Tivat on Yugoslavia's Adriatic coast. Both were subject to severe limitations.

To compensate for the lack of bases, the USSR has established a number of anchorages in areas where the sea is shallow enough to drop anchor. In the early 1980s there were half a dozen such anchorages in the East Mediterranean, including south and east of the island of Crete and near the Aegean island of Limnos. The Aegean, with its fortified Greek islands and threat of a Greco–Turkish confrontation, was a favorite patrol area for Soviet warships and electronic spy ships. At the height of the summer season, the spectacle was often incongruous: massive Soviet cruisers, with helmeted sailors manning missile stations, brushed past sleek yachts, adorned by bikini-clad beauties from affluent Western society. Occasionally, the dark hull of a Soviet submarine could be seen surfacing, almost silently. It was a somber reminder of the threats and uncertainties of this modern age. Yet, the setting could hardly be more idyllic: the craggy rocks of islands protruding from the emerald water, seaside tavernas smelling of cooking, the sound of bouzouki music, and the multicolored sails.

The Soviet navy was also hampered by regulations governing the use of the Bosporus and Dardanelles. The 1936 Montreaux Convention requires all Black Sea powers to give eight-days' notice before sending warships through the straits. (Other countries need a 15-day advance warning.) The trip must be completed in daylight; all submarines must move on the surface only. Although the convention bans transit by aircraft carriers, the Soviets have circumvented the measure by using the nomenclature of antisubmarine cruisers. Obviously, the Turkish authorities wanted no confrontation over the issue.

While to the USSR the Mediterranean is the "politically unreliable path to its back door,"[6] to the United States the sea is also of vital importance. Not only is it part of NATO's southeastern flank (the largest and perhaps most unstable of the alliance's three major European theaters), it is also a barometer of the international political climate, a testing ground for ideologies, and a maritime route for 17 countries.

The Soviet squadron in the Mediterranean is very much on its own, far from home bases, its supply routes under Turkish control. Among the countries regarded as NATO's friends and possible allies in the event of a major conflict are Morocco, Tunisia, Egypt, and Israel. The alliance considers Algeria, Libya, and Syria as possible opponents—although officials are careful about evaluating Algeria's attitude. To the north, Yugloslavia presents an enigma. The country is known to have cooperated with the USSR during several airlifts of Soviet materiel to the Middle East. In 1981 it considerably bolstered its trade relations with the Soviet bloc. During 1982 it was beset by a host of ideological problems, which put the whole Titoist doctrine under considerable strain. At best, NATO could regard Yugoslavia as nonaligned.

NATO listed its and other "friendly" forces in the Mediterranean as 2,100,000 peacetime troops, backed by 15,000 tanks and 1,700 combat aircraft. The strength of the naval forces of these countries was estimated at 77 submarines, 72 destroyers, five aircraft carriers, and over 1,000 other vessels.

The pro-Soviet or nonaligned forces consisted (1981 assessment) of half a million men, with 8,500 tanks and 1,400 combat aircraft. The total number of combat and support ships, including those of the Soviet squadron, was 240.

The comparison of NATO and Warsaw Pact forces in the so-called southern region looked less encouraging. A NATO study published in May 1982, claimed that

> approximately 33 Soviet, Romanian and Bulgarian divisions are available in the area north of Greece and Turkish Thrace. These forces are largely mechanized and are equipped with a total of

6,900 tanks and 5,300 artillery and mortar pieces. They are on terrain suitable for armored offensive operations and could be reinforced by amphibious forces and by the Warsaw Pact airborne/air mobile divisions. . . . NATO's 25 Greek and Turkish divisions in the area are mainly infantry. Their task is rendered difficult for defensive operations by the narrowness of the area between the borders and the Aegean.[7]

The report asserted that the USSR could commit 19 divisions against Eastern Turkey, backed by 4,100 tanks and approximately 4,000 artillery pieces. Turkey at the time had eight divisions in the northeastern part of the country plus four divisions that could be transferred from southeastern areas. NATO estimated the number of Warsaw Pact fighter bombers in the south at 340 versus NATO's 610 but the number of intercepters at 1,775 compared to NATO's 295.

The most up-to-date and combat-ready Western force in the Mediterranean was unquestionably the U.S. Sixth Fleet. Despite the assignment of some of its units to Indian Ocean duty in 1981, the Sixth Fleet was a powerful armada of some 45 ships, 275 combat aircraft, and 60,000 men. Its backbone consisted of two carrier task forces, each with about 90 aircraft. In addition, there were two task forces (TF–61 and TF–62) giving the fleet assault and amphibious landing capability. Some of the U.S. submarines in the Mediterranean carried Poseidon missiles capable of hitting targets in the heart of the USSR.

There is no question that defense planning in the East Mediterranean has been complicated by Greco–Turkish difficulties. Much of NATO's time was consumed in efforts to devise a command structure palatable to the protagonists and their contradictory objectives. There have been periods when the defense of the West was regarded as secondary by the defenders of the flank, whose military preparedness was aimed at each other.

Turkey applied for NATO membership in 1950, when the alliance was one year old. Since some allies opposed Turkish membership, Turkey was invited to participate in "the planning work of the organization, with regard to Mediterranean defense." It was at best "a consolation prize, tantamount to a rejection of her application for full membership. The British and French governments, especially the latter, were opposed to the admission of Turkey because of their unwillingness to guarantee a country so much on Russia's doorstep, the justification being that Turkey was in no sense a North Atlantic power."[8] However, a year later in July 1951, when Turkish troops had been engaged on the Korean battlefield for nine months, the

United Kingdom announced it favored Turkey's full membership in NATO. Other countries lifted their objections, and the NATO parliament ratified Turkish membership by February 1952. Greece had been a member (at the alliance's invitation) since 1951.

On July 16, 1952, NATO announced the creation of a new southeast European command, with headquarters in the Aegean port of Izmir. The command initially included Turkish and Greek forces and was responsible to the Southern European command in Naples.

Under NATO's initial concept, the role of Greece was to protect its northern frontiers from any attack likely to penetrate the Mediterranean theater. It soon became apparent, however, that the Greeks regarded that frontier of secondary importance to their border with Turkey in Thrace. The incompatibility of the two allies became glaring following the Turkish intervention in Cyprus in July 1974; as a result Greece withdrew its forces from NATO's unified command. COMLANDSOUTH EAST (NATO Command of Land Forces in the Southeast) in Izmir eventually became a purely Turkish operation under a Turkish general. There were, as usual, liaison officers from other NATO countries.

For practical purposes, at least as far as NATO was concerned, Greek frontiers with Yugoslavia and Bulgaria were left unprotected. The network of NATO early-warning stations, known as the NATO air defense ground environment (NADGE), was paralyzed. Yet, the United States continued to provide arms for the Greek armed forces and the joint U.S. military advisory group (JUSMAG) operated in Greece—just as did the U.S. installations on the mainland and on Crete.

When he was NATO supreme commander, General Alexander Haig suggested a number of compromise formulas under which Greece would rejoin the military wing. The effort was pursued by his successor, General Bernard Rogers. Their thrust was to assuage the national sensitivities of Greece and Turkey and get the two nations to cooperate as partners in the alliance. One of the most difficult problems was the division of responsibility for the defense of the Aegean.

This involved the so-called flight information regions (FIR) and their division between Athens and Istanbul, shattered during the Turkish intervention in Cyprus (see Chapter 2). Also included were the claims of the protagonists concerning the Aegean seashelf, which the Turks regard as an extension of the Anatolian land mass.

The longer Greece stayed outside NATO's military structure, the more difficult the negotiations became. In February 1980, Greece rejected a plan referred to in the press as the "Rogers plan." Details of the plan were never officially disclosed, but there were leaks by the Greek side that NATO never denied. According to the Athens newspaper, *Kathimerini,* Rogers had proposed dividing the Aegean into three zones: a Greek zone (to be defended by the Greek air force), a Turkish zone, and international waters under a U.S. command based in Crete. The Greeks rejected the Rogers plan, apparently preferring a formula previously suggested by General Haig in talks with the former commander of the Greek armed forces, General Ioannis Davos.

The Haig–Davos formula called for Greek reintegration, basically leaving the solution of the Aegean defense to further negotiations. It also called for the creation of a separate Greek NATO command at Larisa (in central Greece). The Greek government saw the Rogers plan as a step backwards, apparently because it gave the Turkish airforce more command responsibility than the Greek side was prepared to accept. Still smarting from the Turkish invasion of Cyprus, which Athens regards as "Hellenic," the Greek feared that an increased share in the defense of the Aegean could be used by Turkey as a pretext to territorial claims in the area.

In the end, yet another formula was agreed upon, this one involving the Turkish generals who had seized control of the country in September 1980. It combined various previous suggestions, leaving the final apportionment of the Aegean defense to the discretion of the NATO command for Southern Europe. It was assumed that the NATO commander for Southern Europe would give appropriate defense instructions, depending on the nature of the threat. Constantine Mitsotakis, Greek foreign minister at the time, further clarified the compromise in parliament by explaining that it provided for a full and unlimited exchange of information between the Greek and Turkish air forces in the 48-kilometer zone on both sides of the Greek–Turkish separation line in the Aegean, east of its Greek islands. The Greek and Turkish commanders in the area, according to the clarification, were to be in close contact with NATO's Southern Europe air force commander. This compromise brought Greece back under NATO's military wing in October 1980. It did not heal Greco–Turkish animosity, which continued its debilitating impact on NATO's strategy, despite a considerable softening of the Turkish attitude.

The Turkish military establishment appeared genuinely concerned that Greece should be a valid member of NATO, perhaps for no other reason than the fact that to a great extent Turkish defenses against any Warsaw Pact thrust depended on Greece. Yet, the Turks were unwilling to make any significant gesture in the dispute over the Aegean seabed, and their proposals on Cyprus for a loose bizonal federation were not palatable to the Greeks. NATO appeared stymied, but then it was in no position to solve issues which had divided generations of diplomats in Greece and Turkey. What the alliance tried to do was close its ranks and hope for the best in a hardly enviable situation.

The Greek reentry into NATO's military establishment was basically a sign of considerable concern about security by the conservative government of Premier George Rallis. Rallis himself said, "The policy followed by the Greek government strengthens the position and the security of the country. The strengthening of Greece's international position which will ensue from re-integration into the alliance is certain to help Cyprus, which Greece will be able to support in a better way."[9] A year later, the situation had changed dramatically. The Rallis government was replaced by Papandreou's socialists, with their publicly stated belief that U.S. bases on Greek territory as well as a military commitment to NATO represent an "invitation to disaster." Although preparations went ahead with the setting up of the Greek NATO command in Larisa, there was little rejoicing in the alliance. As if the Greco–Turkish difficulties were not enough, NATO also had to seriously consider the prospect of losing Greece. Perhaps the most reassuring factor during Papandreou's first nine months in office was that he promised no "adventures," and did not seem to be in a hurry to either press for a special status within NATO or start negotiations about the fate of the U.S. bases in Greece.*

However, the Socialist government did not wait long to show the alliance that it was not going to be an easy partner. At the annual NATO ministerial meeting in December 1981, Papandreou—acting as his own defense minister—announced a partial suspension of some alliance commitments. "The process of disengagement is on its way," Papandreou said. There were no additional clarifications, and none were to be published during the following six months. It was an uneasy period during which some high NATO officials felt that "not all was lost" and that Papandreou would merely press for a special status for Greece within the alliance's military structure.

At the same meeting, Papandreou insisted that the final communiqué include a paragraph specifying the alliance's guarantees to

---

*Preliminary talks on a new approach to the problem of the bases started in August 1982 amidst some official optimism.

Greece in the event of aggression by Turkey. Such a clause would be contrary to the very principles on which the alliance was based and, as expected, was rejected by Turkey. For the first time in NATO's 32 years, the defense ministers parted without a communiqué. In the words of *The New York Times* columnist Flora Lewis, "The difficulty of sober explanation of complex Western defense issues has never been more obvious and more important. And premier Andreas Papandreou has shown how to make a mockery of the effort among 15 countries with different histories, cultural backgrounds and politics."

By contrast, on the eve of the Brussels meeting, the United States and Turkey announced that they would form a high-level joint military group "to enlarge and improve defense cooperation." Turkey was clearly emerging as the more reliable of the East Mediterranean allies. Still, the United States had to keep all options open and bear in mind the highly complex personality of the new Greek premier as well as his PASOK Socialist party's platform and the mood of the electorate. The strain on the alliance was expected to increase rather than diminish. At the same time, U.S. support for the Ankara military regime appeared to be a divisive factor within NATO, with some Western European members unhappy about the slow process of Turkey's return to democratic rule. The U.S. view was that Turkey's role as the linchpin of the southeastern flank had grown precisely because of the uncertainty shrouding the attitude of Greece. Furthermore, the United States felt that with the precarious situation on NATO's outer perimeter, particularly in the Persian Gulf, only a strong Turkey could provide a valid deterrent against a possible Soviet effort to reach the Arab oil fields.

Turkey's own attitude was obscure mainly because of the political pressure of some NATO allies as well as its growing effort to establish more solid links with the Arab world. In such a context, Turkey was loath to get involved in contingency planning for a possible operation in the gulf that might—and most likely would—antagonize much of the Arab world. To the generals in power in Ankara, stopping a Soviet attack was one thing, but serving as a possible springboard for the U.S. Rapid Deployment Force (RDF) in the gulf was a totally different matter.

The issue was discussed with considerable frankness by Taner Baytok, director-general for Strategic Research and Disarmament in the Turkish foreign affairs ministry. "The Iran–Iraq war has demonstrated the potential for conflict within the Middle East and Gulf regions and the danger they pose for Western interests," he wrote. "However, in shaping its policy, Turkey cannot overlook its crucial stake in peace and stability in the Middle East and in the maintenance and further promotion of its traditional ties with Arab and Islamic countries in the region."[10] Thus, it looked as though even the more reliable of the southeastern flank defenders had some reservations concerning the alliance's possible involvement in a Middle East emergency.

There were areas dramatically undermanned in the vast Mediterranean theater. One such area was Turkey's 370-mile frontier with the USSR. On the whole, it is probably the least talked about NATO frontier, despite the fact that it is there (in addition to Norway) that NATO directly confronts Soviet forces. In 1982 Turkey claimed that Soviet forces deployed there were far larger than required for defense against either Turkey or Iran. It was perhaps significant that the first Soviet maneuvers after the Helsinki Agreement of 1975 took place along the Turkish border in February 1976. The Turks themselves conducted periodic exercises in harsh winter conditions in that daunting mountain terrain. Although the nature of the desolate area is likely to favor defense by hardened Turkish troops, there was no compensation for the Soviet *masse de manoeuvre* and its ability to strike with comparatively little warning. Above all, the Turkish forces deployed along the border were at the end of a long and tenuous line of NATO communications.

Following a visit to Turkey in December 1981 by U.S. Secretary of Defense Caspar W. Weinberger, there was a feeling that more U.S. funds would be forthcoming to bolster the Turkish armed forces or at least partially alleviate their shortage of modern equipment. This was presumably the main reason for the creation of a joint military working group. A statement by Weinberger and Turkish Defense Minister Haluk Bayulken at the time said that a military and economically strong Turkey is "vital to the deterrent capabilities of NATO and will constitute an important element of stability in the region."[11]

However. when Secretary of State Haig visited Ankara in May 1982, he could offer no tangible evidence that the United States was in a position to increase its military aid, at least in the foreseeable future. The Turks had to be content with his praise of the military regime's efficiency and progress, but with little else. In Ankara, officials attributed it to an increased role of the so-called Greek lobby as a result of pressures by the Socialist government in Athens. Nonetheless, Turkey reiterated its commitment to NATO and the West.

In mid-1982 NATO's deterrent on the southeastern flank was a relatively feeble proposition. General Rogers, supreme allied commander in Europe, put it:

Of all the challenges facing NATO, the most fundamental, in my opinion, is to convince the peoples of our nations that it is a very critical period, especially the first half of this decade. They must understand that to be effective our security efforts will require sizeable amounts of resources which could otherwise be devoted to other national needs, such as social services. And they must understand that if we do not accomplish these security imperatives, the social and political gains of our democracies may be short-lived.[12]

Convincing public opinion in the Mediterranean countries of NATO's security imperatives was a daunting task. Greece and Turkey, the two main problem countries, had different views on the situation. The Greek Socialist government was not quite convinced that NATO membership was the best thing for its security, while the Turks were not happy about U.S. amends after the disastrous arms embargo.

In the words of Farouk Şahinbaş, assistant secretary-general for defense affairs in the Turkish ministry, the embargo "was a most disastrous decision. . . . It was a hostile act. It strengthened the position of those who oppose good Turkish–U.S. relations."[13] At the time when Turkish generals were drawing up a shopping list for their crippled armed forces, Şahinbaş pointed out that "the present generation of Turks differs considerably from the soldiers who died in Korea for 60 cents a day. Today the Turks cannot be pacified by backslapping." Another foreign office official, Ayhan Kamel, director general for political affairs, described the embargo as a paradox. "The United States expected Turkey's contribution to NATO but deprived it of the means to carry out this task. . . . The embargo aggravated Turkey's social and economic problems—hence undermined democracy."[14] These words proved prophetic enough.

Within a year of the conversation, Turkey's civil strife reached the proportion of a civil war, and the military stepped in. As far as many U.S. diplomats were concerned, it was not a moment too soon. According to one senior member of the U.S. embassy in Ankara at the time of the military takeover, "alienation of the Turkish masses from the West has been the most serious, dramatic and dangerous development during the past few years. To become part of the West was a major historic decision. But the Turks feel that the West has not reciprocated. The embargo was a glaring illustration of this attitude."[15]

While the Reagan administration was determined to overcome congressional reluctance and considerably boost military grants to Turkey, Western European allies appeared more concerned about the stifling of democracy in that country, albeit temporarily. At the time of the December (1981) NATO ministerial meeting, there were numerous backstage discussions between the United States and its NATO partners about the attitude toward Ankara's military rulers. The United States was all for giving them time to purge the country and install a new political system. Meanwhile, U.S. officials argued, Turkey should not be deprived of support if it was to carry out its role in Western plans to deter any possible Soviet military push toward the Persian Gulf or even Iran. Only with the help of a stronger Turkey could the West create a credible strategy in the face of unstable Southwest Asia, according to this argument.

Because of Turkish sensitivities vis-à-vis the Arab world, as mentioned earlier, none of this was put into a formal policy commitment. However, it was disclosed at the time that some U.S. aid was already being directed to improve air base facilities in the easternmost areas of Turkey, particularly in Van Province. At the same time, such NATO countries as the Federal Republic of Germany (FRG) and Denmark were suspending credits to Turkey, mainly as a result of the sentencing of former premier Bülent Ecevit, who had become a symbol of resistance to the military rulers, at least abroad (see Chapter 3). Perhaps ironically, many politicians in those two countries who defended Ecevit were among his most vocal critics when he ordered the invasion of Cyprus in 1974.

Thus, the attitude of the alliance was hardly unanimous, at least at that juncture. *The Times* (London) claimed it was "uncomfortably reminiscent" of the time when the United States and its Western European partners differed over policy toward Greece during the seven-year rule of the military junta.[16] As the Reagan administration urged a greater financial effort on behalf of Turkey, the split risked becoming perhaps even wider.

To U.S. strategists there was little doubt in 1982 that Greece's role in protecting its northern frontiers from a Warsaw Pact attack had definitely become secondary to that of protecting itself from Turkey. Officially, of course, the United States continued to describe both countries as equally vital to NATO. In terms of manpower and quantity of hardware, Turkey towered over Greece. But Turkish equipment—at least most of it—was antiquated, while Greece had considerably modernized its armed forces, particularly during the U.S. arms embargo against Turkey. Yet, it was obvious that the increasing turbulence in Southwest Asia on the doorstep of the southeastern flank and the Soviet interest in that area had made Turkey more strategically important.

Still, there was no getting away from the fact that as long as Greece and Turkey remained at daggers drawn, the defense of the southeastern flank was being constructed on flimsy foundations. Consequently, a strategic readjustment was likely, with the center of gravity eventually shifting toward Turkey. That country (Western by vocation but Eastern by history, tradition, religion, and to some extent mentality) could hardly be expected to bear the main responsibility for the defense of the West, which criticized and, in some cases, disavowed it.

It was a situation fraught with danger which few Western politicians understood. There was little time and desire in the hectic atmosphere of the West in the 1970s and 1980s to ponder the factors that led to the Greco–Turkish feud and created the enormous problem for NATO. The feud involved national prejudices and sensitivities, old and new claims, quarrels over the interpretation of international law, the division of Cyprus, and historic scars that refused to heal. A closer look at each of these problems might help to at least alleviate some misconceptions and shed new light on the conflicting claims.

Notes

1. Official text of a speech given before the U.S., Senate, Committee on Foreign Relations on May 22, 1978.

2. Author's notes, February 20, 1981.

3. Reuter's dispatch, *Cyprus Mail,* February 23, 1981.

4. Jesse W. Lewis, *The Strategic Balance in the Mediterranean* (Washington, D.C.: American Enterprise Institute for Public Policy Research, 1977).

5. Joseph M.A.H. Luns, "Political Military Implications of Soviet Naval Expansion," *NATO Review* (February 1982), pp. 1–2.

6. Lewis, *Strategic Balance.*

7. North Atlantic Treaty Organization, *NATO and the Warsaw Pact* (Brussels: NATO, 1982), pp. 21–23.

8. Geoffrey Lewis, *Modern Turkey* (London: Ernest Benn, 1974), p. 198.

9. Official text of a statement made on October 20, 1980 in Athens.

10. Taner Baytok, "Recent Developments in the Middle East and Southwest Asia," *NATO Review* (August 1981), p. 11.

11. Official communique, December 5, 1981.

12. General Bernard Rogers, "Increasing Threats to NATO's Security Call for Sustained Response," *NATO Review* (August 1981), p. 11.

13. In conversation with the author in 1980.

14. Ibid.

15. Ibid.

16. *The Times* (London), December 5, 1981.

Chapter 2

A HERITAGE OF HATE

We are in the hands of the foe; for the sake of God,
*   O countrymen, Enough!*
Let us indeed renounce every personal wish
*   and desire.*

Namik Kemal
Turkish poet
(nineteenth century)

They came out of the heart of Asia Minor, little known descendants of the Turkoman nomads. For centuries they identified themselves with the dynasties ruling them (such as Ummayyad, Abbasid, Seljuk, and, finally, Ottoman) rather than by their own names. To the outside world they were the Turks, confirmed enemies of Christianity and propagators of Islam. Their armies swept through the Balkans and twice knocked on the very gates of Vienna. On the southern side of the Mediterranean they conquered vast portions of Arab land. In 1453 Constantinople fell into their hands, and an era came to an end. The Turks were at the peak of their power.

Western historians are rarely kind to the Turks and their conquests. Such terms as "central Asian hordes" are frequently used in a derogatory sense. The word *horde* itself stems from the Turkish *ordu*, meaning army. The "Turkish hordes" came to personify savagery, looting, and conquest.

One of the conquered areas was what today constitutes Greece, at the time a poor country of villages scattered throughout the rocky mountains or dotting the sinuous coastline. For many years Greece lay under Ottoman rule, as did Serbia, Macedonia, and other parts of of the Balkans and the Middle East. However, long after the end of the Turkish occupation and the collapse of the Ottoman Empire, no other country maintained such a burning hatred toward Turkey as did Greece.

To most outsiders there is little rationale in the modern world for this obsession. The two countries last confronted each other on the battlefield in the early 1920s; that confrontation was caused by the Greek invasion of war-weary Turkey.* To some extent the Turks have an inferiority complex about the Greeks, chiefly because they seem to consider them more Western. However, in Greece most things evil and aggressive are identified with Turkey and the Turks. Forced by political circumstances, however, the two countries have cooperated within NATO, but with considerable mistrust. In the late 1970s and early 1980s, much of their military preparedness and spending was aimed against each other rather than toward their roles as the defenders of NATO's exposed southeastern flank.

The Greek hostility toward Turkey is unquestionably rooted in the Ottoman occupation and the bloody struggle for independence, which culminated in a Greek victory. It was accentuated by various subsequent armed conflicts, usually accompanied by mutual atrocities. Perhaps the worst followed the abortive Greek invasion of Turkey; the result was that hundreds of thousands of Greeks fled western Anatolia in tragic circumstances. As years went by, the obsession about Turkey survived, with varying degrees of intensity. Perhaps the most logical explanation is that of fear—fear of a much bigger neighbor with a history of conquest and consequently of animosity toward Greece. One does not have to be a strategist to see that, faced with some 45 million Turks, 9 million Greeks would have little chance. The Turkish armed forces may suffer from various shortages and outdated equipment but would, in any conflict, be capable of inflicting serious damage on Greece. This realization led to various Greek demands on NATO allies for guarantees against Turkey.

---

*In military terms, the Turkish invasion of Cyprus in 1974 was a relatively minor event. In any case, the strength of the Greek mainland contingent on the island plus that of military advisers was barely 1,500 men.

To understand the feud that has so damaged the West's defensive posture as well as the two countries involved, an outline of their conflict and dividing issues is essential. The Ottoman Empire had reached the limits of its European expansion toward the end of the seventeenth century, when its armies were repelled from the walls of Vienna, mainly the result of a massive charge of heavy Polish cavalry, which had come to help save Christendom.*

> It was after the halting of the Ottoman advance that the lag began to appear between the standards of training and equipment of Ottoman and European armies. . . . The decline in alertness, in readiness to accept new techniques, is an aspect—perhaps the most dangerous —of what became a general deterioration in professional and moral standards of the armed forces, parallel to that of the bureaucratic and religious classes. . . . It led directly to what must be accounted, in the Ottoman as in the Roman empire, as one of the principal causes of decline—the loss of territory to more powerful foreign enemies.[1]

One by one the conquered provinces began to rise against the Turkish occupiers. At the same time, the empire was also plagued by serious economic difficulties, accentuated by the fall of the world price of silver and the rise of that of gold. "Turkish raw materials became very cheap for European traders, and were exported in great quantities—including, despite prohibitions, corn. Local industries began to decline, and the import of European manufacturers expanded. Fiscal pressure and economic dislocation, accentuated by large-scale speculation and usury, brought distress and then ruin to large sections of the population."[2] This was the general setting in which conquered Greeks began to stir and clamor for their long-lost freedom.

There is little doubt that the erosion of Ottoman power spurred Hellenic nationalism to more vigorous action. The *klephts,* initially bands of brigands who were used by the Ottomans in parts of the conquered Greek territory as local police, gradually turned into freedom fighters. In the turmoil of growing conflict, their history of oppression of Greek peasantry was generally forgotten, mainly because of their militant hostility to Turkish rule. Perhaps ironically,

---

*To this day the Polish king, Jan Sobieski, who directed the rescue, is not regarded too kindly in Turkish textbooks.

a sense of nationhood among scattered villages of the Peloponnese was fostered by outlaws and highway robbers.

When the Greeks finally rose in 1821, there was no mercy for the often benevolent Turkish colonizers. The Turkish settlers in what today is Greece were the first victims of Greek wrath.

> They were killed deliberately, without qualm or scruple, and there were no regrets either then or later. Turkish families living in single farms or small isolated communities were summarily put to death. . . . In the smaller towns, the Turkish communities barricaded their houses and attempted to defend themselves as best they could, but few survived. . . . All over the Peloponnese roamed mobs of Greeks armed with clubs, scythes, and a few firearms, killing, plundering and burning. They were often led by Christian priests, who exhorted them to greater effort in their holy work.[3]

Yet, historians agree that on the whole, particularly during the years just before the outbreak, the lot of the Greek population under the Ottomans was not a particularly difficult one. As elsewhere in their possession, the Ottoman rulers were mainly interested in collecting taxes. In the case of Greece, this used to be done by the Greeks themselves, who then handed the funds over to the imperial treasurer. The Turkish conquest of Greece was a gradual process and, inevitably, had to be accompanied by bloodshed. In the end, the Turks gave free reign to local Greek officials and to the influential Orthodox church, which was part of the empire's administrative system. Their occupation forces, "relatively small and confined to garrison towns and strategic points, had left to the Greeks and to other subject peoples a considerable degree of autonomy which had increased as time went by."[4] Moreover, the Turks also used Greeks as administrators of other conquered provinces, having considerable respect for their various skills. An affluent Greek merchant class existed in several thriving ports, unhindered or even encouraged by the aloof colonizers.

Of course, there is always the other side of the story. The taxes were usually excessive, and Turkish overlords were often corrupt. Some of the best land was owned by the colonizers and their descendants. The Greek Christians were regarded as inferior citizens by the Turkish Muslims. Consequently, the awakening of Greek nationalism was intimately linked with religion. Many Greeks felt that in addition to fighting for freedom, they were also fighting for their Christian faith. In more than one way, the rising of 1821 was regarded as a holy war against Islam. As the war of independence escalated, religious differences began to play an increasing role. Places of worship were desecrated by both sides. Each side regarded the other as heretics "abhorrent to God and deserving of total extirpation."[5]

The Turkish reprisals to the Greek rampage were predictably merciless and cruel. Gregorios, the Orthodox patriarch of Constantinople, was hanged and his body dragged through the streets to be thrown into the sea, despite the fact that he had denounced the rebels. Hundreds of other Greeks—priests, merchants, and officials— were either hanged or beheaded before cheering crowds. Others were sent as slave labor to the mines, a fate often worse than sudden death. The executions and banishments were personally dictated by Sultan Mahmoud, thus aggravating the growing feud between Greek and Turk, which was to plague both countries for years. The victims were not chosen because of their complicity or support for the rebellion, but simply because they were Christian Greeks. The Ottoman authorities allowed mobs to participate in the vengeance, and the Greek quarter of Constantinople became a blazing inferno for three days, the streets littered with corpses of men, women, and children. Thousands were massacred in Smyrna (today Izmir), a thriving port city on the Aegean Sea, and in other areas of the empire with Greek populations. In Cyprus, virtually the entire Orthodox hierarchy (consisting of an archbishop, five bishops, and 36 priests) was executed.

Such acts are not easily forgotten, and to this day Greek history books portray them in lurid colors. They contributed to the further tarnishing of Turkey's image in the West. To much of the West, the Christian Greeks had become martyrs at the hands of the "barbarian" Turks. This image has survived more than a century, particularly in Greece. For example, when in early March 1982 Greek Premier Papandreou visited Cyprus and unveiled a memorial to the 44 dead and 61 missing members of the Greek contingent during the 1974 Turkish landing, the unit's commander spoke of the "barbarous invasion by the age-old enemy of our race."[6]

Western sympathy toward Greece increased following its hard-won independence from the Ottomans. France and the United Kingdom became protecting powers of modern Greece, which, in July 1832, was finally recognized by the sultan as an independent kingdom. Obviously, the recognition did not heal the wounds. The flames of hatred continued burning, particularly in Greece; the Turks were preoccupied with the decay of their shrinking empire and the steady erosion of their military might. Periodically, Greek and Turk clashed on various battlefields.

The empire collapsed in the wake of World War I. When, in 1919, British, French, and Italian forces were occupying parts of Anatolia, Syria, and Iraq, the Greeks invaded the western district of Smyrna, at that time housing a considerable Greek population. Reports—some true and some exaggerated—of atrocities against the Turkish population in the area soon galvanized the rest of the country; already reeling from a series of disasters, Mustafa Kemal (later to be known as Atatürk) defied the sultan, convened a grand national assembly in Angora (later renamed Ankara), and repudiated the Treaty of Sèvres, under which the allies were to partition Turkey, leaving it a mere stump in the heart of Anatolia. He then gathered his weary and demoralized forces and managed to lead them into what turned out to be a victorious war against the Greek invaders.

The war was not confined to the battlefield. As the Turkish troops pushed the retreating Greeks toward the sea, there were further mutual accusations of atrocities. Captured Smyrna was put to fire, and hundreds of thousands of destitute Greeks fled by boat for the safety of their distant—and to most of them unknown—homeland. They took with them hatred for their conquerors, who were able to demand and obtain concessions from the Allies, including an end to foreign military presence in Turkey. A new Turkey was born, and for a while it seemed as though the two countries would be able to coexist in peace.

While Atatürk instituted his reforms, aimed at turning Turkey into a secular, modern, and Western state, Greece struggled against a host of internal political adversities, culminated in the Italian and Nazi invasions during World War II and a bitter civil war. Although the obsession with the Turkish threat receded into the background, historical animosity remained. Many Greeks maintained that Turkey was an expansionist state, bent on recapturing its lost Greek possessions, particularly Salonika. Equally, some Turks attributed to Greece the *megali* (greater Greece) idea, which was supposed to put Istanbul under Greek rule.

Of course, not all Greeks and Turks were determined to propagate the spirit of vengeance because of the excesses of the past. A number of intellectuals in both countries sought contact as a way of attenuating tensions, which they frequently blamed on politicians. Despite the often strident or even virulent tone of the press in Greece and Turkey, editors and journalists were eager to attend joint conferences, and various cultural exchanges were arranged. Diplomats—optimists by the very nature of their profession—were particularly active in affirming the feasibility of a fruitful cooperation between the two countries, at the same time voicing their often contradictory demands and views.

There was, indeed, a sort of Greco–Turkish "honeymoon" in the 1950s, after the two countries joined NATO. Unfortunately it was spoiled by the start of the turmoil in Cyprus.

The Greek Cypriot struggle for independence from British rule in that East Mediterranean island was watched with alarm by the Turkish minority, which generally cooperated with the United Kingdom, thus planting another seed of discord in its future relationship with the Hellenic majority. There was the usual chain reaction; for example, when in 1955 the United Kingdom sought a solution to Cyprus at the so-called London Conference, a bomb exploded outside the Turkish consulate in Salonika. It triggered anti-Greek riots in Istanbul and Izmir, with considerable damage to property. Later it turned out that the Salonika bomb was planted by the Turks themselves in order to provoke the riots. When enough evidence of this was shown, Turkey apologized to Greece and offered to pay for the damage.

The relationship between Turkey and Greece deteriorated further with the outbreak of intercommunal strife in Cyprus in December 1963, three-and-a-half years after independence; during subsequent months, a U.N. peacekeeping force was dispatched to Cyprus (see Chapter 5). On several occasions the Turks used air strikes from mainland bases to help their beleaguered compatriots, particularly during the battle of the Turkish Cypriot enclave of Kokkina in August 1964. This prompted an influx of troops from Greece to Cyprus, which eventually swelled to between 7,000 and 9,000. As usual, there were reprisals against the Greek inhabitants in Turkey. Expulsions of Greeks accelerated, and by early 1965 some 6,000 Greeks had been forced to leave Turkey, while the property of an estimated 8,000 Greeks, particularly those in Istanbul, was seized (ostensibly as a guarantee for the payment of taxes). At the same time, the Turkish government clamped down on Greek schools, including an orphanage on the island of Prinkipo in the Sea of Marmara. "Some 200 children were thrown out at forty-eight hours' notice, and had to take refuge in two neighboring monasteries. The Greek government, to its credit, did not retaliate against Turkish citizens or the Turkish minority in Greece."[7]

In November 1967 the tension reached dangerous proportions following the Greek Cypriot assault on a Turkish Cypriot village. during which at least 25 Turkish Cypriots were killed, Ankara alerted its armed forces for a move to Cyprus. It took skilled diplomacy by

U.S. special envoy Cyrus Vance to defuse the crisis; the result was that most of the Greek troops were evacuated from the island. The relaxation of tension, following the start of intercommunal talks in 1968, was accompanied by an improvement in the relationship between Ankara and Athens, the capitals to which the Cypriot protagonists always looked for support. However, what progress existed was shattered by the Athens coup in Cyprus on July 15, 1974; the Turks responded by landing an expeditionary force on the north of the island, which moved in mid-August to occupy 36 percent of Cyprus. Faced with the physical impossibility of helping distant Cyprus and the lack of any intervention by the United Kingdom, the third guarantor power, or the United States, Greece withdrew from NATO's military wing. It was yet another example of how the Greco–Turkish tug of war could affect the alliance.

There was some improvement in October 1980, when the generals in power in Ankara lifted their previous objections, and Greece was able to rejoin NATO's military structure. This act, however, was put in jeopardy by the Socialist victory in the 1981 Greek elections, which brought to power Papandreou, with his anti-NATO pronouncements and heady slogans of a Hellenic crusade in Cyprus. In the spring of 1982 the Turkish press hurled abuse at Papandreou and his "reckless policy." There were few signs that a reconciliation was possible in the nervous political climate. Still, in the summer of 1982 the two countries declared a two-month "moratorium" in the propaganda war to prepare the ground for political dialogue. Its outcome was difficult to assess initially.

The Papandreou government was also accused of intensifying oppression of the Turkish minority in the eastern province of Thrace. At a conference in Ankara in December 1981, Mumtaz Soysal, regarded as one of Turkey's leading constitutional experts, accused the Socialist government of Greece of "increasing acts of repression, in disregard of basic human rights" against the 120,000 Turks living in Thrace. According to Soysal and several other Turkish academics attending the conference, the Greek authorities jammed Turkish radio and television programs and limited the number of Turkish teachers in the schools in Thrace. The Turkish minority complained of limited secondary education possibilities, with only 200 places available in the whole of western Thrace. "Even coffee shops don't escape the pressure and discrimination, and are used as recruiting grounds by police and party officials who try to persuade the people to renounce their national heritage."[8] In March 1982 Turkish Premier Bülent Ulusu told a news conference in Ankara that Greece was uprooting ethnic Turks in Thrace and generally pursuing a racist policy in the province. It was, probably, the most outspoken statement by a high Turkish official on this delicate subject.

The Greeks countered such accusations by pointing out that in 1923 there were 300,000 Greeks living in Constantinople (Istanbul) and 110,000 Turks living in Thrace. In 1982 there were barely 10,000 Greeks in Istanbul and 120,000 Turks in Thrace. As usual, the attitudes of both sides were difficult to reconcile.

In May 1982 several hundred Turkish farmers in the Thrace area of Xánthi started plowing their fields in defiance of a court order officially expropriating their land. The Turkish press intensified attacks on Greece, while the Greek press repeated the old charges that Ankara used the land expropriation issue to press its claims to Greek territory. Mufti Mustafa Hilmi of Xánthi appealed to the United Nations Commission on Human Rights for help, with little result.

On the whole, the problem of the Turks in Thrace was secondary to the issue of Cyprus. Still, despite the deadlock in the negotiations on the island's future, some officials remained hopeful. However, there were no visible prospects for a solution of the differences between Greece and Turkey over the Aegean Sea.

Throughout the years there has been periodic speculation of a possible "package deal" between Greece and Turkey, involving Cyprus and the Aegean. Papandreou denied it formally during his 1982 visit to Cyprus. Equally, Turkish officials were adamant that Turkey would not drop the Aegean question in exchange for a Cyprus settlement, even on its own terms.

The Aegean lies between the western coast of Turkey and the eastern coast of Greece. It is dotted with Greek islands, some of them mere rocks protruding from the emerald water. In the summer, it is crisscrossed by private yachts and cruise ships. But under the facade of idyllic charm lie the tensions of the two traditional foes. The tension is accentuated by the occasional appearance of the dark silhouette of a Soviet warship, a reminder of the Soviet navy's presence in that sensitive part of the world. "Calm as a slumbering babe, tremendous ocean lies," wrote Homer of the Aegean millenniums ago. The Aegean is not an ocean and can be rough in the rainy winter months. Above all, it is a potential flashpoint, which a single shot could ignite.

The problem is a complex one. It involves a dispute as to what constitutes the continental shelf and the control of the sea and air space between the Greek and Turkish mainlands. It was exacerbated by the discovery in 1974 by the Greeks of oil in apparently commercially exploitable quantities. The proximity of the Greek islands to the Turkish coastline—both bristling with guns—makes the situation even more precarious.

There are some 3,000 Greek islands in the Aegean, of which 130 are inhabited. Greece claims 34 percent of the sea's area and Turkey, which controls two islands, claims 8.5 percent. The rest is in international waters. Since early 1974 the Greeks have been threatening to extend the limits of their territorial waters from 6 to 12 miles. The Turks, who apply the 12-mile limit in the Black Sea and the Mediterranean, hinted they would do the same, thus overlapping the Greek limits. The threats represented political dynamite.

As far as Greece is concerned, the main problem is Turkey's claim that the eastern Aegean is part of the Anatolian continental shelf. Turkey would like the line dividing control over the sea to be somewhere in the middle of the islands. To the Greeks, this is tantamount to a precedent for claiming possession of the islands. The Greeks say that under the 1958 Geneva Convention on the Continental Shelf, islands have a right to their own such shelves. According to this interpretation, almost the entire continental shelf under the Aegean should be Greek.

The dispute took on more dramatic aspects in 1970, when Greece granted oil exploration rights in the eastern Aegean. In 1973 the Turks replied in kind and sent the survey ship *Candarli* to the area under the protection of warships. Relations between the two protagonists took a turn for the worse. However, in May 1974, Greece announced it was ready to discuss with Turkey the question of the Aegean seabed. Ecevit, Turkey's premier at the time, described the offer as a positive development but warned that "Turkey is always prepared for any eventuality." The same year the Greeks started building fortifications on the Dodecanese Islands, which hug the Turkish coastline. A military force of some 25,000 troops, backed by armor, was quickly implanted. The Turks charged that this measure violated the 1923 Lausanne Treaty, which ended the last Greco–Turkish war and specified that the Dodecanese (the 12 islands between Samos and Kos) should be demilitarized.

In 1975, Turkey created a fourth army, also known as the army of the Aegean, with headquarters in Izmir. It was there that a powerful armada of landing craft was amassed. In August 1976, under strong political pressure, the Turkish government sent out another petroleum research ship, *Sismik I.* The Greeks replied by dispatching their own vessel, the *Nautilus.* Tension ran high, with both sides watching each other through gunsights. Eventually, both countries accepted a U.N. Security Council resolution urging them to show restraint and to resort to negotiation rather than confrontation. This, however, did not resolve the key issue, mainly that international law gives any country the right to explore for minerals on its continental shelf, and that both Greece and Turkey have been claiming the same area of the Aegean as their seabed.

The dispute went to the World Court in The Hague. In January 1979, the court ruled that because of Turkey's refusal to recognize the court's right to settle the dispute, it had no jurisdiction over the case. Another point of Greco–Turkish friction was left festering.

The conflict over the Aegean seabed was inevitably linked with the dispute over the air space. This feud, which caused serious complications to NATO as far as the division of command responsibility is concerned, had two basic aspects: the size of the national air space claimed by Greece in the area occupied by its islands, and reporting requirements concerning the so-called Flight Information Regions (FIR) set up by the International Civil Aviation Organization (ICAO).

The issue is complicated to the layman; perhaps the most concise explanation was contained in the 1980 staff report to the Committee on Foreign Relations of the U.S. Senate; It points out that

> Greece exercises a ten-mile air space margin around each of its Aegean islands. The United States and Turkey recognize only a six-mile national zone in the Aegean. The Turks have protested the Greek claim since 1974 by flying military aircraft through the contested four-mile zones. . . . Differences over FIR reporting requirements are more complex. In 1952 an ICAO regional conference with Greece and Turkey participating decided to establish a Flight Information Region demarcation line dividing the Athens and Istanbul FIR along a line roughly equal to the outer edge of the Turkish territorial sea. Greece, thus, received responsibility for civil and some military air traffic control over virtually all of the Aegean.[9]

The line (which has no relation to any territorial claims) proved to be a fragile one when the Turks landed on Cyprus in 1974.

> Turkey was unable to receive what it considered to be adequate information about aircraft approaching the Aegean coastline. On August 6, 1974, Turkey issued a notice to airmen (NOTAM 714) which required all eastbound aircraft under ICAO jurisdiction to report their flight plans to Istanbul FIR when they reached the midpoint of the Aegean. The Turks argued that this would provide their air defense with only 10–15 minutes warning of an attack. The new

reporting line, however, had important implications for the entire Aegean dispute because it was similar to the Turkish claim for the continental shelf.[10]

To the Greeks NOTAM 714 was yet further proof of Turkish efforts to assert their jurisdiction over the islands of the Aegean. The Greek government instructed pilots to disregard the Turkish NOTAM and issued one of its own (NOTAM 1157) on September 13, 1974, which closed air routes over the area as unsafe. Negotiations on the issue went on without result; direct links between Athens and Istanbul were severed. Finally, in February 1980, Turkey withdrew its NOTAM; Greece followed suit. Direct commercial flights between the two countries were resumed, and the stage was set for talks leading to Greek reintegration in NATO (October 1980).

Both sides have strong views on all issues concerning the Aegean and its problems, which years of negotiation have not changed. In October 1980, the then secretary-general of the Greek foreign ministry, Vedor Theodoropoulos, said "the delineation of the continental shelf is the most complex problem. We've been talking about it for five years without getting closer."[11]

Papandreou's electoral victory appears to have increased the problem almost from the beginning. The outspoken Socialist premier made it clear that Greece would stick to its guns and was unlikely to consider the various Turkish claims in the Aegean. In early March 1982 Papandreou said that both the Cyprus and Aegean issues were "the products of Turkish expansionism which the West had failed to bridle."[12] A few days earlier, in an interview with *The Financial Times,* Papandreou said, "Since the invasion of Cyprus in 1974, there has been an escalation of the Turkish claims in the Aegean. This is less so since the military regime in Turkey took over in September 1980, but their Aegean army now has at least 120,000 men and 180 landing craft. Further, Turkey has challenged Greece in denying in substance that the islands have their own continental shelf." In the same interview Papandreou stressed that "even more important in our opinion is the question of operational control of the Aegean airspace."

Such statements caused a warning by the Turkish foreign minister, Ilter Turkmen, against any unilateral Greek action in the Aegean (February 18, 1982). Turkmen instructed Turkish ambassadors to alert NATO allies to the seriousness of the situation. Premier Ulusu, at his March 13 Ankara press conference (during which he spoke of the persecution of Turks in Thrace), also warned about serious repercussions to Greek plans to extend the limit of Aegean territorial waters. It was all too clear that the two countries were as distant as ever in their interpretation of the dispute. Moreover, the crisis was not being helped by bellicose statements by the protagonists. In fact, it looked as though the Aegean was a more likely point of explosion than Cyprus.

In an interview with the weekly *Tachydromos* in November 1977, Herman Kahn, head of the Hudson Institute and a well-known U.S. futurist, said he envisaged no less than 20 scenarios for war between Greece and Turkey. According to Kahn's analysis, regardless of who starts the hostilities or where, "if war breaks out it will be a brief war. Something will occur and it will stop very soon. An armistice will be declared quickly since these kinds of wars do not reach any specific results."

That much is apparent to anybody who looks at a map of the East Mediterranean and studies the respective troop deployments of the protagonists. Their forces could effectively defend their countries' territories for some time, but not without heavy casualties and severe damage to industry and installations from air attacks. The Turks would be in a position to perhaps capture some of the Aegean islands. The Greeks are confident that their troops concentrated in Thrace could hold that narrow marshy front even against a superior Turkish force. Greek forces permanently deployed in Thrace are estimated at some 40,000 front-line and reserve troops, backed by some 450 tanks. The big question is why two countries condemned to live side by side should waste a large portion of their resources and military budgets on contingency preparations against each other. Granted that their differences are difficult to reconcile; granted that historic animosity is strong, perhaps with reason, on both sides.

Many other historic feuds have been forgotten. They include the initial German opposition to the granting of the Oder–Neisse territory to Poland and the Franco–German quarrel over Alsace, just to mention two. Frontier adjustments have been part of the international scene for years, obviously with mixed results. But it is difficult to argue that Salonika should be Turkish or that twentieth-century Greece has legal rights to Istanbul.

On some Aegean islands, what once were Turkish mosques have been converted into shopping areas. Many Christian churches have also been desecrated in Turkey and in the Turkish-controlled portions of Cyprus.

Religion is a strong dividing factor, although these days perhaps less so in secular Turkey than in Greece, where the Orthodox church is very much a national institution, often linked with the ruling establishment. One example is the 1969 constitution, which spells out the role of the church and its relationship to the state. It was drawn up by Archbishop Ieronymos and the Holy Synod but was submitted to the general meeting of the hierarchy by the head of the military junta ruling Greece at the time, Prime Minister George Papadopoulos.

However, there were strong indications in mid-1982 that the Socialist government in Greece was determined to change the relationship between church and state. Its plans called for a clear separation as well as expropriation of much of the land owned by the church. It was a highly sensitive issue in Greece and likely to cause serious internal problems. Its impact on the Greco–Turkish feud was uncertain.

The Turks are no longer dedicated to the advancement or defense of the Muslim faith. The faith is there but not as a state institution. One of the factors that precipitated the military takeover of 1980 was signs of stirring by a minority of Islamic fundamentalists, apparently influenced by the revolution in nearby Iran (see Chapter 3). Turkey has been making a strong effort to be a part of the Western community and can no longer be considered by Greeks as either the scourge or the enemy of Christendom. As far as Greek claims of Turkish expansionism are concerned, since the collapse of the Ottoman Empire, Turkey has made no territorial claims on any country. There is no formal proof that Turkish demands for the delineation of the continental shelf in the Aegean are a prelude to the occupation of the islands on the eastern side of the line. Equally, while some Greeks speak with nationalistic fervor about acquisition of Turkish territory, there has never been a formal government policy endorsing such an idea. Pamphlets and books propagating the *megali* concept are the work of an insignificant group and should not serve as a pretext for intensifying hostility.

The hostility is there, often under the surface but ready to explode at the slightest opportunity. When in the summer of 1980 ferryboat links were resumed between Turkey and the Greek island of Rhodes, crowds rioted, throwing Molotov cocktails and battling with the police. Specially trained riot squads had to be flown in from Athens. Organizers described it as a protest against the continued Turkish presence in Cyprus (91 people were injured). The ferryboat, *Tzemlik,* was a mere trigger. Ironically, the demonstrations coincided with the signing of an agreement on tourist exchanges between Greece and Turkey. It was yet another illustration of the contradictions that have marred relations between the two countries.

Notes

1. Bernard Lewis, *The Emergence of Modern Turkey* (London: Oxford University Press, 1968), p. 26.

2. Ibid., p. 29.

3. William St. Clair, *That Greece Might Still Be Free* (London: Oxford University Press, 1972), p. 1.

4. John T. A. Koumoulides, *Greece in Transition* (London: Zeno, 1977), p. 23.

5. St. Clair, *That Greece Might Still Be Free*, p. 39.

6. Author's notes, March 1, 1982.

7. Robert Stephens, *Cyprus, A Place of Arms* (London: Pall Mall, 1966), p. 196.

8. Conference statements made available to the author, December 1981.

9. U.S., Congress, Senate, *Turkey, Greece and NATO: The Strained Alliance*, a staff report to the Committee on Foreign Relations (Washington, D.C.; U.S. Government Printing Office, 1980), pp. 57–58.

10. Ibid., p. 58.

11. In conversation with the author.

12. *The Times* (London), March 2, 1982.

Chapter 3

A CRIPPLED POWER

*Greatness consists of deciding only what is necessary for the welfare
of the country, and making straight for the goal.*

Mustafa Kemal Ataturk

In the massive building of Turkey's former Grand National
Assembly in the heart of Ankara, five women and 155 men applauded
a balding general with seven rows of medal ribbons on his chest. The
men wore dark suits; most were middle aged. The date was October
21, 1981, the year of the centennial of the birth of Mustafa Kemal
Atatürk, founder of modern Turkey.

Exactly 13 months and 10 days before, the Turkish armed
forces had seized power from the feuding politicians, filling prisons
with culprits and suspects and moving with determination and military precision to release the grip of fratricidal terror on the strategic
country. Together with the four generals and one admiral of the
ruling National Security Council (NSC), the assembly was charged
with the drafting of a new constitution, which would open a new
era for Turkey, free of extremism and partisan squabbling.

To General Kenan Evren, head of the NSC, the formation of
the assembly was "the first step on the road to the new democracy."
He was applauded on that October day with short, disciplined bursts,
watched from the balcony by his colleagues, General Sedat Celasun,
General Nurettin Ersin, General Tahsin Sahinkaya, and Admiral Nejat

Tumer. Among them they represented all the branches of Turkey's massive armed forces—the nation's pride.

Much of the Western world took little notice of the ceremony, regarded as being of little consequence. Considerably more attention was given by the international media to the October 16 decree by the military rulers dissolving the discredited political parties to pave the way for a new system. The decree was regarded as yet another proof of an uncompromising military dictatorship, whose image was further tarnished internationally·by legal proceedings against former premier Bülent Ecevit.

The Western media deplored the move, but then the West has largely been ignorant about Turkey, its problems, and its objectives. As late as 1950, when Turkey applied for membership in the North Atlantic Treaty Organization (NATO), the respected *Times* (London) objected on the grounds that Turkey used the Arabic alphabet, obviously unaware of Atatürks' sweeping reforms. Equally indicative of Western misconceptions about Turkey was the widespread conviction that Turkey was part of the Arab world. The Turks are considered dour, xenophobic, and violent, the latter hard to dispute given the years of relentless terror. Still, it is hardly fair to judge a nation by extremists pursuing obscure aims. Compounding Turkey's poor reputation in the West were centuries of Ottoman conquest and rule, during which the Turks came to be regarded as the scourge of Christendom. In the sixteenth century Martin Luther compared the Turks to the devil. It was a reputation hard to live down, and it has weighed heavily upon modern Turkey's efforts to be accepted as a European nation.

Turkey's performance during the Korean War attenuated somewhat its image in the West, but only to a modest degree. Yet, Ankara answered the United Nations call for military contingents promptly, eventually increasing the strength of the Turkish brigade there to some 7,000 men. All told 25,000 Turks saw duty in Korea, leaving on the battlefield 617 men killed and 2,156 wounded. Officers and soldiers of other armies who fought alongside the Turks came back with descriptions of fierce Turkish fighters, excelling in hand-to-hand combat and apparently oblivious to danger.

To some extent the Turks share the blame for Western ignorance of their fascinating country. Their public relations apparatus has been notoriously hopeless, and the comparatively few objective accounts of modern Turkey were written by devoted scholars and journalists fighting considerable obstacles. During much of the 1970s all the outside world knew about Turkey was the landing and occupation of northern Cyprus and the rising toll of men and women shot down as extremist gangs did battle with machine guns and grenades. In 1979 some 2,200 people died in political violence, and by September 1980 the death rate averaged 30 a day. Security services had identified at least 47 different underground groups. Turkey's foreign debt had reached 17 billion dollars, and embarrassed officials were jetting around the world asking for a rescheduling of interest payments. Politicians hurled insults at one another, while a total of 1,275 bills awaited parliamentary action.

In the oppressive summer of 1980, with days and nights punctuated by explosions and the chatter of automatic weapons, two documents alarmed the government of Premier Suleyman Demirel, that rotund veteran of the Turkish political scene. One was a list of politicians, including Demirel, slated for assassination by extremists of the Marxist Dev Sol (Revolutionary Left). The other was a letter, signed by Evren and other generals, warning the politicians in no uncertain terms that unless they put the country's interests ahead of their quarrels, the military would have no choice but to seize control.

The warning was ignored. A dejected Western diplomat in Ankara said, "Only drastic surgery can save Turkey and only the armed forces are capable of performing it."[1]

Early in September some 40,000 people massed in the Anatolian city of Konya, known for its famous Whirling Dervishes of the Mevlana cult. Under the banners of Islam, the crowd chanted slogans demanding the establishment of an Islamic state, presumably on the ruins of Kemalism, which the military had sworn to defend. The Islamic revolution in neighboring Iran appeared to be hammering on Turkey's door. In the words of Ankara journalist Metin Munir, "The ties that are binding Turkey are being severed by political extremists. Poor are being driven against rich, Alevi Moslems against Sunnis, Kurds against Turks, workers against bosses, sons against fathers."[2] Turkey, not long ago the "sick man of Europe," had become "the ugly ally of the West."[3]

The coup was swift, well thought out, and bloodless. By dawn on September 12, 1980, troops were in control of the major cities. In clipped military tones, Evren explained the reasons to a nationwide television audience: anarchy, terrorism, foreign (meaning communist) influence, and the inability of Turkey to fulfill its commitment to the West. Within 24 hours, airports were reopened and tourists milled around Istanbul's Topkapi museum.

On September 18, Evren and his colleagues swore themselves in as the country's official leaders and subsequently appointed a technocrat civilian government with a retired admiral, Bülent Ulusu, as premier. To all those who know anything about Turkey, the takeover was not the action of a Latin-type junta, just as Turkey is not a "banana republic." It was, basically, the solution of despair for Kemalist generals watching Atatürk's hereitage being shattered.

Travelers arriving by plane in Istanbul, that spectacular city astride Europe and Asia, see from the air the breath-taking view of lean minarets shooting up toward the sky over the fat domes of mosques and cars streaming over the bridge spanning the Bosporus. On the ground, the reality is often brutal: unsmiling policemen, sullen porters, dejected-looking crowds, ramshackle cars, and weather-stained buildings festooned with a tangle of telephone and electricity wires. Of course, as everywhere in the Mediterranean world, all this looks better in brilliant sunshine than under an autumn drizzle. The arrival in Ankara can often be more depressing: the capital's airport is a dilapidated eyesore, and the trip to Atatürk's city passes groups of shantytowns, the curse of Turkish urban centers.

It takes considerable time to get used to the Turks and to understand their ways. Those who reach that point find them a fascinating people, particularly their scholars and diplomats, who equal and often surpass their Western colleagues. During many conversations with Turkish officials and diplomats, I became convinced that, at least as far as the educated group is concerned, Atatürk did accomplish his aim of turning Turkey into a Western nation.

On the whole, if the Turks want to be successful at something, they usually manage. Their intellectuals often give the impression of having a chip on their shoulder when talking to Western Europeans, and this is understandable: few Westerners have accepted them as part of the Western world. By contrast, NATO officers in contact with the Turkish military are invariably impressed and regard the Turks as worthy and equal partners.

Despite the political turmoil of the 1970s, Turkey's achievements were considerable. Roads were built across the rugged Anatolian land mass; dams began to harness the waters of the Euphrates. New agricultural techniques increased food production; illiteracy was slashed, although it still remained at about 40 percent. For two decades Turkey consistently registered an annual growth in national income of 7 percent. Industry grew, providing the country with 25 percent of its gross national product. Diplomatic dispatches often described the country as "robust" and of having "great potential."

Shortly before the military takeover, a visiting trade delegation from South Korea told Turkish officials that if Korea had Turkey's resources, it could become as strong economically as Japan. Basically, all Turkey needs is organization, proper marketing techniques, more efficient production methods, and above all, political and social peace. And this is precisely what the Turkish armed forces set out to achieve, to the applause of many Turks and amid a barrage of criticism from Western Europe. Ignoring (although inwardly perturbed by) the latter, the generals in power were convinced that they had acted in the spirit of Atatürk. Only time will tell whether they were equal to the daunting task.

No study of contemporary Turkey would be valid without at least a brief look at the founder of the republic, whose adopted name —Atatürk—literally means father Turk. Today pictures of the man, with his penetrating blue gaze, adorn nearly every office, classroom, and shop in the teeming bazaars of Istanbul. His bust and statues dot the Turkish cities and countryside. Volumes have been written about the man who, with an iron will, ordered his country to look westward. Unfortunately, one has to look to foreign publications to find the "real" Atatürk. Turkish documents tend to eulogize him, glossing over some of his weaknesses. But Atatürk was a man, and his various human frailties do not necessarily detract from his achievements.

Some historians have described him as a "shallow" reformer, claiming that most of his edicts were superficial and cosmetic in nature, without profoundly affecting Turkey's character. Granted that the drastic change of a nation's outlook requires at least several generations; but no other modern statesman accomplished as much in such a short span of time. Atatürk instilled tremendous national pride in a country reeling from Ottoman disasters by giving it a military victory over Greece in 1921. He changed the Arabic alphabet into Latin, abolished the supremacy of Islam, freed women from their purdah, and irrevocably moved the country toward Western laws and a Western-type civilization.

It can be argued (and has been) that Western values are not necessarily the ideal answer to Turkey's problems. But Ataturk felt differently, and history so far has proved his vision correct. While beset by a host of problems and still searching for an identity, Turkey has shed the shackles of Ottoman obscuration and established a legitimate claim to being part of the West.

True, only 5 percent of Turkey's territory of 301,000 square miles is now in Europe, and 90 percent of its population lives in Asia. But Turkey's educated population has adopted Ataturk's reforms as the cornerstone of a drive toward a better, more Western future.

Perhaps the most moving description of Atatürk was made by one of the unfortunate military plotters, Major Fethi Gurcan. Sentenced to death in 1963, at his trial Gurcan argued that the country's rulers at the time "deviated from the spirit and idealism of the Kemalist reforms."[4] Before dying, he said:

> It is my belief that Atatürk is not a mere symbol whose vitality and function are exhausted, who is hung on walls and talked about on holidays and anniversaries; nor is he merely a great man to be remembered with feelings of gratitude. He represents an idea, a doctrine, a developing system of government, which can and must be applied to our society. . . . In the face of death and in the presence of God and justice, my conscience is as clear as that of a poet who takes up his pen to write in praise of Atatürk. . . . Atatürk is dead but he has not ceased to exist. I shall now die, but Atatürk's ideas, through my death, will acquire yet higher value.

Those who accuse Atatürk of expanionism should remember that under his rule Turkish territory was not expanded but contracted. Part of this was owing to the realization that Turkey was in no position to acquire more territory; part was a quest to create a solid national monolith, without cumbersome and hostile foreign possessions. But such monoliths are more difficult to create than reforming the alphabet and installing secularism.

There were, understandably, a number of contradictions in the complex personality of Atatürk. In his youth he conformed superficially to the traditions of Islam but regarded religion as a force that held Turkey back. Yet, the soldiers he sent to battle died with the name of Allah on their lips, often carrying the Koran in their rucksacks. Atatürk did not hesitate to use their religious zeal—something they understood better than patriotism—when it suited his grand design.

The complexity of Atatürk's character was, in part, based on his Macedonian origins. Born in Salonika, at the time part of the Ottoman Empire and a throbbing and cosmopolitan city, Atatürk was mesmerized by the nearby West, "with the coldness of her glitter and the price of her wooing."[5] Indeed, he had been wooed by the West since his early youth and throughout his stormy career in the disintegrating army of the last Ottoman sultans. He brooded about his countrymen, their backwardness, their corruption, and the all-embracing mantle of Islam, "which oppressed them and stunted their growth, shutting them off from the more advanced and enlightened ways of the Christian peoples."[6]

Atatürk's reforms, encompassed by the well-known term *Kemalism,* were the guiding light for Evren and his colleagues on the

National Security Council. But while the Gazi* had a clear image of the Turkey that he wanted, in 1982 the generals in Ankara still searched for a specific blueprint that would allow them to restore the country safely to constitutional rule. All they knew was that the previous system had brought Turkey to the brink of catastrophe, and their password was "never again." They wanted reforms, but the first two years of military rule were merely a "wind tunnel," according to Admiral Isik Biren, the NSC's main spokesman.[7] In this respect, they were similar to the 1908 revolutionary Committee of Union and Progress, more commonly known as the Young Turks, who had no specific substitute for the system they opposed.

While after the military takeover the jails were being filled with terrorists and terrorist suspects of all political colors, the martial-law authorities moved to eradicate all signs of activity that had played or could play a destabilizing role. Among the first to go were political slogans, those crudely scribbled initials and signs that disfigured many a Turkish wall in the cities and even in dilapidated villages. Patrols of helmeted troops moved systematically through the streets, splashing thousands of gallons of paint over such slogans as "Dev Sol" (Revolutionary Left) or "Azadi Bo Kurdistan" (Freedom for Kurdistan). It would be safe to say that two months after the coup not a single slogan was intact, at least in the major cities. They were replaced by enormous blotches of white or black paint, depending on the availability of the paint or the color of the graffiti. Turkish paint manufacturers were among the initial beneficiaries of Evren's purification campaign.

The approach to the problem was not as simplistic as it may seem. Without the staring slogans, the banned parties and groups were more likely to pass into oblivion, helped by tough police methods. It was part of the campaign to depoliticize Turkey before allowing any form of political thought to flourish again. Not all was smooth, of course. The military law-enforcement machine, frustrated for so many years under corrupt regimes, did not use an iron fist in any velvet glove. More frequently than not, the fist was of red-hot iron.

In some ways, the paint campaign against political slogans resembled Atatürk's methods for Westernizing Turkey. One of them was his ban of the fez, that colorful headgear that for many years symbolized the Turks to much of the world. To proud and overly

---

*In Turkish Gazi means Victorious Islamic ruler, the title bestowed upon him by the Grand National Assembly during the 1921 war of independence.

sensitive Atatürk, the fez was "backward" and "oriental" and was one of the first things he decided to do away with. It was his fez, worn with his uniform, Ataturk thought, that had caused Sicilian urchins to pelt him with lemon peels. Once in power, he ordered it replaced by the grim cloth cap so familiar to Americans from the photographs of the depression-era breadlines. The Turkish military adopted the standard Western cap with a visor.

The first year of military rule was characterized almost entirely by the "cleansing" of Turkey. Members of the left wing and right wing alike were rounded up under a law that permitted detention for up to three months. They included Necmettin Erbakan, once the "king maker" of Turkish politics and head of the strongly Islamic National Salvation party, and Retired Colonel Alparslan Türkes, founder of the National Action party and its shock troops, the Grey Wolf commandos. The evenhandedness of the generals was impressive indeed, although it soon became evident that they blamed much of the terror that plagued the country on the USSR.

At the end of 1981 Türkes, a former deputy minister, and some 300 followers were on trial for their lives on charges of trying to establish a right-wing dictatorship. In the eastern city of Erzurum more than 500 left-wing militants went before a military tribunal, accused of a violent antistate campaign in that remote region of Turkey near the Iranian and Soviet borders. Most of them were members of the underground organization Dev Yol (Revolutionary Way).

The number of weapons seized during the first seven months of military rule was simply staggering: over 30,000 rifles, 243,000 pistols and revolvers, close to 6,000 automatic weapons, including machine guns, as well as tons of explosives. Once the military tribunals went to work, weapons were quickly abandoned by the thousands by their owners, who did not want to face military justice.

In mid-1982, the military authorities issued even more impressive statistics covering arms seizures from the end of 1978 to April 30, 1982. During that time 86,685 rifles and automatic weapons and no less than 717,486 handguns were seized or found, as well as over 5 million rounds of ammunition of all calibers.

One thing was abundantly clear to the generals: such an arsenal could only have been assembled with outside help. While carefully maintaining reasonably correct relations with their Soviet neighbor, the NSC soon started leaking documents pointing at Soviet subversion. According to the reports made available to some Western embassies, the USSR was said to have spent over 1 billion dollars on weapons and terrorist activities carried out by leftist extremists in Turkey between 1977 and 1980. Most weapons apparently were smuggled in either through Bulgaria or by way of Turkey's Black Sea coast.

The specter of internal and external threat was convincing enough for the generals to justify massive arrests, particularly during the first few months following their seizure of power. Various figures have been quoted as to the number of those held without sufficient proof of illegal activity. It can be assumed, however, that the figure of prisoners either charged or awaiting charges hovered around 33,000 by the end of 1981. They included minor offenders, such as curfew violators or black marketeers. Martial-law authorities initially authorized detention for up to 90 days without charge, but that limit was eventually lowered. In the spring of 1982, more mass trials took place, including that of 248 accused members of Dev Sol in Istanbul and 125 persons described as separatists in the southern city of Adana. Arrests in Istanbul and Ankara included 44 lawyers, journalists, and academics known for their leftist views. The authorities announced in May that 950 suspects were in custody as well as 19,480 detainees and 6,054 convicted terrorists. Those convicted were classified as leftists (51 percent), rightists (14 percent), separatists—meaning Kurds—(5 percent), while 30 percent had no known political affiliation. All told, it is believed that during the first 20 months of martial law, some 100,000 suspects had been through Turkish jails under martial-law regulations.

Under the watchful eye of the retired officers put in charge of Turkey's vast and often cumbersome administrative apparatus, the country acquired a different look. Policemen trimmed their often unkempt mustaches; there were unprecedented seizures of drugs smuggled across Turkey from the Golden Crescent (Afghanistan, Pakistan, and Iran); even traffic in the cities moved in a more orderly fashion. The purification campaign extended to entertainment and pornography. In Adana, the martial-law command banned semipornographic films and nude photographs on the grounds that they were "against our customs and traditions and against the structure of the Turkish family." Transvestite actors were hauled out of Istanbul's dingy cabarets and deported to obscure villages. An exception was made for one of the most popular singers, Bülent Ersoy, who underwent surgery to change sex. But Ersoy had to promise that "I will wear normal clothes while practising my art and will not indulge in acts and manners which would offend the eye."

Turkey's Western European partners were increasingly unhappy. They wanted to see a democratic Turkey, not a country ruled by stern generals. While warnings and threats of suspending aid multiplied, Turkish reaction was predictable. To quote Evren at a public rally in November 1981, "If we are pressured from abroad we may tell them to keep their aid to themselves, that we can manage with our own resources." Replying to charges by Amnesty International that torture was practiced in Turkish jails, Evren snapped, "Where was this organization before September [1980] when 20 to 30 people were losing their lives daily?" Nonetheless, the authorities did admit the possibility of brutality by police and the paramilitary *jandarma,* and investigations were launched.

Eventually, the authorities acknowledged 15 deaths in prison, which apparently occurred during interrogations (compared to Amnesty International's figure of 70). Reacting sharply to Western criticism, Ankara stopped visits to Turkey by officials of the 21-nation Council of Europe, a Strasbourg-based consultative organization. In March 1982 Leo Tindemans, at the time chairman of the European Economic Community (EEC) council of ministers, personally conveyed to the generals the community's concern over arrests and torture accusations. Evren responded on April 4th by confirming his determination to go ahead with plans for a new constitution and rejecting any outside interference. "The new constitution will prohibit communism, fascism and a theocratic regime," he said. "We will not leave any unsolved problems behind."[8] There was also a stern warning to the country's former politicians: "They should stop having fantasies. The nation has liberated itself from them and does not want to be led by the same persons. If they do not find this warning sufficient, we will not hesitate to take very strong and severe measures."[9]

One of the leading victims of this policy was Ecevit, head of the disbanded Republican People's party (RPP) and three times premier. In October 1981 Ecevit distributed stinging criticism of the military regime in a statement to foreign newsmen. "In view of my own conception of democracy, I cannot bring myself to approve the present mode of administration in Turkey or the regime that is being stipulated for Turkey by the current administration," the poet-politician wrote, adding a somewhat oblique statement that "one should categorically refrain from behavior which can be construed as a stand against the army, because the army is the army of us all."[10]

The statement clearly violated the martial-law regulations imposed by the junta. Ecevit was sentenced to four months in jail (of which he only served two), a sentence upheld by Ankara martial-law authorities. The sentencing and jailing caused a predictable chorus of criticism from Western European sociodemocrats, who saw in it yet another sign of military oppression.

European displeasure was followed by suspension of EEC economic aid to Turkey, a gesture which basically showed ignorance of Evren's aims and of his country's political and psychological makeup. Evren could not have overlooked Ecevit's violation of the law, albeit imposed by the military. To have done so would have shown weakness, and Turkey has rarely pardoned weak rulers.

But Ecevit remained undaunted, or, as one Western diplomat put it, "apparently bent on martyrdom." In April 1982 he was accused by martial-law authorities of twice violating a decree banning former politicians from commenting on past, present, or future government policies. According to the prosecution, he had made false statements in an interview with Dutch television and in an article for the West German magazine, *Der Spiegel.* He was placed in Manak military prison pending trial. If convicted, he could face five years in prison. Again there was a predictable outcry in the West, which did not help the image of Evren and his colleagues. Ecevit, editorialized *The Washington Post* (April 15), "is no terrorist of the sort whose depredations forced the generals to seize power in 1980. He is a certified democrat, humanist and lover of liberty, the single Turk who most represents the values Turks share with the West."

Turkey's rulers received a welcome and badly needed shot in the arm from the United States in December 1981, when Secretary of Defense Weinberger visited Ankara. It was not only the decision to set up joint military groups to "enlarge and improve defense cooperation" that pleased the Turks; it was psychologically even more important that Weinberger made a statement expressing admiration for the reestablishment of law and order in Turkey. He elaborated that "we feel Turkey first of all embarked upon the course that will bring it a democratic government. They have many of those principles in effect now and are working very diligently to secure a new constitution."

Weinberger was supported by Secretary of State Haig in May 1982, when, after a two-day Ankara visit, he spoke warmly of "my friend Evren" and praised Turkey's economic recovery, its security effort, and its timetable for a return to constitutional rule.

The process to which Weinberger and Haig referred consisted mainly of the creation of the consultative assembly. There was little doubt that the assembly was hand-picked by the military. The candidates had to be over 30 years of age and have some form of higher education (being a retired officer apparently was considered as such). The NSC directly named 40 members; the others were selected from among Turkey's provinces, their dossiers carefully studied. All former politicians were banned from participation in this group of "fresh blood and new faces."

In addition to drafting the constitution, the assembly was to prepare a new electoral law as well as a law governing the formation and functioning of political parties. As expected, the initial draft prepared by the assembly invested sweeping powers in the president to the detriment of those of parliament. Elected for seven years by the one-chamber assembly of 400 members, the president would be the supreme arbiter, with the authority to suspend personal freedoms, and dissolve parliament if he deemed it necessary. Assembly members would be elected for five years. To facilitate discussion on the draft, two martial law decrees banning public political debate were lifted. Almost immediately, the constitution project was criticized by the left as giving the president excessive powers, limiting personal freedoms of the citizens as well as the right of association that would affect political parties and trade unions. The constitution draft of some 200 articles clearly specified that political parties with communist, fascist, or Islamic links would not be allowed. There were persistent reports that a new Kemalist party was going to be launched, strongly linked with the military establishment.

Evren himself remained cryptic about his own intentions, although it was generally believed that he would be the first president under the new system. To news correspondents who questioned him about plans to run for president, he kept replying, "I will do whatever the nation wants." Of his reaction to Western European criticism of the assembly's composition and its overall military supervision, Evren commented, "We have presented a program and we have said we would return to the democratic system within this program. . . . Years ago the Turkish nation adopted a parliamentary system which suited its own needs, and not those of foreign countries. . . . Now we are looking for a new system of the kind we need. We are moving step by step and we are making progress."[11]

To much of the world, Turkey appeared to be in step behind the junta. Foreigners familiar with the country were much less perturbed by the all-pervasive military grip than Western sociodemocrats, who looked at Turkey according to different values and concepts—and from a considerable distance. Former U.S. ambassador to Turkey, James Spain, believed that "the present efforts, seemingly undemocratic, might in the end bring back democracy."[12]

There was little popular pressure within Turkey itself to speed up the process. One reason was that political activity was banned, but what perhaps mattered more to the average Turk was a new sense of security. Mothers stopped worrying about sending children to school;

wives did not panic when husbands were late from work. To a nation harrassed by terror for so many years, the military regime represented, above all, peace and order.

The regime was particularly sensitive about any comparison to the state of martial law imposed in Poland on December 13, 1981. The Polish generals acted to stop the budding movement of freedom to safeguard the discredited Communist party committed to Moscow's interests. The clandestine opposition and rioting which followed the imposition of Polish martial law were outspoken demonstrations of general hostility. In Turkey the military stepped in to stop national slaughter, which successive democratic governments had been unable to prevent. Their harsh measures against the politicians had widespread backing, at least during the first two years of their rule.

There was seemingly very little of the iron-fisted, autocratic dictator in Evren, who was put in power because, as he himself said, "I happened to be chief of staff and such was the verdict of the nation." Within a few months of being invested by his uniformed colleagues with the country's supreme powers, Evren had become a well-known figure as he toured the country by helicopter, visiting the wind-swept villages of Anatolia in his first-hand attempt at popularity. True, the gatherings were held in check by green-uniformed police with white pistol holsters, duly cleaned up after the coup. But the police did not need to intervene. To men in tattered pseudo-Western suits and heavy cloth caps and to women in flowery dresses holding up children, Evren was the man who stopped terrorism. "Don't bring the politicians back," they shouted at him in November 1980 in Corlu, Corum, Tuzlam, Gölcük, and Eskişehir. The demonstrations were not staged, although the turnout most certainly must have been encouraged; certainly the presence of the crowds close to the ribbon-bedecked chest of the *orgeneral* was an easy target for a terrorist's bullet.

In the clichéd language of many Western newspapers, Evren soon became a father figure. That highly flattering image was inevitably tarnished by the prolongation of military rule and by the no-nonsense treatment of terrorist suspects, curfew violators, and former politicians, such as Ecevit.

As the military rule neared the end of its second year, Evren was still, on the whole, a benign dictator. More often than not he acted not so much as leader but as spokesman for the National Security Council. True, his consultative assembly was a tame and carefully screened body that was unlikely to challenge the military regime, even if given the opportunity. But history has not recorded Evren as having the same outspoken contempt for parliamentarians as that demonstrated by his illustrious mentor, Atatürk. To the Gazi, the Grand National Assembly was often a "zoo."

Evren was a Western general, carefully combining the military lore acquired from abroad with his deep-rooted Turkish traditions. Atatürk did not hesitate to divorce, by decree, his wife, Latife, the woman who raised her admiring eyes to the face of the conqueror of Smyrna (Izmir), illuminated by the flames of the burning city abandoned by the Greeks. Evren had no need for personal fiats or conquests by fire. Yet, Atatürk has passed into history as a courageous reformer with a vision, the founder of the republic. History—at least Western history— is not likely to be so kind to Evren.

U.S. concern about the stability and economic viability of Turkey was based mainly on that country's importance to NATO and as home of six major and 21 smaller U.S. military facilities, manned in 1982 by an estimated 5,000 U.S. servicemen. The facilities include Incirlik air base near Adana, perhaps the closest runway to the Middle East, where the United States maintains a squadron of F–4 fighters said to have nuclear capability. However, Incirlik is primarily a NATO base, and Turkish permission is needed to use it for other tasks. The base has been stocked with an array of equipment and spare parts and could play a vital role in the event of any Middle East emergency. Its primary task, however, is deterrence against the USSR.

Under the 1980 agreement, the United States also had access to Turkish air force facilities at Esenboga (near Ankara) and Cigil (near Izmir) but only in time of war. At Kargaburun, on the Sea of Marmara, the U.S. Navy has a station to assist naval units through long-range electronic radio-navigational devices. At Sinop, on the Black Sea, there is a highly sensitive intelligence base monitoring large parts of the USSR. Near Diyarbakir, in southeastern Turkey, an important long-range radar and communications complex exists, where a support air base is located. Near the capital of Ankara, at Belbasi, the United States maintains a seismographic detection base.

There are also various storage depots, including one at Iskenderun, where an estimated 20 percent of the fuel used by the Sixth Fleet is kept. Other facilities consist of ammunition dumps; 14 early-warning radar sites, operated mainly by Turkish personnel on behalf of NATO; and 20 defense communications system sites, also working for NATO.

These installations, scattered throughout the country from the Black Sea to the Syrian border, keep an electronic eye on the USSR and its Black Sea fleet and provide an infrastructure in the event of conflict. Under surveillance are the activities of the Soviet Baikonur cosmodrome near Leninsk, the nuclear testing ground at Semipalatinsk, and the missile launching pad at Kapustin Yar. The loss of intelligence-gathering facilities in neighboring Iran has made the Turkish ones even more vital.

The effectiveness of the military coup of 1980 lay in the popularity of the Turkish armed forces as a national institution. Few other countries have such a profound respect for the military uniform. One only had to watch a parade through Ankara's broad boulevards following the landing in Cyprus in 1974 to realize the enormity of the army's prestige. Many men and women had tears of joy in their eyes; they applauded the precise march of the troops, particularly of the crack commandos flown from Cyprus for the occasion. The crowds knew little about that fumbling operation, the intricacies of faulty intelligence, and the other flaws in its planning. All they saw were Turkish troops returning from a victorious war.

The Cyprus intervention apart, it should be stressed that the modern Turkish army has a reputation as a tough combat force, known for the endurance and discipline of the common soldier. It proved itself during the World War I Gallipoli campaign, in the subsequent "war of liberation" against Greece, and, 30 years later, by the performance of the Turkish contingent in Korea. Led by devoted and underpaid cadres, the armed forces are an institution above suspicion in Turkey, despite their political plotting as far back as the Young Turks. But the plotting was mainly against inefficiency and corruption and in favor of democracy. In fact, all reformist movements in Turkey were started and carried out by the military. They included two coups (1960 and 1971), after which the troops returned to barracks, frustrated at their inability to carry out profound changes.

The aura of the military can, perhaps, be graced to the inner Turkish nostalgia for power, exercised for so many centuries over vast portions of land by the Ottoman sultans. Be that as it may, the army is not a retrogressive but a dynamic force, an educational institution, where illiterate conscripts are taught to read and write as well as the first elements of patriotism. "One Turk is worth the whole world!" roar recruits with shaven heads at morning parade. This approach is perhaps naive, but it appears to work.

Few foreigners have understood the somewhat contrary role played by the Turkish military, "the watchdog of Kemalism" with a "genuine passion for democracy."[13] Born out of the tattered remnants of the defeated Ottoman armies, honed during the vicious campaign for the consolidation of modern Turkey, the army is unquestionably the country's pride. "I am not ordering you to attack, I am ordering you to die," wrote Atatürk in an order of the day before the 57th Turkish Infantry Regiment charged the Australian-New Zealand Army Corps (ANZACs) during the Gallipoli campaign in 1915. Indeed, almost the entire regiment was wiped out, winning immortality in Turkish military history,

In 1982 the Turkish armed forces consisted of 556,000 men in the three services and were the second largest in NATO, after those of the United States. Their weakness was obsolete equipment, Korean War heavy weapons, and psychological scars on the cadres caused by the disastrous U.S. arms embargo imposed between 1975 and 1978, a response to the use of U.S. arms in the Cyprus operation.

When the embargo was lifted, a Western report described the Turkish air force as barely "50 percent operational" and most of the navy's ships—World War II British and U.S. hand-me-downs—as a "year beyond the scrapyard stage."[14] The army was capable of police-type operations in the imposition of martial law; of limited actions, such as in Cyprus; but little more. Two months after the military takeover, the situation had changed little. A U.S. report claimed that "basically the Turkish armed forces are in such a state that they do not fulfill their NATO role. . . . The problem is how to maintain a NATO-standard force in a poor country. Turkey, at this point, manages to feed and clothe its armed forces but hardly more."[15]

In the winter of 1981, the Turks invited a group of foreign observers to watch maneuvers of the Third Army along the sensitive "silent frontier" with the USSR. Vintage tanks rolled through snowdrifts; officers, drinking tea from small cups, watched the precision fire of howitzers; a young infantryman had an aching tooth extracted in a makeshift open-air clinic before stupefied foreigners. In the view of Western specialists, the exercise went well—according to 1950 standards. The Third Army, according to some Western diplomatic reports, "lacked almost everything—modern tanks, antitank weapons, even field radio sets."[16]

Throughout 1981 intense negotiations went on between the Turkish government and several NATO countries, mainly the United States and the Federal Republic of Germany (FRG). The issue was how to modernize the Turkish military machine at the lowest possible cost—a formidable task, given that a complete modernization, in the eyes of U.S. specialists, would cost between 10 and 15 billion dollars. No country in the world—or group of countries—were prepared to spend that kind of money on Turkish defenses, regardless of their role in NATO. The United States also invoked the limited Turkish "absorption capability"; to introduce new weapons systems, a whole new infrastructure was needed. The average Turkish soldier, while perfectly capable of carrying out strenuous tasks, lacked the appropriate educational background to handle the more sophisticated weapons.

Consequently, it looked as though Turkey had to settle for the phasing out of the old M–47 tanks and the conversion of M–48 to diesel engines and their "upgunning" from 90 mm. to 105 mm. cannon. Even then, the Turks would still have old tanks, likely to be under fire before reaching assault positions. There were strong indications that several hundred U.S. M–60 tanks would be forthcoming, and an advance consignment of the promised 200 West German Leopards reportedly arrived in the latter part of 1981.

For some years U.S. military experts argued that the Turks should considerably reduce their tank force of some 3,500 in favor of cheaper and more useful units of mobile antitank missiles. The Turkish generals appeared reluctant to get rid of their heavy armor— a formidable weapon on parade and against unruly mobs but not against a modern assault force. Still, it looked as though a compromise had been reached.

The Turks were making a strong bid to have a self-sustaining defense industry. At the end of 1981, the United States was helping in the production in Turkey of several types of weapon and military equipment. In November of that year, Turkey and Pakistan decided to develop a joint defense industry, with self-sufficiency as the ultimate aim—something that Western observers seriously doubt despite Pakistan's comparatively advanced military technology. Another reform concerned the Turkish navy, with the United States pressing for the replacement of World War II warships with smaller and cheaper missile-equipped patrol vessels. The Turkish air force—by far the most modern branch of the armed forces—started receiving U.S.-made F–4s from several NATO countries, who were replacing them with F–16s. The Turkish general staff designated the air force as top priority in the modernization program.

Despite its technical obsolescence, the Turkish army was still regarded by the West as a deterrent, particularly in the rugged area along the Soviet frontier. "They would fall back but fall back fighting," according to one U.S. specialist.[17] Indeed, there was little doubt that the Turkish soldier would fight and die if ordered to do so. Every Turkish officer is taught Atatürk's famous order of the day of the War of Liberation: "The whole country is a defense area. Not an inch of it is to be given up until it is wet with Turkish blood. Any unit, large or small, may be thrown out of its position. But it will face the enemy and continue to fight. . . ."[18]

At the beginning of 1982 the Turkish army consisted of some 400,000 men, grouped in 17 divisions and 19 independent brigades. The air force had nearly 400 combat planes. The navy included 16 submarines, 13 destroyers, two frigates, and a number of support ships and smaller craft—a total of 183 vessels. The ground forces were grouped in four land armies, of which one (the Third Army) was deployed along the Soviet frontier; one, known as the Army of the Aegean, faced the Greek islands hugging Turkey's coastline. The air force had a tactical air command, air training command, and various support units. The navy was divided into a northern and southern naval command, submarine fleet command, and landing units command, the latter concentrated mainly in the Aegean and at the southern naval base of Mersin.

Despite Atatürk's sweeping reforms, aimed at changing Turkey into a Western nation, the country's origins, religion, and location have kept it to some extent a part of the Middle East. Turkey may officially be considered a part of Europe, but few Europeans regard it as such. While no one disputes the historic scope of Kemalism, few nations can undergo a really profound transformation in the space of 50-odd years. Many Turkish intellectuals have found it extremely frustrating to demonstrate their European vocation, particularly in the face of rebukes by the EEC. Turkey's hope for EEC membership before the end of the century was a source of acute embarrassment— almost a nightmare—to many Eurocrats. Torn by internecine quarrels over such issues as farm subsidies, the price of butter, and preferential treatment for the former colonies of member nations, the community was hardly in a position to throw its doors wide open to yet another poor member. Turkey's economic ills appeared daunting, and jails packed with terrorists and curfew violators were an unlikely recommendation for membership in the European club.

The EEC clearly saw Turkey as a major risk, a financial drain, and a source of endless problems. When, in 1963, an agreement of association between Turkey and the EEC was signed. Walter Hallstein, at the time president of the European Commission, said, "Turkey is part of Europe. This means that Turkey is establishing a constitutional relationship with the European Community." This resounding phrase was soon conveniently forgotten or at least hardly mentioned. The Turks themselves provided the EEC with an excuse to shelve the unpleasant issue: Turkey was hardly in a position to push for EEC membership while under military rule.

But the fact that Greece became a full member on January 1, 1981, rankled Ankara. Greece was the traditional foe; its economy was not dramatically different from Turkey's. While the Turks had some hope of overcoming European reluctance before 1980, it all but evaporated with Greek membership. After all, Turkish exports of fruit, vegetables, cotton, olive oil, and wine would duplicate those of Greece (and of two other prospective Mediterranean members, Spain and Portugal). In 1981 three was a distinct feeling in Ankara that the 626,000 Turkish workers in Western Europe (over 2 million including their families) would eventually be squeezed out of that lucrative labor market. The economic recession of that period did not help, and the imposition of visas on Turks by a number of Western European countries was seen as a slap in the proud Turkish face.

On the other hand, the Arab East, once a part of the Ottoman Empire, loomed more and more enticing. The Arabs did not have to court anyone; they were being courted (prior to the 1982 oil glut). They controlled a good portion of one of the world's most coveted commodities: oil. While Western Europe heaped criticism on the Turkish military rulers and threatened economic sanctions, the Arabs and other Islamic countries remained discreetly silent. After all, their own political systems were not that different.

Thus, a reassessment of Turkey's orientation and links appeared inevitable. It did not automatically imply a reduced role within NATO, although such threats were made by the government headed by Ecevit in the mid-1970s. Evren and his generals were too deeply committed to the idea of the West and its defenses to even contemplate it, despite such Western actions as the punitive U.S. arms embargo. What Turkey is likely to do as time goes by is to increase its trade and cultural relations with the Islamic countries and reduce its reliance on Western Europe. There appears to be no valid substitute for Turkey's military dependence on the United States and NATO.

The stronger pro-Arab orientation was inevitably accompanied by the cooling of Turkey's relations with Israel. In the summer of 1979, the Palestine Liberation Organization (PLO) opened an office in Ankara. The PLO mission soon became a vocal and influential diplomatic force in the Turkish capital. At the same time, the Israeli embassy was reduced to a barely acceptable minimum of two low-ranking diplomats, a move regretted by many Turkish intellectuals. In a formal statement, Turkey's permanent representative at the United Nations said that "any efforts at finding a solution to the Middle Eastern problem without the PLO are bound to be meaningless."

While warning about a Soviet buildup along the 370-mile border, Turkish generals were much more discrete in discussing growing U.S. military contingency plans for the Middle East. At least in public, the rulers in Ankara scoffed at any suggestion that bases in Turkey might be used as transit points or back-up facilities for the Rapid Deployment Force (RDF) in the Persian Gulf. The reasons were fairly obvious: Turkey did not want to harm its improving relations with the Arab world, having succeeded to a large degree in overcoming the residue of Ottoman colonialism. The joining by Turkey in the Islamic Conference in 1968 was an important step. What was more significant was that Turkey, a nation committed to Kemalist secularism, appeared to be putting a greater accent on Islam while keeping it in check at home. Thus, during a visit to Pakistan in late November 1981, General Evren called for "greater cooperation among members of the Islamic Conference," with Turkey and Pakistan playing a "more effective role" in that organization. The statement, which caused a flurry of excitement among Ankara's foreign diplomats, was seen as an effort to woo the Islamic world while keeping the domestic Muslim militants in Turkey reasonably happy.

Evren and Pakistani leader Zia ul-Haq have a lot in common. Both are generals who have been criticized in the West for their right-wing tendencies; both rely on U.S. aid; both are leaders of countries bordering on revolutionary Iran; and both are equally concerned about Soviet involvement in Afghanistan. Consequently, it was not surprising when they announced plans for military cooperation, including the creation of a joint weapons industry. Turkey was clearly "hedging its bets." Having found a difficult partner in Western Europe, it was looking for solace in Southwest Asia and, to some extent, in the Middle East.

The Middle Eastern connection was mainly economic, and its increase was impressive. Turkish construction firms have moved in force into such Arab countries as Libya and to a lesser extent into Syria, Iraq, Tunisia, and Jordan. At the end of 1981 the value of construction contracts in Libya alone was 6 billion dollars, with forecasts of 10 billion by 1983. In 1982 Turkey expected to sell Iraq 800 million dollars worth of goods, compared to 559 million in 1981.

A number of Turkish economists felt that Turkey, the historic link between Europe and Asia, could carve a solid niche for itself in the growing and frequently lucrative Arab market. While Turkish finished products are not competitive in Western Europe, they are perfectly acceptable in Arab countries. With proper marketing and transportation techniques, Turkey could easily become the Middle

East's major supplier of fruit and vegetables. In the early 1980s, Turkey also emerged as a serious supplier of skilled and semiskilled labor for Arab countries, with over 100,000 Turkish workers on short-term contracts. But while the Turkish *Gastarbeiter* in Western Europe tend to settle down with their families where they work and repatriate barely one-fourth of their earnings, those who work in the Middle East send the bulk home. The growing number of Turkish workers in the Arab Middle East has thus become an important source of badly needed foreign currency.

The Turkish economic push into the Arab world was accompanied by a diplomatic effort, including the strengthening of existing missions and the opening of new ones, particularly in the Persian Gulf area. By all indications, it was a healthy move, bound to improve the country's economic posture and diplomatic leeway. However, only time will tell whether closer bonds with such strongly Islamic countries as Libya or Saudi Arabia will have any impact on Turkey's own religious scene. While the strength of Islam in Turkey should not be underestimated, there was no evidence that it threatened the secular nature of the state. While some Arab countries would like to see stronger religious fervor in Turkey, there were no signs of any pressure or conditions tied to various loans or economic agreements.

It would be erroneous to pretend that Turkey, a nation of 45 million or perhaps more (current figures are unavailable at this writing), is a monolith. It may try to present such an image to the outside world, but inside there are serious sectarian and, to some extent, national rifts. In a country where 98% of the population adheres to Islam, the sectarian feud pits the Sunnis against the Shiites (known in Turkey as Alevis). On the surface the difference of the question of succession to the Prophet Muhammad may seem petty. Over the centuries, however, other differences have developed, making the Alevis in some areas of Turkey a people very much apart, generally less affluent than the majority Sunnis. Inevitably, the differences involve politics, with the Alevis tending to lean to the left. This was one of the causes of the sectarian explosion in the city of Kahramanmaras in December 1978, which forced the government of then Premier Ecevit to impose martial law on 13 of the country's 67 provinces.

The national rift centers mainly on the Kurds, that unhappy nation-tribe of 16 million divided among Turkey, Iraq, Iran, and Syria. Their late leader, Mulla Mustafa Barzani, called them the orphans of the universe. Their numerous rising have been drowned in blood in Iraq, Iran, and Turkey. The closests the Kurds have come to having a country of their own was in 1920, when the Treaty of Sèvres (by which the Western powers intended to dismember Turkey) provided for a Kurdistan in the predominantly Kurdish areas. Atatürk abrogated the treaty, and three Kurdish uprisings (in 1925, 1931, and 1937) were mercilessly stamped out.

Today *Kurd* does not appear in the official Turkish vocabulary, just *mountain Turk.* The ban on the printing of the Kurdish language and the overall restriction on Kurdish cultural traditions have not destroyed the indomitable spirit of the Kurds; in fact, it continues to fuel it against almost impossible odds. General Evren's regime followed the attitude of his predecessors by turning down all Kurdish autonomist claims. "All separatist tendencies will be stamped out without mercy," Evren said in May 1981. At that time the centuries-old "wound of Kurdistan" was opened again in the bleak mountains of eastern Turkey. After a spate of terrorist attacks by Kurdish nationalists, the local Kurdish leadership was decapitated, and hundreds were arrested. In the city of Diyarbakir, a total of 447 Kurds went on trial by martial-law authorities on charges of terrorism, subversion, and efforts to set up a separate Kurdish state "along Marxist lines." Over 2,000 other Kurds awaited interrogation in crowded jails (125 of them went on trial in Adana in the spring of 1982).

Yet, the bulk of the people in what is known as the Kurdish belt welcomed the military takeover, which ended more than three years of bloodshed, turmoil, and political quarreling. Evren himself was at first greeted with applause as he descended from his helicopter in the miserable Kurdish villages. But Evren is a Turkish nationalist and, like many other Turks, regards the Kurdish problem as potential dynamite in the Turkish republic. It appears highly unlikely that major concessions will be made to the Kurds.

This does not mean that the Turkish state opposes Kurdish assimilation—quite to the contrary. There have been Kurdish judges, cabinet ministers, and members of parliament. There has been some intermarriage but mainly in the urban centers, where ethnic Kurds rarely use their native language. The problem exists mainly in the rural, poverty-stricken areas, where a dozen nationalist Kurdish organizations have been exploiting the frustration caused by poverty and suppression of the Kurdish heritage. Some of these organizations demand an independent Kurdistan, an elusive aim. Many would settle for a form of autonomy, and others would simply like free Kurdish cultural expression.

The Turkish authorities do not recognize the Kurds as a minority. According to the official version, the minorities are "Greeks, Armenians and Jews who benefit not only from the rights of minorities assigned to them in the treaty of Lausanne (1923) but also from all rights and freedoms accorded them by the laws which apply to Turkish citizens."[19] Indeed, the Turkish Jews have few complaints about discrimination. The attitude toward Greeks has already been discussed. The Armenian problem continued to haunt the Turkish leadership in the early 1980s, harming the country's international prestige. Since 1975, attacks by Armenian nationalists trying to avenge the 1915 massacres have been decimating the ranks of Turkish diplomats in foreign capitals. The issue is mired in accusations and denials, surrounded by a web of intrigue involving alleged Greek and Soviet interference, and kept alive by fierce Armenian nationalism, which refuses to forgive or forget.

It is not the object of this study to analyze the causes of a problem now a part of history. The Armenians claim that over a million men, women, and children were killed in World War I massacres by the Turks. The Turks admit the loss of some 200,000 Armenian lives during a forcible resettlement of the Armenian minority in Ottoman-occupied Syria. Whatever the facts, the issue is very much alive after the military takeover and perhaps even gaining in intensity. By early 1982, 21 Turkish diplomats abroad had been killed in precision attacks by Armenian terrorists. The underground Secret Army for the Liberation of Armenia claimed 51 attacks against Turkish lives and property between 1976 and 1981. A manifesto distributed in Turkey and abroad said, "The period of meaningless and naive hope has come to an end. The crucial hour has arrived for the Armenian people to prove that they are still the masters of their destiny as well as of human dignity."[20] Perhaps the boldest and bloodiest attack by the Secret Army inside Turkey took place on August 7, 1982, at Ankara's Esenboga airport. Two Armenian nationalists hurled a grenade into the departure lounge and sprayed the passengers with submachine gun fire. All told nine persons were killed—including one of the attackers—and 74 were wounded. Security forces brought an end to the carnage. The Armenian terror campaign caused a predictable, almost hysterical, reaction on the part of the Turkish media. A typical example was a column by Levon Panos Dabagyan, obviously of Armenian origin, writing in *Son Havadis*. "Read this, you degenerate pseudo-Armenians," said the headline, followed by rather contradictory statements. "I have nothing to tell you at all because you are not worth talking to. Not even detailed medical tests can discern the generation, the race or the demonic order you belong to. You are the sons of basest creatures belonging to no race. . . . It is for this reason that I do not have a single word to spend on such brainless creatures."[21] The article continued in this vein for about 600 words.

There were in 1982 an estimated 40,000 to 50,000 Armenians living in Turkey, compared to 1,250,000 under the Ottoman Empire in 1882 (according to official Turkish statistics). Many of them have become assimilated, and very few openly demonstrated any nationalistic tendencies. The Turkish system, Article 12 of the 1961 constitution notwithstanding, does not lend itself to militant nationalism other than Turkish.*

While the Armenian problem can be contained and controlled, at least within the boundaries of Turkey, the religious rift is far more complex and elusive. No one knows the exact number of Alevis. The most frequently quoted figures are between five and eight million or, at most, one-sixth of the population. Some Western scholars of Turkey claimed there could be as many as 15 million Alevis, a figure impossible to verify. The Alevis frequently conceal adherence to their sect on the basis of *tagiye*, a concept allowing for their anonymity. Not all, of course, are anonymous. In such areas of Turkey as the mountain chain stretching from Bingöl through Elâziğ, Malatya down to Kahramanmaras, many villages are divided into Sunni and Alevi portions. Many Sunnis regard the Alevis as heretics, what with their mysticism, which includes bits of Christianity and shamanism brought by the Turkmen from Central Asia. The Alevis frequently do not go to mosques but have prayer meetings. This in itself exacerbates their separatism.

The world became aware of the Turkish sectarian conflict during the bloody 1978 Kahramanmaras clashes, which killed 108 persons and destroyed 210 primitive homes. The victims were mainly Alevis who had drifted from the countryside to the comparatively affluent city near the Syrian border. As the cause and effect of the rioting had considerable impact on subsequent developments in Turkey, it deserves more than a passing mention.

Kahramanmaras sprawls around a hill dominated by an ancient castle. It has two distinct quarters: the relatively prosperous one inhabited by the Sunnis and a collection of miserable Alevi shacks in an area known as Yorukselim. On the nearby highway leading toward Syria, heavy trucks with Bulgarian and Yugoslav license plates rumble by. Brown water cascades from the mountains dotted with shrubs

---

*Article 12 specifies that "all individuals are equal before law, irrespective of language, race, sex, political opinion, philosophical views, or religion or religious sect."

and sturdy local pine. In the winter the only touches of color are the red roofs over houses in need of repair.

The Sunni quarter has shops stacked with local goods; garages and the main boulevard bear Atatürk's name. The Alevi part is a rabbit warren of narrow alleys infested with refuse, stalked by mangy dogs and skeletal cats. The town's Sunni majority always resented the newcomers—heretics to boot. This feeling was easily exploited by the subsequently banned National Action party (NAP) of Retired Colonel Türkes. (Ironically, Türkes's Grey Wolf commandos, who had clamored for military rule, were among the first victims of the 1980 takeover; hundreds of them were rounded up and put on trial.)

When, on December 20, 1978, three Sunni pupils of a Kahramanmaras secondary school were dismissed for disciplinary reasons, two Alevi teachers were assassinated the following day. The funerals started a chain of events, pitting Turk against Turk. Children's skulls were crushed against the walls; fires were set indiscriminately to Alevi houses. "Kill them! Kill the heretics! Kill the communists! Kill the devils!" a Sunni *imam* (priest) shouted through a loudspeaker as mobs rampaged through the city. (The impoverished Alevis lean politically to the left; hence, the epithet "communists.")

It took an estimated 15,000 Turkish troops, including crack commando units, to restore order in the city. Many of the 1,000-odd wounded were flown by helicopter to nearby Gaziantep. When I reached Kahramanmaras, it resembled an armed camp. Steel-helmeted troops patrolled the streets, pelted by rain mixed with snow. Soldiers manning roadblocks searched every car, every bus, every passenger. A dusk-to-dawn curfew froze all life in the city. Under strong political and military pressure, Ecevit had to clamp martial law on 13 provinces inhabited by one-third of Turkey's population. This was later extended to 16 provinces but did not spare the country from intensified strife between political factions.

Six months after the Kahramanmaras rioting, 807 men, women, and teenagers sat on uncomfortable iron chairs inside a sports stadium in the southern Turkish wheat-belt city of Adana. The area was surrounded by a ring of blue-bereted paratroopers in splotched camouflage uniforms. Behind a long table facing the crowd, six army judges painstakingly went through the indictment, consisting of 240 pages, charging "armed insurrection and massacre." The press called it Turkey's trial of the century.

It was the trial of Turkish reality, which was leading the country toward the brink of civil war. The accused themselves represented Turkey in microcosm; they included shopkeepers, construction workers, and mule drivers. Two were deaf mutes; almost half were illiterate. The prosecution demanded death sentences for 350 of them, including 10 mothers who had 40 children among them. In the end only 22 were sentenced to death. As, under Turkish law, parliament has to approve each death sentence, dissolution of the legislature in September 1980 postponed the executions. A total of 411 persons were acquitted, 14 were sentenced to life imprisonment, and others received lesser sentences.

During that period Iran was swept by Islamic revolutionary hysteria, with shock waves approaching Turkey. But those Western correspondents looking for a Turkish Khomeini were wasting their time. The religious issue does exist, but it explodes only in conjunction with social and political problems. The military takeover dealt an enormous blow to the tension, without, however, eliminating its roots. Still, as long as the Kemalist Turkish army controls the country, no religious riots are likely and no Turkish imam can electrify mobs to fight for an Islamic state.

On the whole sociologists feel that religion was only a secondary issue in the tension that exploded in Kahramanmaras. They tend to blame the events on the uncontrolled drift to the cities, which trebled the urban population between 1968 and 1978, leading to the creation of mushrooming shantytowns known throughout Turkey as *gecekondu.*

The *gecekondu* (the term literally means built overnight) are the bane of modern Turkey. The collections of shacks, often built from old crates, oil drums, and discarded metal sheets, now surround nearly every major city. They spread out into the polluted industrial wasteland, constantly swelled by a mass of landless peasants drifting to the cities in search of employment. In early 1982, the inhabitants of the gecekondu constituted about one-half of Turkey's urban population of 18 million.

If the present birthrate of 2.4 percent—among the highest in the world—is maintained, Turkey will have 87 million people by the end of this century. The population of Istanbul alone is expected to surpass that of the whole of Greece. Comforting as it may seem to the believers of Pan–Turanism (a movement to unite all Turkish-speaking people in the world, with the ultimate aim of creating a "greater Turkey"), the very idea is an economist's nightmare. It means that the gecekondu population would automatically double, creating disease-breeding belts swarming with miserable humanity around all the urban centers.

The gecekondu were blamed to some extent on the terrorist campaign, which had brought Turkey to the brink of civil war and resulted in the military takeover. The shantytowns, surrounded by putrid smells, not only were breeding grounds for despair and political extremism but convenient hideouts for hit-and-run urban guerrilla gangs. Divided into racial and religious ghettoes (according to the origins of their inhabitants), the gecekondu gave shelter to extremists on the run. Weapons and explosives were stored in the maze of alleys, which police rarely penetrated.

While the military rulers succeeded to some extent in depoliticizing the gecekondu, little has been done about the problem itself. The shantytowns have remained, staring the visitor in the eye—a painful reminder of Turkey's poverty. A nation which has not undergone an industrial revolution appears unable to cope with the millions of impoverished peasants attracted by the magnet of the cities, caused to some extent by the government's promise of rapid industrialization in the 1950s. Because Turkish law forbids the destruction of a building with a roof on, the shacks had to be built at night and finished before dawn, when the police would come. Hence the term *gecekondu.*

The original gecekondu dwellers have taken root, building more permanent houses, often with colored walls and tiled roofs. These generation-old settlements have acquired a degree of municipal services, including electricity and sewage. A whole "parallel civilization" was thus created next to the cities, which remain the main employers of the gecekondu dweller. There are artisans and tradesmen who specialize in gecekondu—a suspect and often gruesome world for the average inhabitant of Turkish cities.

The real problem is the new gecekondu, created during the late 1970s. Their inhabitants have had little opportunity to organize themselves, and many are jobless. They are settlements without hope and basic amenities, where many children suffer from rickets and sullen men and women stare at strangers with hostility.

Although the generals who ruled Turkey after 1980 and most sociologists were perfectly aware of the magnitude of the problem and its potential impact, few practical and lasting measures were undertaken. One solution would have been a vigorous birth control program, something that should not have been too difficult in a country accustomed to secularism and, on the whole, not shackled by too many religious taboos. But while preventative measures or sterilization are comparatively easy in industrial Western countries, in Turkey they are much more difficult to carry out. One of the main reasons is a dramatic shortage of trained medical personnel. In 1981 Turkey had only 23,000 physicians (the acceptable minimum for its population would be 60,000) and some 20,000 registered nurses—

one-fourth of the number needed by the hospitals. Nonetheless, in early 1982 the government decided to approve a law authorizing abortion. A similar law proposed in 1978 was blocked in parliament by the small rightist and Islamic parties. However, the military regime had no such constraints. Moreover, legalizing abortion was favored by most educated Turks; the practice had been widespread, mostly in clandestine and unhygienic conditions. According to semi-official estimates in early 1982, every year some half a million Turkish women had abortions, with about 10,000 deaths eventually resulting from complications. The new bill, according to Kaya Kilic-turgay, minister of health, was going to be "more liberal than in any Moslem country and perhaps even in Europe."[22]

Few of the 200,000 children born every year under the corrugated iron roofs of the gecekondu are delivered with the help of a doctor. There are gecekondu midwives, but most babies are born simply with the assistance of neighbors. The child grows up playing on dirt floors, scrambling more often than not in refuse. The monotony of the day is interrupted by the five Moslem prayers boomed by loudspeakers. In the evening the more affluent families gather around a television set, usually the most cherished possession. In the summer, the insides of the shacks are stiflingly hot. During the bitter Turkish winter, temperatures drop below zero and icy winds howl through the many gaping holes in the shacks.

Aside from the glaring poverty of the urban shantytowns, to much of the world, Turkey's economic potential is an unknown quantity. Everybody agrees that the country is rich agriculturally, but marketing and distribution techniques are yet to be worked out. There are deposits of high-grade bituminuous coal along the Black Sea coast, lignite in eastern Thrace, iron in southeastern Turkey, and chrome in several parts of the country. Still the bulk of the Anatolian land mass is yet to be properly surveyed to assess the country's real possibilities. Before this monumental task is carried out, the country will rely mainly on exports of foodstuffs; a variety of finished products, which are attractively designed but rarely meet Western standards; the shipment of goods to and from the Middle East; and, more recently, of quickly developing and increasingly profitable construction projects in several Arab countries. In Western Europe, throughout the 1970s and early 1980s, the image of Turkey was reflected by a mass of Turkish "guest workers," a euphemism covering the westward drift of helpless people unable to find satisfactory employment at home. Their remittances surpassed 2 billion dollars a year ($2.6 billion in 1981), the biggest single Turkish source of foreign currency.

Excluding the "guest workers" and military personnel, Turkey's labor force was estimated in 1982 at over 17 million persons; 60 percent were either employed or semiemployed in the agricultural sector and only 17 percent in industry. Unemployment, as usually defined in the West, has stood at between 20 percent and 26 percent of the labor force for much of the recent decade.

The turmoil, which reached its peak in the summer of 1980, was closely interlocked with the economic scene. It is hard to establish which came first: political and sectarian extremism or the economic decline. The whole created a daunting combination. Labor unions had become highly politicized; strikes and power cuts plagued industry, which at times operated at 50 percent capacity. Before the military takeover, the inflation rate passed the 100 percent mark. While in a relatively rich agricultural country such as Turkey no home-grown produce was ever lacking, a drastic curb on imports had to be imposed to stop further draining of the meager foreign currency reserves. Thus, coffee disappeared from the market until early 1982, along with such luxury goods as whisky and a variety of other items. During the bleak winter of 1979 and 1980, Turkish cities suffered frequent power cuts to save costly fuel. In 1979 Turkey's bill for imported oil (close to 3 billion dollars) passed its export earning capability.

It would be false to claim that the relative recovery which followed military rule was caused entirely by the iron hand of the generals. What is remarkable is that the Turkish military saw considerable value in the economic plan announced eight months before their coup and prepared in detail by one of Turkey's top economists, Turgut Özal, who became deputy premier for economic affairs in the technocratic government under the military National Security Council.*

Özal's objective was to eliminate the perpetual crisis by stimulating economic growth through a tight fiscal policy, expanded exports, and a campaign to encourage foreign investment. The first result of the program was a dramatic (by Turkish standards) drop in the inflation rate, to about 40 percent. It was followed by a sharp rise in exports and Turkish business activity in the Arab world. U.S. economists felt Özal needed about five years to fulfill most of his

---

*Ozal resigned in July 1982, casting doubt on the future course of Turkey's economic and fiscal policies.

goals and that he was on the right track. Some fields, of course looked better than others, and one had to take with a pinch of salt a statement by Premier Bülent Ulusu in December 1981 that the progress was "miraculous because of popular support in an atmosphere of economic and social security." This official euphoria aside, there was no doubt that the situation was improving. In fact, Özal was so confident that on December 7, 1981, he announced that Turkey's requirements for government-to-government financial aid from major industrial nations would be virtually eliminated by the end of 1983.[23]

Turkey would still have to rely on loans from the International Monetary Fund (IMF), the World Bank, and other international agencies. What Özal hoped to eliminate was aid arranged directly with countries such as the United States and the FRG and assistance under the auspices of the Organization for Economic Cooperation Development (OECD), mainly to cover the deficit in Turkey's balance of payments. The OECD package dropped from 1.2 billion dollars in 1980 to 960 million dollars in 1981.

One of the factors responsible for the increase in exports and the intensified economic performance was a ban on labor union activity under the state of martial law, thus eliminating strikes. Before the takeover, work stoppages often paralyzed entire sectors, such as tourism, shipping, or glass manufacturing. During the last three-month period before the coup, Turkey lost 250 million dollars in glass exports alone to Arab countries because of strikes.[24] It was thus inevitable that the military rulers should launch a frontal attack on organized labor, mercilessly clamping down on such left-wing unions as DISK (Turkish initials for "The Confederation of Revolutionary Labor Unions") which claimed a membership of half a million, decidedly leaning to the left. The regime authorized the existence of the relatively moderate Turk Is (Turkish Labor) but without rights to conduct any significant activity, including the recruitment of new members.

Such an approach, while beneficial in the short term, might contain a germ of unrest. The military rulers compensated their fiat by granting immediate wage increases of up to 70 percent, implementing long-dormant tax reforms, adjusted to the rate of inflation; and taxing agricultural incomes for the first time. The measure affected some wealthy landowners, who had never before paid taxes on their agricultural earnings. The whole tax-collecting apparatus was tightened up; evasion was made more difficult. There was an atmosphere of considerable relaxation in Turkish cities in early 1982.

The bulk of the population continued to feel the pinch; and, as a Western economist summed up, "economically the trend is good but all the basic problems still exist."

Notes

1. In conversation with the author, August 1980.

2. In conversation with the author, August, 1980.

3. Claudia Wright, "The Ugly Ally of The West," *MacLean's*, August 4, 1980, pp. 20–23.

4. David Hotham, *The Turks* (London: John Murray, 1978), p. 51.

5. Leon Sciaky, *Farewell To Salonika* (London: 1946).

6. Lord Kinross, *Atatürk* (New York: William Morrow, 1965), p. 24.

7. Author's notes, May 1, 1982.

8. Ibid, April 5, 1982.

9. Ibid, April 5, 1980.

10. Ibid, October 23, 1981.

11. Author's dispatch to the *Atlanta Constitution,* July 21, 1981.

12. Author's notes, April 29, 1981.

13. Hotham, *The Turks,* p. 56.

14. Author's notes, December 1978.

15. Confidential document made available to the author, April, 1981.

16. Author's dispatch to the *Atlanta Sunday Journal-Constitution,* November 22, 1980.

17. In conversation with the author, April 1981.

18. Geoffrey Lewis, *Modern Turkey* (London: Ernest Benn, 1974), p. 82.

19. State Information Organization of Turkey, *Facts about Turkey* (Ankara, 1971), p. 1.

20. From the text, November 1981.

21. *Son Havadis,* March 1981.

22. Author's notes, February 8, 1982.

23. *International Herald Tribune* (Paris), December 8, 1981.

24. Figure supplied by the Turkish foreign ministry.

Chapter 4

HELLENISM IN TRANSITION

*The Greeks have survived in spite of all the world could do against
them, and all they could do against themselves.*

Sir Winston Churchill

The warm autumnal night of October 18, 1981, in Athens exploded with shouts of joy and the blaring of automobile horns.
Thousands locked arms and danced *syrtaki* in Constitution Square.
Others massed around their leader's villa in the suburb of Kastri,
roaring the socialist hymn "Kalimera Elios" ("Greetings to the Rising
Sun"). In Ormonia Square, a coffin was raised over the heads of a
cheering crowd, with the inscription, "Tonight the Right has died."

The future will show whether the right wing really died after
the first Socialist government in the history of Greece was swept to
power. The electoral victory of the Pan-Hellenic Socialist Movement
(PASOK), led by Andreas Papandreou, was impressive but by no
means a record; it won 48 percent of the popular vote and 172 seats
in the 300-member parliament. The majority certainly was comfort-
able, and Papandreou had reason to beam at the wellwishers. It
seemed that it was, indeed, the time for *alaghi* (change), that oft-
repeated slogan of PASOK's electoral campaign.

The Socialist victory had been anticipated by most, although
not all, seasoned observers of the Greek scene. Three days before the
vote took place, a cable from the U.S. embassy in Athens still specu-
lated about the various coalition possibilities that could result from

an inconclusive election. But the electoral trend was already clear shortly after the polls closed. Less than three hours later, an ashen-faced Premier Rallis, head of the conservative New Democracy (*Neo Dimokratia*) party conceded the election. "The people have decided, I hope they are not proven wrong," Rallis told the massed foreign and Greek newsmen. As he walked out of the building into Venizelou Street, he was observed by an arriving official of the U.S. embassy. "What's Rallis doing here?" the diplomat asked. When told that the premier had just conceded, he exclaimed, "Jesus Christ! I got to call the embassy."[1]

U.S. concern was understandable; the euphoria of PASOK sup-porters spelled trouble to Washington and other North Atlantic Treaty Organization (NATO) members. A pivotal ally, Greece has rarely been a convenient partner. A year before the Socialist election, it agreed to rejoin NATO's military structure after a six-year boycott caused by the Turkish occupation of the north of Cyprus. Four key U.S. defense installations on Greek territory were operating on a pro-visional agreement of the outgoing conservative government, after talks on a permanent treaty broke down in June 1981. Papandreou campaigned on a platform of withdrawal from NATO's military structure and removal of U.S. bases. Like many politicians, the former U.S. citizen, who graduated from Harvard and later taught economics at several U.S. universities, did modify his stand somewhat. He con-ceded that the United States had vital interests in the Mediterranean and that he did not want a confrontation over the bases. "There will be no adventures, no unilateral moves," he said after the election.[2]

While an uneasy Washington waited with concern and a number of contradictory statements by various officials were issued, Papan-dreou further clarified his stand on the bases. In the event they remain on Greek territory, "we should like to have complete control, so that we can prevent the launching of some military operation from Greek soil against a third country with which we maintain good rela-tions."[3] This was not exactly according to PASOK's platform, but most Greeks accepted that politicians usually change their views once they have been propelled to power. In any case, Papandreou initially showed considerable verbal flexibility, depending upon his audience.

Greece did not elect PASOK because of NATO, the European Economic Community (EEC), and other rather distant foreign problems. The average Greek was either indifferent or vaguely hostile to NATO (according to one opinion poll in the Athens area, only 12 percent supported military reintegration). PASOK won because of simple bread-and-butter issues, widespread suspicion of corruption by the conservative establishment and its internecine quarrels, and the lack of badly needed changes in the country's social and economic structure. Essentially the Greeks wanted *alaghi* and that's what Papandreou capitalized on. Besides, Andrea* had a reputation as a man who could stand up to the United States. It did not mean that the Greeks wanted him to do anything dramatic. What they did not want was for their country to be considered anyone's satellite. During the 1967–74 military regime, there was the distinct feeling throughout Greece that Washington (namely the Central Intelligence Agency) was pulling all the strings. This impression did not disappear during the subsequent New Democracy governments. Andrea was going to change this.

Papandreou certainly stood out in a crowd of generally colorless or ossified politicians vying for the support of the Greeks and not merely because of his height (over six feet). He was a flexible and lively speaker, who knew how to gauge the mood of his audiences and how to respond. Years of university lecturing have been of considerable help in his rise to power in his native country. If there was a charismatic leader in Greece in the early 1980s, it certainly was the popular Andrea.

His past groomed him well for the role he assumed in October 1981. Born on the island of Khíos off the coast of Turkey, he is the son of former premier George Papandreou. During the stormy years of World War II, Andreas was imprisoned and tortured. Eventually released, he managed to go to the United States, where he obtained a Ph.D. in economics at Harvard in 1943. He held a number of posts as a lecturer (at Harvard, the University of Minnesota, Northwestern University, and the University of California at Berkeley, where he was dean of the faculty from 1956 to 1959). He returned to Greece in 1959 and served as an adviser to the Bank of Greece in 1961–62. In 1964 he was elected to parliament on the ticket of his father's Center Union party, becoming a "minister to the prime minister" (his father) and then deputy minister of coordination (1964–65). Following the military coup of April 21, 1967, Papandreou was arrested and imprisoned. Upon his release, he once again went into exile, first to Sweden, then to Canada, where he pursued his career as a professor of economics. When the junta resigned after the Turkish intervention in Cyprus in 1974, Papandreou returned home and founded PASOK. The party gained popularity steadily until its 1981

---

*Diminutive of Andreas.

electoral victory, which put Papandreou in the coveted prime minister's chair.

With his background as an economist, Papandreou seemed eminently qualified to steer Greece at a time of major economic structural adjustments. But academics deal in theories rarely put into practice. Papandreou's performance could not be judged conclusively on the basis of his first nine months in office (when this study was completed).

Papandreou's Greece was a mixed picture of hectic and polluted Athens; colorful villages, where men gathered in tavernas to watch television; monasteries where bearded monks offered hospitality to impecunious tourists; and increasingly chaotic automobile traffic. Despite the growing urbanization, it had one of the lowest crime rates in the world. To foreigners it offered the sun, the sea, the scenic islands, and the excitement of ancient ruins. To the average Greek, life was becoming increasingly difficult and expensive, particularly in urban areas. Young people were leaving the countryside in search of better opportunities in Athens, Salonika, and a few other industrial centers. Most remained frustrated by the growing cost of living and the slim chances for improvement. Urban congestion was reaching alarming proportions. In 1981 some 40 percent of the population of 9 million lived in the Athens metropolitan area, which also contained half of the country's industry and 400,000 of its 700,000 automobiles. The strain of living there was such that, according to sociologist Dimitrios Vranopoulos, 75 percent of the capital's young women "are incapable of experiencing sexual enthusiasm."[4]

Politically, Greece was very much a self-centered country. It felt it merited international attention and support as the proverbial cradle of democracy. In fact, until the mid-nineteenth century, most Greeks knew little of their glorious ancient past, which had made Greece a magnet for Western scholars and travelers.

> By the beginning of the 19th century the travelling gentleman, with his pocket version of the classics, became a permanent feature of the Greek scene. These confident and successful men were amazed at the ignorance they found. They began to lecture the Greeks about their ancient history and established a regular circuit of famous sites to be visited. The Greeks picked up scraps of history and legend and repeated them back to subsequent visitors. In the towns frequented by tourists a superficial knowledge of Ancient Greece thus appeared, derived mainly from the West, but believed by many of the visitors, much to their delight, to be a genuine tradition from ancient times.[5]

Understandably, Greece had the sympathy of the Western world in its struggle against the Ottomans and subsequent conflicts with Turkey. In the first place, Greece was usually allied with the United Kingdom and France and made a strong contribution to the Entente in World War I and to the Allies in the second world conflict. Turkey's image was tarnished by its military forays against Europe, the primitive oriental nature of the Ottoman rule, and its xenophobia (in which most Westerners believed). Although many Europeans and Americans traveled to Greece, few bothered to look at Turkey. While Turkey remained beyond the pale, Greece was increasingly regarded as a strongly pro–Western country, committed to European ideas and civilization.

This image grew after World War II, despite the carnage of the civil war. It was fueled by Athens correspondents representing foreign newspapers, many of them either Greeks or Greek-Americans. Until the 1967 coup, most readers in the West received a positive, frequently enthusiastic, picture of Greece, regardless of its vicissitudes. The trend basically continued during the military rule, mainly owing to efficient control over correspondents resident in Athens. It gained in intensity following 1974, with most dispatches analyzing Greco–Turkish relations being written in the Greek capital.

One could easily claim that Hellenism was fumbling during the rule of the conservatives, torn between heady Greek nationalism and their own commitment to the United States and NATO. Once in power, Papandreou certainly put more stress on the nationalistic facets of Greek policy, antagonizing the West, without, however, giving any concrete meaning or direction to Hellenism besides slogans and elusive promises. At least during the first period of Papandreou's leadership, Hellenism was in a stage of transition, with its outcome uncertain. During that period trying to guess Papandreou's intentions was a difficult task, and Western capitals remained "tensed with wary discretion."[6] Indeed, Papandreou took tension with him wherever he went: to the EEC summit, to the annual NATO ministerial meeting (as his own defense minister), and to Cyprus.

Soon Papandreou gained a reputation, at least in Western newspaper headlines, as a troublemaker.[7] Some newspapers, such as *The Washington Post,* urged "patience with Greece," (November 30, 1981), saying, "Although we hesitate to put an anti-American tag on Mr. Papandreou, or on Greeks in general, a policy that will sound anti-American to many American ears can now be expected out of Athens. It is a good time for Americans to be patient while Greeks straighten themselves out." There were few signs of any straightening out in the U.S. direction. On December 17, 1981, *The New York*

Times editorialized, "He [Papandreou] came to power talking neutralism and needs to prove he meant it. So he threatens Greek 'disengagement' from NATO, unless he gets what the alliance cannot give: a guarantee of Greek territory against 'aggression' by Turkey, another NATO ally."

To quote *The Economist* (of London)—simply because it has been interpreting Papandreou and Greece with amazing accuracy— "Greece's foreign policy is becoming increasingly erratic under its new Socialist prime minister, Mr. Andreas Papandreou. The latest example is a bizarre maneuver over Cyprus, which suggests that Mr. Papandreou is more interested in making bellicose declarations than in advancing the cause of Greece in that unhappy island" (February 27, 1982). The weekly was referring to Papandreou's three-day visit to Cyprus, marked by an avalanche of platitudes, such as "I shall remain on the bastions of this struggle until final victory."

In late spring, however, there were some indications that Papandreou had become aware of the hostility his statements had created in the West. A series of careful signals went out of Athens, implying a desire to reach a modus vivendi with NATO, the EEC, and the United States on the bases issue. Few details were available, however. Some ambassadors accredited to Athens felt that Papandreou had to tread carefully in order not to antagonize his supporters by a radical departure from the electoral platform of PASOK. Already PASOK was under attack from the Communist party for "backsliding and procrastination" as well as "failure to establish a truly independent policy." Clearly, Papandreou's task was a difficult one, and some diplomats believed that he was being pulled in different directions by his various advisers as well as by political currents.

Keeping NATO allies and Greece's EEC partners on edge was one way of centering international attention on Athens. Of course, there was nothing dramatically new in this approach. Historically, the Greeks have frequently looked for foreign scapegoats for their various problems and enjoyed any attention they could get. "Andrea" has given his countrymen a new sense of importance without—at least initially—doing anything concrete. The professor simply continued lecturing and trying out his various theories, this time before a worldwide audience. He even endorsed the long-standing proposal for a nuclear-free Balkan zone, presumably knowing well that all previous efforts to create any semblance of Balkan unity or consensus have ended in failure. Predictably, Papandreou never specified how he envisaged bringing about any lasting agreement that would include isolated Albania; pro-Soviet Bulgaria; Yugoslavia, with its own brand of Titoist communism; reluctant Romania; and Greece—

not to mention Turkey, which should, in principle, be included among the Balkan nations. Presumably, in fostering yet another abortive Balkan idea, Papandreou followed one of his campaign statements in which he said, "We see Greece as part of the Balkans, the Mediterranean and Europe and we want a foreign policy to meet these criteria."

Such criteria represented a tall order, indeed, even for a man with Papandreou's ambitions. In fact, some Greeks had begun to wonder whether this barrage of unfeasible ideas would not lead to an internal upheaval, particularly once the right-wing opposition succeeded in healing old wounds and closing its ranks.

There was always the possibility that conservative President Constantine Karamanlis might resort to the drastic act of dissolving parliament and declaring a state of emergency. Karamanlis, the supreme arbiter of the Greek political scene, initially heard Papandreou's statements with little official comment, presumably so as not to provoke an open clash. However, his friends and confidants reported an increasing concern by the man whose whole life has been devoted to making Greece a constructive member of the West.

Political strife and sudden upheavals have been part of the Greek scene since the end of Ottoman rule. A monarchy replaced a republic in 1832, as the nation was making its first hesitant independent steps. Barely a hundred years later, a republic returned, then a monarchy again, confirmed by a referendum. King George II returned from exile and, in 1936, appointed General Iannis Metaxas as premier. With dictatorships getting an increasing grip on a number of European nations, Metaxas soon showed his true colors. Faced with political opposition and bolstered by the king's backing, Metaxas staged a coup in August 1936, which formally installed a military dictatorship in Greece. Officially, that period was called the Third Greek Civilization, the term ominously evocative of Hitler's Third Reich. However, Metaxas and his associates never developed a strong ideology and relied mainly on political suppression, slogans, glorification of the monarchy, and "Christian values." For all practical purposes, Greece had become an anticommunist, antiparliamentarian, totalitarian state. The style of regime was to be repeated later, when in 1967 a group of embittered colonels seized power, claiming to forestall political chaos and communism.

It is not the purpose of this study to trace in detail the tortuous developments in Greece on the eve of and during World War II, culminating in the refusal of an Italian ultimatum in October 1940, by the single proud word, 'Okhi"—"no." While the Greek armed forces fought valiantly against the resulting Italian invasion, they were simply not strong enough to resist Hitler's onslaught. It was during the somber days of Nazi rule that the communist-dominated National Liberation Front (EAM) and its Popular Liberation Army (ELAS) became the focus of resistance. By the end of 1944, the communists claimed the backing of 1.5 million Greeks and controlled about two-thirds of the country's territory. This was accomplished "by organizing relief in the urban centers and by keeping alive the spirit of resistance to the Germans in defiance of the Greek puppet government."[8] The strength of the communists and the weakness of the democratic forces contained the germ of the fratricidal war that was to follow. As World War II was drawing to a close, Greece was a political and administrative shambles, with most essential government work handled by British missions. Between the start of 1945 and April 1946, the country saw no less than eight ineffective governments.

The summer of 1947 is usually regarded as the start of the civil war. By December a "provisional democratic government" was formed, and the "Democratic army" received supplies and instructors from neighboring Yugoslavia, which also offered a haven whenever the communist forces were pushed to the border.

The defeat of the communists can be traced not only to massive U.S. aid, which poured into Greece, but also to the fact that, following its expulsion from the Soviet bloc for "Titoist heresy," Yugoslavia sealed the frontier and stopped giving succor to the Greek communists.

The civil war marked a new period in the hisotry of modern Greece, that of involvement with the United States. With the United Kingdom worn out after its war effort and grappling with the first waves of independence battering its empire, the United States was the only logical source of help for the Greek anticommunist forces. Thus was born the doctrine that later bore the name of its founder, President Harry S. Truman. As he himself explained in his memoirs, (Vol. II, Years of Trial and Hope), "Greece needed aid and needed it quickly and in substantial amounts. The alternative was the loss of Greece and the extension of the iron curtain across the eastern Mediterranean. If Greece was lost, Turkey would become an untenable outpost in a sea of communism. Similarly, if Turkey yielded to Soviet demands, the position of Greece would be extremely endangered."

Thus, the United States took over Britain's role in Greece. The country mourned some 80,000 civil war dead, hundreds of thousands of injured, and the thousands of villages turned to rubble. According to General George Grivas, who later founded the Cypriot terrorist

National Organization of Cypriot Fighters (EOKA), "Greece was devastated, her economy ruined, her people starving and her honor stained by the atrocities which the communists committed against their innocent countrymen."[9] But while physical scars of the war mended reasonably quickly, the psychological impact continued to weigh over Greece's political life, making it a weak and unstable ally on which to anchor Western defenses in the East Mediterranean.

Traditionally, the political scene in Greece was what some newspapers call "a family affair." In practical terms it meant that the levers of power were almost exclusively in the hands of a small group of usually wealthy families. It was a government by an elite which controlled loyal fiefs. Inevitably, the *vouli* (parliament) reflected the clanishness and personality feuds opposing the various "dynasties." They included such names as Venizelos, Rallis, Tsatsos, and Tsaldaris; streets throughout Greece were named after them. More often than not, major economic and political decisions were made in private caucus, often in cafes around Athens' Kolonaki Square. It was an "old boys" network on a grand scale. According to political commentator George Stalios, "Everyone knows everyone, that is everyone who matters. At the end of the war, Athens was a city of less than a million. Then there was a massive influx of refugees from the war. Industrial units were expanded and the countryside was abandoned. Of course, the ruling class did not increase proportionately."[10]

There were, as usual, notable exceptions. They included Karamanlis, the son of a modest family, who headed the first democratic government after the collapse of the military junta in 1974 and took Greece into the European Economic Community, eventually becoming president (1980).

Against such a setting, political crises came and went, parties and alliances were formed and dissolved. In 1956 Karamanlis formed National Radical Union party (ERE), which won 165 of 300 parliament seats. The new premier showed considerable administrative efficiency, but Greece remained paralyzed by its antiquated system. Migratory workers traveled in droves to such industrial nations as the Federal Republic of Germany; the Greek countryside stagnated. A Greek proverb says, "When God finished making the world, he had a sack of stones left and used them to make Greece." That bit of peasant wisdom held true virtually until the early 1960s, despite considerable progress in many fields. To most foreigners, Greece was a beach suburb of industrial Europe, an accessible and cheap place, where sunburned tourists dined on octopus and fried aubergines, listening to *bouzouki* music. Needless to say, by the early 1980s the picture had changed dramatically. Greece was plagued by inflation. Athens was shrouded by a pall of polluted air, its streets jammed by chaotic traffic. One had to travel to distant islands to find the old charm of the seaside tavernas.

The problems facing Karamanlis in the 1950s were not so much caused by the internal situation but by events in the British colony of Cyprus, whose Hellenic majority wanted *enosis* (union with Greece). Feeling that the government acted in a manner subservient to NATO and particularly to the United States, many ERE members started deserting the premier's party. Once again Karamanlis went to the voters (1958), this time under a new "reinforced proportional representation system," which worked against political coalitions.

Although ERE lost popular votes, it gained seats in parliament. However, the opposition Democratic Union (EDA) became the second largest party in parliament. Right-wing zealots proceeded to form paramilitary organizations, such as the Battalions of National Security, whose aim was to rid the country of ETA supporters. The quarreling liberal politicians eventually formed a new party, the Center Union, under George Papandreou. Still, in the 1961 elections, which were plagued by a campaign of terror in the villages, ERE emerged victorious, with 176 seats versus the Center Union's 100. EDA got the remaining 24.

Following the vote, Papandreou launched an all-out attack on the ruling establishment, accusing it of manipulating the electoral law, dominating the press, interfering in political campaigning, and using the army to ensure its victory. The political tension was exacerbated in May 1963 by the assassination in Salonika of Demetrius Lambrakis, a popular EDA deputy. The country seethed with unrest. Mass demonstrations took place in the cities, often turning into riots. In June 1963 Karamanlis resigned and left the country. Elections held in November of that year gave a victory to Papandreou, despite the hasty return of Karamanlis, who tried to revitalize his battered party. The unhappy leader left Greece again, vowing to give up political activity.

With Papandreou's Center Union controlling only 138 seats and political tensions high, the parliament was too fragmented to be capable of any coherent action. One answer would have been a Center Union–EDA coalition, but Papandreou refused to hear of it. Instead, he dissolved parliament, and Greece once again went back to the polls in February 1964.

This time the Center Union got 52.7 percent of the vote and 171 seats. In his contribution to *Greece in Transition,* Yanis Yanoulopoulos describes the activities of the new government.

> Despite his overwhelming support in the country, Papandreou was
> to follow a policy marked for its inconsistency. He disbanded a num-
> ber of para–state organizations set up during the rule of ERE, re-
> leased most of the political prisoners, relaxed the application of
> certain civil war laws and tried, with some success, to restrict the
> police to its normal duties. . . . In the economic field his son, Andreas
> Papandreou, made an effort to stimulate growth in response to in-
> creased demand by a policy of moderate wage increases and agricul-
> tural subsidies. He failed, however, to introduce any substantial mea-
> sures to curb the unconstitutional power of the parallel state. . . . His
> half-hearted attempts to bring the Greek Central Intelligence Ser-
> vice (KYP)—directly financed by the CIA—under the effective
> authority of the government proved unsuccessful.[11]

The reason for the above outline of the postwar political events
in Greece is to illustrate the setting in which a military conspiracy
was hatched. The first conspiracy was discovered in 1965 and consisted of some 20 junior officers forming an organization called
Aspida (Shield). According to Yanoulopoulos, "almost all of these
officers had themselves been associated with KYP at the time when
the Center Union government attempted to acquire some measure
of control over the CIA activities in the Greek secret service and the
army communications system. Some among them were said to regard
Andreas Papandreou as the future leader of Greece."[12]

Confusion followed the discovery of the plot, with troops moving into the vicinity of Athens without the government's knowledge.
King Constantine, faced with personality clashes of government
members and rising dissatisfaction in the army, virtually dismissed
Papandreou and sought to form a government based on a coalition of
ERE and Center Union defectors. Eventually, Stefanos Stefanopoulos
managed to obtain a slight parliamentary majority, but the popularity
of Papandreou continued unabated. To break the deadlock, an agreement was made to hold elections on May 28, 1967. The king himself, to quote Yanoulopoulos again, "was prepared to resort to
'official' military intervention under his direct or indirect command
and to proclaim a 'state of emergency'."

Whatever the monarch's planning was, it was soon overtaken by
events. On April 21, a group of colonels, said to have U.S. backing,
activated an operational plan, code-named Prometheus. Tanks rum-
bled through the streets of Athens in the predawn hours. Troops surrounded key buildings and hauled political figures out of their homes.
The bloodless operation took a mere five hours. The head of the junta
was Colonel George Papadopoulos, assisted by Nicolaos Makarezos,

another colonel, and Brigadier Stylianos Pattakos. The king remained in his palace, a weak figurehead monarch. Throughout Greece, troops painted a new slogan on the walls: "zito o stratos" ("long live the army"). Perfectly aware of the stark political realities, the king cooperated with the junta to the degree of swearing in an appointed technocratic government.

Apparently annoyed by his diminishing prestige, Constantine launched a vague "royal countercoup" in December 1967 by appealing over the radio to the country and the armed forces to disobey the junta and follow him. The broadcast was heard only in parts of Greece. The fumbling monarch left the country and, 24 hours after the abortive attempt, Greece went back to work as though nothing had happened. The exiled king was noted Christmas shopping in Rome only a few days after coming close to plunging his country into a civil war. His wife, Danish-born Queen Anne–Marie, summoned dressmakers and models to her residence to decide on a new winter wardrobe. In Athens, the junta appointed a regent, conducted a wave of arrests, and announced that the 1968 budget was ready on time for the first time in years. A new constitution was outlined, in theory guaranteeing democratic freedoms—provided they were not aimed at the military regime. The constitution was adopted six months later. The colonels were firmly in power.

Their symbol was the phoenix, the mythical bird that, after living for centuries in the desert, burned itself and rose from the ashes with new vigor. The colonels wanted a new Greece—pure, strong, and vigorous. In this sense they were not unlike the Turkish generals who followed in their footsteps 13 years later. Most military plotters throughout the world act either to eradicate corruption or to restore their countries' glorious past. It would seem that despair rather than a lust for power motivates them, at least initially.

The Greek phoenix was crudely painted, spreading its wings over the dark silhouette of a helmeted soldier—that guardian of the *epanastesis* (revolution). A scarlet flame enveloped both. This symbol was hoisted on public buildings, displayed on billboards and even on matchboxes and children's copybooks, reminding all that the *syndamatarche* (colonels) were in power. But their power lacked a program and a doctrine, except for the belief that "Greek political life had become cancerous and that surgery of this drastic variety was essential to prevent anarchy and the possibility of a communist takeover."[13] The colonels dreamed of a vague corporate system along the lines of Mussolini's Italy but lacked the means to put it into effect. Anticommunist, they nonetheless recruited a number of former Communists to help them in the transformation of Greece.

A typical example was George Georgalas, who for 10 years studied Marxism in Eastern Europe, a Communist exile from Greece with a 20-year jail sentence on his head. The colonels made him undersecretary for information, directly responsible to Premier Papadopoulos himself. Among the regime's chief theorists were two other former Communists: Theofylactos Papaconstantinou, author of *The Manual of Democracy,* and Savvas Constantopoulos. Apologists of the junta explained such an incongruous relationship by the military's inability to provide solid thinkers. Georgalas himself, a pleasant, multilingual man, had a tendency to speak in cliches. He would stress the "all-embracing nature" of the regime's reforms and explain the coup of 1967 as "a reaction of the healthy parts of the national organism against the sickness ruining it, against the decadence of the Greek political life."[14]

Junta members tried to deflect worldwide hostility to their coup by painting a picture of an increasingly healthy economy. The economic overlord was former artillery Colonel Makarezos, who delighted in showing visitors neat graphs illustrating the rise in productivity, industrial potential, tourism, shipbuilding, and road construction. "Economic progress depends on stability," he would repeat. "We have brought stability and the country is now reaping the profits."[15] Indeed, the short, stocky colonel had his facts and figures right: in 1969, two years after the military takeover, Greece registered an 8.3 percent growth rate, the highest in Europe. Three years after the military takeover, salaries of low-paid workers had risen 26 percent, while the cost of living climbed only 6 percent—the lowest such increase in Europe.

There is no doubt that the economic picture was helped by the system of political rigidity imposed by the junta, although the elements of prosperity were there before. Between 1947 and 1966, the United States pumped in a massive dose of 3.7 billion dollars in grants and loans. Thus, progress was eventually reaching the distant villages perched on the rocky mountainsides. The merchant fleet grew; new industries were created; power grids were constructed. However, much of this progress was hampered by political agitation rocking the country. By putting an iron lid on Greece, the colonels were able to allow the nation to "reap the profits," in the words of Makarezos. The colonels pushed an ambitious road construction and irrigation program and, by the end of 1970, electrified some 3,000 villages. Their Chicago-born minister of finance, Adamantios Androutsopoulos, revised the taxation system: taxes were lowered by 13 percent, but the government's revenues were increased by a more efficient collecting apparatus, under the watchful eye of the military.

Part of the junta's economic success was attributed to its alliance with two internationally known shipping magnates, Aristotle Onassis and Stavros Niarchos. Both had pledged their money to an intense investment program. All this eventually filtered down to the poorest peasants and harrassed workmen. The fact is that the junta, a sinister and oppressive force to much of the world, was not regarded in such negative terms by many Greeks. In this sense the situation was similar to that in Turkey following the 1980 army coup.

In a detailed survey of Greece entitled "The Gods Smiled at Last," *The Economist* (September 20, 1975) quotes the testimony of an unidentified young man, who was 15 when the colonels took over.

> They were not all bad, and those who say they were are hypocrites. In my town of 50,000 people, under an hour's bus ride from the center of Athens, we had no paved roads, no running water in the houses and no high school. Now we have them all, and a wonderful square and a sports ground. Of course I believe in democracy, but it would not be honest to say the junta did nothing. It put in some good mayors who got things done in many towns and the people were grateful.

Apart from the junta's well-known record of political oppression, the colonels failed to implement one of the key elements of their program: a profound reform of governmental structure. When they seized power, they claimed the system was corrupt and antiquated. Yet, during seven years without any parliamentary hindrance they did little to slash the web of inefficiency and red tape which pervaded in Greece. Yes, here and there things moved more smoothly and construction progressed. But on the whole, Greece remained shackled by bureaucracy and outdated concepts, without political freedoms. It was a feeling of frustration and political immobility that sent Athens polytechnic students into the streets in November 1973. Eight months later the junta, by then under General Dimitrios Ioannides, caused the Turkish invasion of Cyprus through its coup against Archbishop Makarios. The Greek scene was ripe for a major upheaval. Democracy returned to its proverbial birthplace.

The transition from military dictatorship to civilian rule was exceptionally orderly. Political commentators described it as "one of the most remarkable and surprising episodes" in Greek history. The junta collapsed mainly because of the Turkish war against Hellenism in Cyprus; the Turkish landing had a sobering and incongruously salutary impact on the Greek political scene. As *The Economist* put it (September 20, 1975), "In a dangerous situation Greeks chose to revert to their former democratic structure, albeit with subtle and important changes, and not to seek to change the country's social, economic, and political institutions radically. And the army concurred."

Inevitably, the army had to suffer from the return of democratic rule. After the toppling of the junta, 1,263 officers were dismissed, including 14 generals. In the years that followed, the army maintained discipline and its fighting ability was considerably bolstered by intense modernization. However, the mood of the cadres was uncertain and often dispirited, exacerbated by Greece's withdrawal from NATO's military wing, a result of the Turkish landing in Cyprus. With former junta members under lock and key pending trial (the leaders received death sentences, later commuted to life imprisonment), political events moved swiftly.

Karamanlis conveniently forgot his earlier pledge to stay out of politics and promptly answered the call of President Phaidon Giziks to form a government. He created a new political force, aptly named New Democracy (Neo Dimokratia). It was to give Greece clean and free air after seven years of regimentation. Predictably, Greeks of all walks of life attacked the "infamous era," forgetting that while the regime of the colonels was in power, there was little opposition or resistance. The anger spilled into the streets of Athens only when it was clear that the junta had undermined its own foundations through fumbling and indecisiveness. By the end of 1973 the junta was losing support even among the most devoted right wingers. "They could have done something beautiful, they could have shown the world that conservatism is a vibrant force," complained a frustrated Athenian rightwinger.

From the beginning of the new era, Karamanlis unquestionably dominated the Greek political scene. He was many things to many Greeks. Tall, urbane, stubborn, proud, and often secretive, Karamanlis was not part of the traditional political Greek network. Born in 1907 in the village of Prote in the Greek tobacco belt (then under Turkish rule) and the son of a schoolteacher, Karamanlis moved through life the hard way. From early days, he was practically obsessed by political ambition. In 1935, at the age of 28, he managed to be elected to parliament. In 1955 he was prime minister for a comparatively brief spell, during which he demonstrated considerable shrewdness as well as fits of bad temper. "To the devil!" he shouted when offended by a politician.

This fiery, elegant politician led New Democracy to a brilliant victory in the general elections in November 1974 (220 seats in the

300-member parliament). It was a record in the history of modern Greece, and church bells pealed throughout the mainland and myriad islands. "Costa" promptly proceeded to a referendum, which confirmed the end of the monarchy already abolished by the colonels in June 1973 after an abortive naval mutiny. He then set out to accomplish his life-long dream: to turn Greece from a backward country on the fringes of Europe into a full-fledged European nation. This was to be culminated by membership of the European Economic Community (EEC), the achievement Karamanlis watched from the height of the nation's presidency.

The doctrine of Karamanlis and his party was that "Greece belongs to the West—ideologically, historically, organizationally." It was a comparatively popular theory in a country where communism had become a minimal force. The main difficulty was that, as far as the internal scene was concerned, it was easier said than done. Countless politicians before Karamanlis had promised reforms and failed. Soon it became only too apparent that Karamanlis and New Democracy were really doing little that was new. Red tape and corruption continued; in fact Athens buzzed with rumors of ministers paid by that traditional scapegoat, the CIA. While Karamanlis made an unquestionably positive impact on the international scene, there was little concrete movement inside Greece. This was reflected in the 1977 elections, when Papandreou's socialist PASOK doubled its popular vote to 25.4 percent (compared to 12 percent in 1974) and seized 93 parliament seats. The conservative establishment was losing popularity. Increasingly, the socialists, with their promises of sweeping internal reforms and an improved economy, loomed as a more dynamic force.

Before he ceded premiership to Rallis in May 1980 to become president, Karamanlis relentlessly moved to tie Greece closely to the democratic nations of Western Europe. He genuinely felt that by joining the EEC the threat of military coups and other dramatic political upheavals would be eliminated, or, at least, considerably diminished. Thus, when Greece became the community's tenth full-fledged member on January 1, 1981, it was clear that the decision was of a political rather than economic nature. According to Manolis Kothris, the president of the parliamentary committee on foreign affairs, "Karamanlis has painstakingly completed the political and economic sides of the Greek pyramid. But unless the military side is built too, the pyramid may crumble." The military side of the Greek pyramid was constructed when, in October 1980, the generals in power in Turkey lifted some of their objections; the parliament, still dominated by New Democracy, voted to return to NATO's military structure. To Premier Rallis, the move represented a guarantee of security. To Papandreou it meant "an invitation to national destruction."

Papandreou continued on this theme as the preparations for the electoral campaign gained momentum in 1981. His stance against the presence of U.S. bases on Greek territory was bolstered by the fact that the Rallis government was unable to sign an agreement with the United States before the summer's parliamentary recess.

The U.S. bases in Greece consist of four major and several smaller installations. Their task is twofold: to provide electronic intelligence from the area and give direct operational support to the U.S. Sixth Fleet. In short, they offer port facilities, supply depots, transportation infrastructure (used during the evacuation of U.S. nationals from Iran after the Islamic revolution), and information.

Perhaps the most important installations are on the island of Crete. At Souda Bay, there is a large anchorage, storage areas, and a backup airfield. There is also a missile firing range nearby. Official U.S. documents describe the facility as "difficult to replace." The Iraklion Air Station is a major electronic surveillance base monitoring the activities of the Soviet fleet in the East Mediterranean. The United States also has the use of Athens' Hellenikon air base for transport and reconnaissance flights. At Néa Makri, north of Athens, the United States maintains a large fleet communications center. There are five NATO air defense ground environment (NADGE) early-warning sites throughout Greece, but their activities are related directly to NATO.

Leaving the question of the bases up in the air was a blow to U.S. hopes. A few days after the Greek reentry into NATO's military wing, U.S. ambassador to Athens at the time, Robert McCloskey, told me he expected a treaty before the end of 1980. By June 1981 it was clear that the U.S. and Greek sides were no nearer any form of agreement. A break-off followed, with the U.S. department of state playing it down as a suspension, although it was obvious that regardless who won the October elections, the whole issue would have to be negotiated from scratch.

The breakdown was caused by a U.S. refusal to agree to several Greek demands. They included a suggested clause under which the treaty governing the use of the bases could be abrogated by Greece unilaterally, the limitation of the activities of the bases by placing them under Greek command, and, above all, formal acceptance by Washington of a 10 to 7 ratio of aid between Turkey and Greece. Following the break-off, the Rallis government announced that "the status of the American military facilities in Greece will remain in force until the government, after the forthcoming elections, takes up the matter." Predictably, it was a new Socialist government that was faced with the matter. Its terms were likely to be stiffer than those of its conservative predecessors.

On June 17, 1981, *The Economist* (London) commented that the talks collapsed "thanks to a serious miscalculation by the Greek government. It had been confident that the Americans would pay almost anything to wrap up a deal on the bases now rather than risk having to negotiate with a xenophobic Socialist government under Mr. Andreas Papandreou, who could win the Greek elections this autumn."

Not surprisingly, Papandreou proceeded to modify PASOK's platform on the bases question. Instead of threats to remove the installations unequivocally, Papandreou was merely saying that he would negotiate a timetable for their withdrawal. While the bases remained in Greece, his government would seek a sustained program of U.S. arms sales. "The decisive issue," said the Socialist candidate, "is the full satisfaction of the country's defensive requirements to ensure the absolute efficiency of our armed forces in confronting the threat from the East" (meaning Turkey).[16] Within weeks of his electoral victory, it became apparent that if Papandreou was going to do something about the bases, he certainly was not in a hurry. The issue was obscured by speculation, trial balloons, and often contradictory statements. There was no question Papandreou regarded Turkey as his country's main potential enemy—to the point of obsession.

"Why should we be in NATO, when the alliance protects against a 'threat' from Third World countries we do not perceive, but not from a very real threat from another member of the alliance?" he asked in one of his preelection speeches.[17] "Over the past seven years Turkey has made claims on our airspace, seaspace and continental shelf [in the Aegean]. Turkey has a strong army called "The Army of the Aegean" which does not face the north but us in the west. It has 150 landing craft. What for? The Black sea?" (A staff report to the U.S., Senate, Committee on Foreign Relations published in 1980 places the number of landing craft of the entire Turkish armed forces at 72.)

It should be stressed here that Papandreou was not the only Greek politician who wanted NATO and specifically U.S. protection against Turkey. Ever since Turkey and Greece came near an explosion over the Aegean in 1976, Greece has been seeking U.S. military guarantees in the event of a Greco–Turkish conflict. Yet, somewhat incongruously, Papandreou saw the NATO umbrella not as protection but as a possible cause for Warsaw Pact intervention. This view was shared and strongly propagated by his U.S.-born wife, the former Margaret Chant of Chicago. (Some Athenians believed that Mrs. Papandreou was more of a socialist than her husband.)

"From the Greek point of view, having U.S. bases here makes us a target for nuclear holocaust," she said three days after her husband's victory. "What has NATO done for us to cause Greece to remain in the alliance? It doesn't even want to protect us against Turkey, the most likely agressor." Referring to general speculation about which campaign promises Papandreou would honor, she said testily: "Andreas is a man of his word. . . . He will do everything he promised. His program is fully developed. Only the tactics remain to be worked out."[18]

The Socialist takeover in Greece was watched carefully by the military government in Ankara, with understandable concern. Initially, the generals said merely that the assessment of the Papandreou government would be made after a full clarification of its program. But they did allow the controlled Turkish press to give vent to the country's suspicion of the Greeks. After a series of nationalistic statements by Papandreou, Turkish headlines charged that he was "poisoning the atmosphere" and "fanning the flames of the Greco-Turkish dispute." The Istanbul daily, *Hurriyet,* went as far as to say that "war clouds began to circle over the Turkish and Greek communities in Cyprus.

On the whole, the sparring between Athens and Ankara had few immediate consequences except for the considerable cooling of their relations. Neither side wanted to slam the door on the possibility of dialogue. In fact Papandreou's aides felt that, on the whole, it was easier to deal with Evren than with the previous governments, hindered by parliamentary and emotional partisan considerations.

Cyprus remained the most emotion-charged issue, with no indication that the two countries were making any progress toward closing the gap in their contradictory views. Almost from the start of his premiership, Papandreou became involved in a close relationship with Greek Cypriot President Spyros Kyprianou, who rushed to Athens on the heels of the Socialist landslide to seek succor.* Afterwards Papandreou described the Cyprus problem as a "crucial international

---

*This relationship was marred somewhat by a dispute over an electoral coalition in Cyprus between Kyprianou's Democratic Party and the Communist party (AKEL) in the spring of 1982.

issue" and said that Greece would support any move to rid the island of "foreign troops." In one speech he called Cyprus part of the national space of Greece, triggering speculation that he might revive the idea of *enosis*. Still, the Socialist premier canceled a trip to Cyprus scheduled for January 1982 and only agreed to visit the island at the end of February after strong pressure by Kyprianou. It was a low-key visit, with mass rallies canceled and only a brief policy speech before the 35-member Greek Cypriot house of representatives. There were the usual slogans of Hellenism (always dear to the Greek Cypriots) and references to the Turkish military presence in the north of the island. Papandreou promised the Cypriot Hellenes his backing but made no other concrete gesture. In the final analysis, it was another disappointing performance by the "motherland" for those Greek Cypriots who still believed that Athens was capable of exercising any leverage. The best Papandreou could promise was a vague idea of an international conference once the intercommunal dialogue proved unproductive.* Most Cypriots knew that the dialogue had not produced a single concrete result since the Turkish intervention. In 1982, the Cyprus problem existed to the Greeks but was basically considered as solved by most Turks.

Immeasurably easier was Papandreou's effort to win friends among the Arab nations. There were several reasons for the various economic and political overtures to the Arab world, started by a formal diplomatic recognition of the Athens representative of the Palestine Liberation Organization (PLO). Papandreou wanted to undermine the important trade inroads made by Turkey in the Middle East, show the Arabs his penchant for nonalignment, and secure the flow of Middle Eastern oil. In early 1982, Greece had long-term oil import agreements with Libya, Saudi Arabia, and the USSR. The flow of oil from Iraq, a traditional supplier, had dropped following the September 1980 Iraqi–Iranian war. In one of his first policy statements, the new Socialist premier told parliament that "in the energy sector, there are great possibilities of cooperation with Arab countries.

At the same time, Papandreou's government made a stormy debut as far as NATO and the EEC were concerned. He demanded a special status for Greece within the EEC, only to be rebuffed. Greece made an attempt to obstruct Spain's application for NATO

---

*An equally low-key visit to the north of Cyprus took place in May by Turkish Premier Ulusu. Predictably, it caused a storm of Greek protests.

membership, achieving little besides annoyance. When NATO, after a month-long hesitation, issued a statement stigmatizing the Soviet-backed military repression in Poland, Greece made "reservations" on five of the 16 points of the resolution. Once again, Papandreou wanted to show that, as a socialist, he was not hostile to the actions of the Socialist bloc.

Typical was a statement by Papandreou in January 1982, when Poland was numbed by a combination of paralyzing winter cold and the iron fist of general Wojciech Jaruzelski's regime. In a conversation with Kyprianou, who continued to commute to Athens, Papandreou is said to have described the West's attitude toward Poland as a big sham. "The West, especially the United States, is shaken these days by the imposition of martial law and the danger of the Soviet invasion of Poland," the Greek premier was quoted as saying. "Not a single word is heard from any responsible lips about the military rule imposed by the Turkish people. Not a word about the savage invasion of Cyprus."[19]

With uncertainty shrouding the sensitive question of continued Greek participation in NATO's military structure, Papandreou sounded another warning bell: his government agreed to service Soviet naval supply ships on the Aegean island of Syros. It repeatedly stressed that such ships would be unarmed; nonetheless, NATO was worried. Once again the alliance was the object of a cat-and-mouse game by Greece. Turkey, which bore the crippling U.S. arms embargo between 1975 and 1978 with amazing stoicism and loyalty, looked increasingly the more stable of the two anchors of the southeastern flank.

During the first year of Papandreou's rule, there was little reaction from the armed forces to the Socialist victory. Needless to say, Papandreou took no chances by personally assuming the portfolio of the defense minister. Within days of being sworn in, he conferred with some of the key generals and promised continued modernization of the armed forces. At that time, the strength of the three services (army, navy, and air force) was 191,000 men, of whom some 150,000 were draftees. The army had 150,000 men organized in 11 infantry divisions, one armored division, one armored brigade, one paratroop brigade, and one marine infantry brigade, plus various support and artillery units. The air force had close to 400 relatively modern combat aircraft. The navy was somewhat more antiquated and consisted of 12 former U.S. destroyers, 4 frigates, 10 submarines, and a number of support vessels.

The military has always been a strong political force in the history of modern Greece, as the 1967 coup clearly demonstrated.

The officer corps was particularly active in politics before World War II.

> In the various military assumptions of power of that pre-war era, officers of the armed forces assumed the role of political manipulators, protectors, and advisors, and they alone made the decisions as to when political conditions were ripe for their sudden intervention. To many people in Greece, however, the officers of the military forces, of the army in particular, appeared to be the only group able to take control of the country in a crisis and in the absence of strong political parties and a strong government.[20]

Obviously, in 1982 PASOK was not a weak political party, and Papandreou's regime was certainly a strong one. There was no question, however, that the armed forces were, "the best organized part of the nation," as outgoing Defense Minister Evanghelos Averoff described them in his farewell address. He added, "You are the foundation of the integrity and the honor of the motherland, as well as of the stability of democracy."

There were no signs that the military establishment objected to any of the reforms outlined with staggering profusion by the Socialist government. The plans were, indeed, wide-ranging but appeared to be falling short of the expectations of some of the more radical PASOK supporters. Averoff, who took over the leadership of New Democracy as the main opposition party, spoke of "the government's contradictory policies on critical domestic and foreign issues and its inability to fulfill its preelection promises." Former Foreign Minister Mitsotakis said, "Papandreou is occasionally compelled to play the lion to give the impression of fulfilling his previous foreign policy threats but in effect he changes nothing."[21]

Among the initial measures were wage increases for old-age pensioners and workers in lower income brackets, index-pegged wages, and a 40-hour work week. Other measures concerned the improvement of prison conditions, equality of the sexes, legalization of abortion, and civil marriage—the latter a bold move in a country dominated by the influential Orthodox church. (Church hierarchy promptly compared the decision to "prostitution and adultery.") The government also proceeded to purge the labor movement as well as state-controlled radio and television, where the showing of U.S. films was drastically reduced.

Perhaps the most daring plan concerned the separation of church and state, including the expropriation of church land holdings. It was, in a way, an attack on a state institution in a country where being Greek is tantamount to being Orthodox. Papandreou, however, felt that the constitution gave the church excessive status and influence. According to the government's program, "total separation will give the church the ability to continue its course freely and independently of worldly authority, allowing it to depend on its own strength and on a healthy and democratic internal organization." At the same time, an amendment to the constitution was to make all other religions equal. The project had the backing of many intellectuals and politicians, but the reaction of the peasant masses was uncertain. The primate of Greece, Archbishop Seraphim, initially accepted the idea as beneficial but wanted ironclad guarantees as to the financing of the church by the state. The question of church land was a delicate one, involving some 300,000 acres. The church in Greece is the second largest property owner, after the state. Its holdings include myriad business ventures, and vast treasures are believed to be kept in the vaults of various monasteries.

Carefully—perhaps too carefully for some of his supporters—Papandreou refrained from nationalization (socialization, according to PASOK's terminology) of Greece's feeble industries. Although such a move was part of PASOK's campaign platform, early in 1982 the government merely said that major industries would be "assisted in management areas" to "conform with the overall economic objectives." Papandreou himself said in a nationwide television address on January 4, 1982, that foreign capital and enterprises would be encouraged to function in Greece as long as they "created new jobs, protected the environment, promoted exports and brought in new technology."

The economic picture in Greece following the Socialist victory was certainly dominated by the hopes, expectations, and problems resulting from the newly acquired EEC membership. The country (covering a rugged area of close to 51,000 square miles) entered the community with an annual 7 billion dollar trade deficit and an inflation rate of 25 percent—twice that of most EEC members. An adjustment of the antiquated business structure to the requirements and competitive ways of the EEC was inevitable. It meant that most small, family-type enterprises were doomed, unable to compete with Western European giants. In 1980 Greece had barely 100 firms employing more than 500 people. This meant higher unemployment, already the bane of the European club, and emigration. U.S. economic experts anticipated that upward of half a million Greeks would be forced to emigrate during the first five years of full community membership.

One of the strongest economic performances was registered by shipping. With some 4,500 ships and a tonnage of 50 million in mid-1981, Greece controlled about 13 percent of the world's commercial shipping, most of it in the hands of powerful magnates with tentacles reaching literally every nook and cranny of the nation's life. A succession of Greek governments, including the military junta, has co-operated with this business oligarchy. There were no indications, at least in 1982, that Papandreou either wanted to curtail the dominant business role of shipping and other tycoons or make a serious attempt at limiting their political influence. There was, of course, a distinct possibility that, as time went by, the Socialist government could come under increasing rank-and-file pressure to equalize national income. Distribution of income has been one of the main problems in Greece since it emerged from the shambles of the civil war. Since those somber days, the progress has been impressive: from $390 in 1961, the per capita gross national product moved to $530 in 1966, and $4,590 by 1980.* But average figures are deceiving, and only a small percentage of the population was responsible for the growth or shared its benefits.

In October 1980, the U.S. department of state estimated that the growth of the Greek economy would decelerate to about 1.5 percent annually, definitely too small for a developing country rather than developed one. One of the main problems was the reliance on imported oil, which kept pushing up the country's trade deficit. In 1980, the fuel bill stood at a hefty $2.5 billion for a country of a little over nine million people. The government hoped that the newly discovered oil field on the northern island of Thasos would supply at least 13 percent of Greece's needs.

As mentioned before, in the early 1980s tourism in Greece had lost much of its proverbial charm. Although easily accessible by road (at least its bulk), Greece had become comparatively expensive for the average holiday maker. Athens, which showed all indications of becoming an urban nightmare, had ceased attracting visitors; many groups stopped there for one or two nights only, preferring sites which were easier on the nerves. Greece also suffered from an overall decrease of tourism caused by the recession in the industrial Western world, and the drop in arrivals during 1981 was close to 20 percent. What the Greek government wanted was quality rather than mass

---

*These figures do not reflect the cost-of-living increase.

tourism—well-heeled visitors who would profit from the opportunities of a fleet of 1,300 charter boats, some of which cost upwards
of $1,000 a day. There was some talk of developing ski resorts on the
slopes of Mount Parnassus and winter tourism on some of the southern islands, including Rhodes and Crete. But winter months can be
capricious in the East Mediterranean, and the steady increase in the
price of airline tickets made that part of the world less and less
tempting to the average traveler. A handful of the rich were unlikely
to help Greece revise its tourist structure or fill its coffers with the
visitors' hard currencies.

Notes

1. Author's notes, October 19, 1981.
2. In an interview on ABC's "Issues and Answers", given October 21, 1981.
3. *8 Days*, November 7, 1981.
4. Author's dispatch to the *Atlanta Constitution,* November 12, 1980.
5. William St. Clair, *That Greece Might Still Be Free* (London: Oxford University Press, 1972), p. 14.
6. *MacLean's*, November 2, 1981.
7. *The Economist*, December 5, 1981.
8. John T. A. Koumoulides, *Greece in Transition* (London: Zeno, 1977).
9. George Grivas, *Memoirs of General Grivas,* (London: Longmans, 1964), p. 10.
10. *International Herald Tribune* (Paris), May 9, 1977.
11. Koumoulides, *Greece in Transition, p.* 85.
12. Ibid., p. 86.
13. Jane Perry Carey and Andrew Galbraith Carey, *The Web of Modern Greek Poli-tics* (New York: Columbia University Press, 1968), p. 2.
14. In conversation with the author, August 1970.
15. Ibid.
16. Author's notes,
17. Ibid.
18. Ibid., October 20, 1981.
19. *Cyprus Weekly,* January 29, 1982.
20. Carey and Carey, *Modern Greek Politics*, p. 3.
21. *The New York Times,* January 26, 1982.

Chapter 5

THE DIVIDED ISLAND

A fool throws a stone into the sea and a hundred wise men cannot find it.

Cypriot proverb

One look at a map shows the strategic importance of Cyprus. It lies some 40 miles off the southern coast of Turkey. Its Karpass panhandle points to the area where the Turkish and Syrian borders meet. Lebanon, flanked by Israel and Syria, is 25 minutes away by commercial jet. The Island of Aphrodite to tourist brochure writers, to strategists Cyprus is the "unsinkable aircraft carrier of the eastern Mediterranean." The Greek Cypriots want it to be Hellenic and non-aligned, although some also talk of enosis. Its Turkish Cypriot minority—18 percent of the 650,000 inhabitants, without counting settlers from the Turkish mainland—wants full and unhindered citizenship rights, its own zone, and the protection of the nearby Turkish mainland. These contradictory aspirations for years thwarted a solution to what has become known as the Cyprus problem. The island's conflict seriously compounded other difficulties dividing Greece and Turkey. It affected U.S. interests by contributing to the weakening of the North Atlantic Treaty Organization (NATO) defensive posture in a highly vulnerable area.

Between 1963 and 1974 Cyprus was mainly a problem of inter-communal strife and of peacekeeping efforts of the United Nations force deployed throughout the island as well as a source of friction between Greece and Turkey. After 1974, when Turkish troops seized the north in answer to an Athens-staged coup, the issue became a major international abscess, with potentially explosive complications. The sequence of events during those years shows clearly the extent of the impact of the Cyprus problem. It was because of the coup that the Turks landed on the island and, thus, caused Greece's withdrawal from NATO's military wing (which was to last six years). The U.S. arms embargo against Turkey followed, further weakening NATO's defenses. Papandreou's electoral victory in Greece in 1981 appeared to have exacerbated the problem, with his references to Cyprus as part of "Greek national space" and threats to suspend intercommunal talks as long as foreign troops remained on the island.

The separation of the feuding ethnic groups, which followed the Turkish invasion, was beneficial insofar as it eliminated constant friction and bloodshed on the island itself. Yet, foreign governments did not regard it as a solution, feeling that the division of the island contained the germ of a wider conflict. To a number of governments, Cyprus also looked like the small and innocent victim of Turkish aggression. The pre-1974 fate of the Turkish minority was seldom considered in such an analysis.

In mid-1982 Cyprus was bristling with guns. North of the so-called Attila line (separating the Greek and Turkish zones) were some 19,000 Turkish troops and 5,000 well-armed conscripts of the Turkish Cypriot security force. In the south there was the Greek Cypriot National Guard of 10,000 men, with 20,000 reservists, a contingent of 950 troops from mainland Greece, a United Nations peacekeeping force of 2,200 men, and some 2,500 soldiers manning two British sovereign bases, Akrotiri and Dhekelia. All of this existed for an area of 3,500 square miles to which, despite its trials and tribulations, tourists flocked in search of the sun and relatively cheap holidays.

From the air, the Cypriot beaches look golden and inviting. The craggy Kyrenia range rises sharply over the northern coastline. In the southwest, the bulk of the Troodos Mountains towers over the island, the peaks covered with snow for part of the winter. Moufflon dart about in the thick forests of pine and cedar. Wild flowers and bright bougainvillea relieve the grey monotony of the central Messaoria Plain, parched in the summer but covered with lush greenery after the autumn's first rains. The sunsets are luxurious against the gleaming waters of the Mediterranean.

Enterprising traders and businessmen, the Cypriots have profited from the United Kingdom's colonial rule by acquiring some British efficiency and, above all, a knowledge of the English language. In their desire to profit from the island's tourist possibilities, they have constructed a number of architectural monstrosities along the beaches, first around Famagusta and then along the southern coast, near Limassol. Eight years after the Turkish landings the Famagusta hotels stood gutted and abandoned, forlorn sentinels of concrete awaiting a settlement. Distressed environmentalists shouted in vain about "the rape of Aphrodite" as new hotels went up in the Greek-controlled south after 1974. The Turkish north, grappling with an assortment of economic ills, was much more restrained in tourist ventures, although not for reasons of taste. Even the hotels abandoned by Greek Cypriots fleeing the Turkish advance in 1974 stood empty much of the year.

One of the most scenic parts of the island is, unquestionably, the northern coastline, where rocks protrude from the emerald waters and pebbled coves are shaded by shrubbery. The ruins of ancient crusader castles stare down from the mountain range. The harbor of Kyrenia is dominated by the massive walls of one of the best preserved castles of that period. Unfortunately, most towns and villages in the Turkish north have been spoiled by gaudy billboards advertising plastic toys and imported whisky. The taste is somewhat better—but not much—in the south. For an aesthete, Cyprus has been spoiled by the inhabitants, who have shown few indications of their interesting cultural past.

What has become known locally as the Cypriot heritage actually has little to do with the Cypriots themselves. The inhabitants of the island have left few original contributions to civilization since the Bronze Age, when the copper industry gave the island its name. After that period it was mainly a succession of conquerors and foreign settlers—ancient Greeks; Phoenicians; the Ptolemies; Romans; Byzantines; Venetians; Lusignans; and, finally, in 1571, the Ottoman Turks, who were to rule the island for some 300 years. Each succeeding wave left its imprint, and to this day the Cypriots take considerable pride in Venetian walls, Byzantine monasteries, Greek and Roman ruins, and a couple of interesting mosques. All this has little to do with Cypriot creativity itself. The diet of the average Cypriot is a simplified version of the Ottoman cuisine. The vineyards dotting the foothills of the Troodos often produce palatable wines, but they are hardly the gourmet's delight portrayed in tourist pamphlets. Perhaps the most original Cypriot product is the delicate Lefkara lace, now an increasingly disappearing commodity, except for machine-produced imitations. More prevalent are crudely manufactured plastic and leather bags decorated with maps of Cyprus, popular with troops of the U.N. contingent. Many foreigners have become attached to the island, some because of its people but most for the climate and the cost of living, which in 1982 was among the lowest in the accessible extremities of Europe. While courteous and friendly and generally helpful to visitors, the Cypriots have antagonized many with their political obsessions, mutual accusations, and excessive bureaucracy (particularly on the Turkish side). After a few months in Cyprus, diplomats usually become exasperated with the Cyprus problem. They hear the same arguments daily: intransigent, bitter, and often self-righteous (mainly on the Greek side). It is enough to spoil the charms of the Island of Aphrodite, that mythical goddess of antiquity who is said to have stepped ashore out of the white Mediterranean foam near Romios. In Cyprus, where legend and fact frequently blend, she was also known as the goddess of adultery and rape.

It is not the purpose of this study to analyze in detail the un-questionably colorful past of Cyprus. But to understand fully the island's role as well as its ambitions and grievances, at least a brief glance at its recent history is essential.

First, it should be stressed that at no time did modern Greece control the island. The predominantly Hellenic character of Cyprus was mainly formed during Turkish rule, much of which was relatively benign. In many ways the Turks encouraged the creation of a pros-perous Greek community in Cyprus as a serious source of the taxes so avidly demanded by the Ottoman rulers. The comparatively small Turkish community which drifted to the island was generally neglect-ed and often lived in the shadow of the more prosperous Greeks and their influential Orthodox church. However, during periods of ten-sion, priests and even bishops were executed by Turkish troops, and many Greek shops were put to fire. Cruel as they were, such methods of revenge or punishment were common throughout the world in that period; Cyprus was not spared.

On the whole, Turkish influence on the island was limited to the traditional administration and tax collecting system, which (as in Greece and other Ottoman possessions) left the inhabitants to their own devices as long as they obeyed the financial rules imposed by Constantinople. The rulers were flexible and, at least in Cyprus, showed little interest in keeping the island as part of the empire. This was confirmed in 1878, when the United Kingdom literally bought Cyprus from Turkey in exchange for some cash and British guaran-tees for Ottoman control of parts of the Middle East. While Disraeli pursued his grand design for an imperial presence in the Levant, Cyprus was an important springboard to that part of the world, just as it was for the crusaders, Venetians, and other Western conquerors.

The arrangement between Turkey and the United Kingdom concerning Cyprus was odd by international standards. Although the British flag flew over the island, Cyprus continued, at least theoretically, to be under Ottoman sovereignty. Only after Turkey entered World War I on the side of the German–Austro–Hungarian coalition did the United Kingdom annex Cyprus. Still, the island was not proclaimed a crown colony until 1925—seven years after the Entente's victory in Europe and four years after the rout of the Greek armies from Asia Minor.

By all standards, the United Kingdom was an enlightened colonizer; to this day many of the island's inhabitants express regret at its departure. Initially, the British presence was welcomed by the Turkish minority (46,000 in 1882), who feared domination by the Greeks (136,000). The Greek community, however, conscious of the friendly relations between the United Kingdom and the Greek mainland, looked forward to the realization of the dream of enosis or union with Greece. The concept was eventually to plague British rule in Cyprus, leading to independence in 1960, after four years of underground struggle by the National Organization of Cypriot Fighters (EOKA).

Pan–Hellenism (that intoxicating concept of a community of all Greek-speaking people) continued to grow before and after World War I, despite the fact that in 1915 Greece declined an outright offer by the British of control over Cyprus. The collapse of the Ottoman Empire further enflamed Greek Cypriot hopes and made relations between the island's ethnic communities increasingly difficult. To the Greek clamor for enosis, the Turkish Cypriots replied with their own slogan of *taksim* (partition).

The United Kingdom fully realized the extent of the problem, but all it could do was keep passions under reasonable control while guaranteeing the rights of the Turkish minority in the face of vocal and hostile Hellenes. As time went by, the British role became more and more difficult. British troops had to quell a number of riots and demonstrations by Greek Cypriots. In 1931, crowds, enflamed by a manifesto of the Orthodox Bishop of Kition, burned down the governor's residence in Nicosia. Troop reinforcements were rushed to the island, and two bishops and a number of other religious and political leaders were sent into exile.

World War II and Greek participation on the side of the Allies rekindled Hellenic aspirations in Cyprus. Many Greek Cypriots were genuinely convinced that after an Allied victory, enosis was inevitable. Although British statesmen, such as Sir Winston Churchill, recognized the predominantly Hellenic character of Cyprus, none went so far as to officially and publicly endorse the calls for enosis. During the war itself, the United Kingdom relaxed its rule in Cyprus and allowed the creation of political parties. Soon the Greeks formed no less than 32 parties, while the Turks had three. Most of the Greek parties demanded "enosis and only enosis."

In 1950, the Greek Cypriots organized a referendum on the question of enosis, with predictable results (96 percent in favor of the union). It was the first political victory of the man who subsequently became Archbishop Makarios III, and later the island's first president. A wily politician and a man with considerable vision, Makarios also shared responsibility for the island's future tragedy and the split between the communities. But Makarios knew his electorate and its burning desire for union with the motherland. Early in 1967, seven years after independence and over three years after the breakdown of the British-designed constitution, the archbishop–president said that "the union of Cyprus with Greece has always been and continues to be the national aspiration of the Greek people of Cyprus."[1]

However, in the 1950s, the march to independence had barely begun. Seeing that the United Kingdom had no apparent intention of giving in to their demands, the Greek Cypriots started organizing the only action capable of bringing results—a campaign of terror. Arms and explosives were smuggled to the island from Greece, and the first freedom fighters were sworn in by a Greek colonel, George Grivas, born in the Cypriot village of Trikomo. In April 1955, Grivas and EOKA struck with bomb attacks against British installations in Cyprus. It was the start of a four-year period of terror and repression, arson, murder, and intercommunal clashes, which eventually led to the creation of a Cypriot republic.

In his memoirs, Grivas succinctly describes the reasons that motivated him.

> When, in the Second World War, the swastika flew over the Acropolis in Athens, our hopes were kept alive by the promises of Britain and America. . . . 30,000 Cypriots were induced to join the British army by assurances that they were fighting for "Greece and freedom". Like every other Cypriot, I believed that we were also fighting for the freedom of Cyprus. But when the war was over and democracy was safe once more, these promises were broken and the principles for which we had struggled were trampled into the dust. As the empty post-war years went by I was forced to realize that only in

one way would the island win the freedom which it sought so long: by fighting for it.[2]

While British troops struggled against EOKA terrorism, the Turkish community also organized for combat. The Turkish Cypriot organization, known as VOLKAN (volcano), began to take a toll among the more vociferous proponents of enosis. Still, it was not until Christmas of 1963, long after independence, that the two ethnic communities clashed head-on, necessitating the dispatch of a United Nations peacekeeping force and turning the island into an open wound.

Makarios himself earned his political martyrdom when he was exiled by the British to the Seychelles Islands in 1956. Released in April 1957, he was not allowed to return to Cyprus because of his alleged contact with Grivas. Instead, the clergyman–politician traveled to Athens, where he was given a tumultuous welcome. The sight of chanting crowds in Athens' Constitution Square apparently convinced Makarios that his horizons should extend beyond his small native island. It was then that Makarios styled himself the leader of Hellenic people, an aim history did not allow him to achieve.

He did, however, achieve the independence of his Cypriot homeland after some 500 deaths (142 of which were British), a frustrating police operation by 30,000 British troops, and a series of negotiating sessions. The compromise was the so-called Zurich Agreement in 1959, which set up a Cypriot republic the following year, with the United Kingdom, Greece, and Turkey as guarantor powers. The settlement included a draft constitution and three subsidiary treaties, under which the United Kingdom retained two sovereign base areas. Under the agreement Greece was to keep 950 and Turkey 650 troops on the island, a clause that was to be violated soon after independence, when Greek troops swelled to some 9,000 and had to be evacuated after strong U.S. diplomatic pressure in 1967.

As far as the United Kingdom was concerned, the settlement was not a bad one. The cumbersome and costly problem seemed over. The Cypriots got their independence and promptly reinforced mutually advantageous commercial links with the former colonial power. English continued to be the working language on the island, and British law was the basis for the law of Cyprus. Eventually, disregarding years of terror and bloodshed, British tourists poured into Cyprus, profiting from the sun, low prices, British-instilled efficiency, and a widespread knowledge of English. Former EOKA terrorists took degrees at British universities; a thriving Cypriot colony took root in

London. Above all, the Union Jack continued flying over 99 square miles of military installations in Cyprus. Even the Turkish Cypriots thrived in the initial stages of independence, which gave them guarantees and privileges far exceeding their numbers. Unfortunately, this disproportion contained the germ of conflict.

The constitution specified that the president of the new republic was to be a Greek Cypriot and the vice-president a Turkish Cypriot. When, on August 16, 1960, the Union Jack was replaced by a white flag showing a yellow map of Cyprus, Makarios became president, assisted by Swiss-educated Dr. Fazil Kuchuk.* The two men were hardly ideal partners. Equally unwieldy was the cabinet, consisting of four Greek and three Turkish ministers. Eventually the pattern became clear to all: most of the voting at cabinet sessions was along national lines. The president and vice-president had the power of veto in foreign affairs and defense.

The Turkish minority, which always felt dwarfed by the Greeks, was favored in a number of fields. Thus, 30 percent of the seats in the house of representatives were allocated to the Turks, who were also to hold 40 percent of the commissions in the island's National Guard. Policemen and civil servants were to be recruited at a 70–30 ratio, despite the fact that according to official statistics the Turkish Cypriots represented only 18 percent of the population.

This arrangement soon came under pressure. There were simply not enough qualified Turks to take over the posts assigned to their ethnic group. Greek Cypriots complained about the budget allocations requested for the education of Turkish children. The heart of the problem was that the two communities had few solid bonds; whatever cooperation existed was strained and superficial. Years later, Rauf Denktash, the first president of the "Turkish Federated State of Kibris" told the author, "There has never been a Cypriot nation—just Turks and Greeks living in Cyprus." The recent history of Cyprus has certainly proved the validity of this statement.

Against such a background, the breakdown of the independence agreement seemed inevitable. It was triggered by Makarios himself in November 1963, when he presented Kuchuk with a memorandum proposing drastic changes in the constitution. The changes were

---

*The flag itself was hardly an emblem likely to rally the new nation. Years later, (February 28, 1982) Colin Smith in *The Observer* described it as "anaemic looking: a yellow island-shaped blob with a sprig of greenery on a white background, something like a runny fried egg served with parsley."

intended to curtail the advantages of the Turks and create a unitary state. Ankara backed Kuchuk's angry rejection, and events raced beyond control, leading to intercommunal strife, which exploded on December 21. Towns and villages were littered with corpses; within months some 24,000 Turkish Cypriots fled their villages to seek protection in larger enclaves. Both sides accused each other of atrocities, but the sheer number of Greeks worked in their favor. Eventually troops from the British sovereign bases had to step in, and in 1964 a multinational United Nations force was dispatched to the island. Cyprus became laced with barbed wire, dotted with gun emplacements, and scarred by burned out and abandoned villages. Places of worship were desecrated; friendships were lost in the turmoil of fratricidal strife.

While useful in preventing a number of small incidents, U.N. troops were generally helpless in the face of major clashes. Thus, they merely stood by in August 1964 when a Greek force attacked the Turkish enclave at Kokkina, whose defenders were eventually aided by air strikes from nearby Turkey.

During the subsequent four years, the Turkish Cypriots were very much living in a state of siege on the island they were supposed to share with the Greeks. The enclaves were deprived of building material and gasoline on the grounds that they were useful for defense purposes (see Appendix A). The Greek Cypriots, who controlled the Nicosia airport and other ports of entry, instituted a ban on arrivals of male Turkish Cypriots of military age. Students wishing to return to their homes from Turkey and elsewhere had to be put ashore by Turkish gunboats off the Kokkina enclave to avoid immigration scrutiny. Letters to Turkish Cypriots were frequently returned; their businesses in mixed communities were often penalized by heavy taxes.

It was during that bloodstained period that the cleavage between the communities became painfully accentuated. In Cyprus, that proverbial island of love, the much larger conflict between Greece and Turkey took on its most ominous and ugliest form. The Greek Cypriots rallied around the blue and white flag of Greece and chanted "enosis" on Greek national holidays. In the Turkish enclave of Nicosia, "Turkish Fighters" in peaked caps marched to drums and pipes, the red flag with the star and crescent snapping in the breeze. The flag of Cyprus was flown on a few courthouses and police stations. To most Cypriots, it meant little.

Nonetheless, a search for some form of solution went on, encouraged by diplomatic efforts from outside. It was complicated by the proponents of enosis, who, spurred by the tireless Grivas, formed a new EOKA, known as EOKA-B. The organization was blamed for the massacre of 25 Turkish Cypriots in November 1967, and Turkish troops were loaded on landing craft at the Mersin naval base. The crisis was averted by the skillful diplomacy of the special U.S. envoy, Cyrus Vance. Greece was forced to evacuate the bulk of its troops from Cyprus. In 1968, intercommunal talks began, with Glafkos Clerides representing the Greek side and Denktash the Turkish. Both men were lawyers and had known each other from school days. On several occasions during their arduous talks a solution seemed within reach. Whenever it was approved by Ankara, however, it was blocked by Athens, which wanted to see Cyprus a unified state under Greek control, particularly after the military coup of 1967. In the end, it was Makarios himself who torpedoed the blueprint for a settlement on the flimsy pretext that it would cost the Greek Cypriot taxpayers too much to support the poorer Turkish community.[3] Perhaps the most tangible outcome of the talks was the relaxation of Greek restrictions on Turkish enclaves. For the first time in years, Turks from Nicosia were allowed to reach the northern beaches during the torrid Cyprus summer. Construction material began to trickle in; many Turks went back to work in the Greek areas. The Turks, however, refused to allow the Greeks into their sectors in Nicosia and Famagusta nor into several smaller enclaves. Travel between the Greek sector of Nicosia and the coastal town of Kyrenia (16 miles north) was under the guidance of a U.N. convoy only. The Turks claimed the measure was essential to prevent spying.

To the outside world, however, the Cyprus problem in early 1974 was not so much the issue between Greeks and Turks but the internal turmoil created by EOKA-B in the name of enosis. The terror campaign was not on the scale of the original EOKA action; nonetheless, bombs exploded on the island again, gunmen were hauled into courts, and arms caches were raided. These actions represented a growing challenge to the authority of Makarios, and the former monk from the Kykko monastery decided to act. In July 1974, in unusually blunt terms, he accused Greece of meddling in the affairs of Cyprus and ordered home the 600 Greek officers and noncommissioned officers who constituted the cadres of the Greek Cypriot National Guard. Enosis, at least as far as the Makarios government was concerned, was not politically convenient at that stage.

It has been established (with some degree of accuracy) that the Athens junta had planned to get rid of Makarios and install a regime favorable to enosis. The coup, apparently, was to take place in October 1974, but Makarios's decision to remove Greek officers required some form of immediate reaction. This occurred on the morn-

THE DIVIDED ISLAND / 99

ing of July 15, 1974, when units of the National Guard, led by Greek officers as well as parts of the official Greek military contingent, took over the radio station and attacked the presidential palace, the archbishopric, and such installations as the telecommunications center. Luck was with Makarios, as it had been during a number of previous assassination attempts: he fled the burning presidential palace and, without his cassock, was driven southwest toward Paphos past columns of rebellious national guardsmen shouting slogans of enosis.

All communications, internal and external, were cut in the classic tradition of all coups. Although the radio station in the hands of the rebels repeatedly stated that Makarios was dead, scattered groups of his supporters resisted for over two days. Troops of the Greek mainland contingent seized the airport outside Nicosia after an exchange of gunfire, and soon planes arrived from Athens bringing more military advisers and policemen. The paralyzing curfew was reduced on the third day, but shots still crackled in parts of Nicosia. By then it was known that Makarios had survived and had been flown to the safety of London from the British base at Akrotiri. Nikos Sampson, a former EOKA gunman saved from a British hangman's noose by a political amnesty, became the president of Cyprus. It was this choice that helped precipitate the decision to send Turkish troops to the island.

Sampson was a simple man, obsessed first by the struggle against British colonial rule, then by his hostility toward Makarios, Rightwing and anticommunist, he nonetheless regarded the USSR with some respect, mainly because of its policy of strength. Although in his capacity as a newspaper owner he was courted by the U.S. embassy in Nicosia and invited to visit the United States as an official guest he delighted in flippant anti-Americanism. Above all, Sampson hated Turks. He was photographed in the ruins of the battered Turkish suburb of Omorphita in 1963, waving the Greek flag. To the Turks in Cyprus and Turkey, Sampson symbolized the enemy.

His initial repression, however, centered on the supporters of Makarios. Thousands were herded into jails; hundreds were summarily executed. On July 17, three days after the coup, when charter planes bringing newsmen were allowed to land, Sampson staged a parody of a press conference at which he attempted to reassure the Turkish community. By then it was clear that Turkish Premier Ecevit considered the coup as inevitably leading to the annexation of Cyprus by Greece. Troops began to converge on the Mersin base. Turkey's efforts to secure the support of the United Kingdom as a guarantor power failed. The United States dispatched Undersecretary of State Joseph Sisco to the East Mediterranean, although it was obvious that the United States had little intention of bringing pressure on Turkey. Besides, it was equally clear that Turkey was not going to be easily persuaded to ignore the Cyprus events again.

On Friday, July 19, as a red sunset swept over the Mediterranean, an armada of 22 Turkish warships and landing craft sailed from Mersin. John Lawton, an enterprising correspondent of the United Press International, managed to get a telephone call out of Mersin despite the military ban on communications. He was the only one with the news, and many capitals remained skeptical. Most Greek Cypriots shrugged off any speculation about a Turkish attack. "They wouldn't dare. They're cowards," laughed the National Guardsmen manning barricades outside Kyrenia. The following day, at dawn, Turkish jets attacked Kyrenia, sinking a Greek Cypriot gunboat. Paratroopers landed on the plain outside Nicosia, and warships loomed off the northern coastline. The invasion of Cyprus had begun.

From a strictly military point of view, the operation was hardly a success. The elite paratroopers dropped from planes or brought in by a steady shuttle of helicopters regrouped in the Turkish Cypriot zone between Gönyeli and Nicosia, with the apparent aim of capturing the airport, defended by a mainland Greek battalion. They were bogged down in a barrage of Greek Cypriot artillery. The spearhead of the seaborne assault force landed at the so-called 5½ Mile Beach west of Kyrenia (hardly more than a cove), dominated by a steep, easy-to-defend slope covered with parched shrubs. It took the Turks 48 hours to get out of the narrow perimeter of the beach, defended by the ragtag National Guard and reinforced by reservists, most manning World War II rifles. At one stage the Greeks boldly attacked St. Hilarion Castle, perching like an eagle's nest on the crest of the Kyrenia range, dominating the sea, and being held by a Turkish Cypriot unit. Only the arrival of Turkish jets at dawn saved the defenders and scattered the attackers.

Greek Cypriot resistance was stubborn and, in many cases, heroic. Turkish aircraft dominated the skies incessantly: their warships pounded Greek Cypriot positions. But when a U.N. imposed cease-fire took effect on July 22, the Turks had captured only a narrow strip of land and managed to implant troops in the Turkish triangle between Nicosia and the Hilarion pass. Despite repeated attacks, they failed to capture Nicosia airport.

In those torrid days of July 1974 there was still a feeble hope of preserving something of Cypriot national unity. The Turks seemed amenable to a solution, under which they would have access to

Cyprus and, above all, to the Turkish sector of Nicosia. They also wanted full Cypriot rights for the Turkish Cypriots. This hope was quickly shattered by two factors: Greek Cypriot behavior toward the Turkish minority during the invasion and its aftermath and the abortive negotiations which took place in Geneva.

While Turkish warships shelled the coastal defenses of northern Cyprus and jets crisscrossed the island's cloudless skies, Greek Cypriot wrath turned on Turkish villages and urban enclaves. The Turkish part of Nicosia was under artillery attack. Fire poured into the walled-in ancient city of Famagusta, deprived of water and electricity by the surrounding Greeks. Mortar shells were rammed into the Turkish quarter of Larnaca, and search parties arrested all able-bodied men, who were subsequently herded into a school building, without food or medical attention.* Thousands of interned Turks camped under the broiling sun in the Limassol sports stadium. Thousands of others rushed for the safety of sovereign British bases, along with Greeks who were fleeing the advancing Turkish troops. Northumberland Fusiliers, colored feathers in their berets, traced neat lines of a huge tent city near Dhekelia, carefully separating the two ethnic groups of an island on fire.

The diplomatic disaster took place in the early part of August in Geneva. The Turks were in a strong position, and their demands reflected it. They wanted a Cypriot federal government with an equal voice for the Turkish minority, Turkish Cypriot administration for scattered Turkish cantons, and other concessions traditionally unpalatable to the Greek side.

Before the conference started, the military government in Athens collapsed, already undermined by the student riots of November 1973. While crowds clamored for death for the infamous colonels, a new administration was groping for ways to reestablish democracy. Greece was unable to cope with 500-mile distant Cyprus or give it any practical help during or after the Turkish military intervention. All Greece did was to announce its withdrawal from NATO's military structure, a gesture whose impact was to damage the alliance in years to come.

Representing the Greek Cypriot side at the Geneva talks was Clerides, a man eminently suited to make a compromise. But the uncompromising directives of Makarios from his London hotel suite

---

*When I visited the school after the cease-fire, the leader of the interned, Alper Faik Genc, said, "All we want is security. If we find it in hell, we'll go there."

weighed heavily over the conference. He was still the elected president of Cyprus, while Clerides, following Sampson's hasty resignation, was variously referred to as "president" or "acting president." Neither Makarios nor the new government in Athens understood the determination and advantages of the Turks, and Clerides could do little by himself. When negotiations started to drag on with few signs of progress, Turkey simply broke them off. At dawn on August 14, 1974, barely four weeks after the first landings, some 30,000 Turkish troops, waiting in the narrow area captured earlier, fanned out east and west of Nicosia, without attacking the Greek sector of the capital. In clouds of dust, tanks raced across the Messaoria Plain toward Famagusta, where some 40,000 Greek Cypriots fled the once thriving modern quarter of Varosha, leaving electric fans whirling and air conditioners turned on. The British bases filled with another wave of refugees. All the Clerides government could do was launch appeals to the world, which eventually resulted in another U.N.-sponsored cease-fire. By then the Turks had reached their objective—the line which continued to divide Cyprus while this work was being written eight years later.

The island reeled under the impact of swift and unpredictable events. Mass graves were discovered filled with Turkish Cypriot bodies; thousands of Greek Cypriot men were shipped to mainland prisons by the conquering Turks. The towns of the Greek-controlled south were filled with hapless refugees mourning their kin and their lost homes. The northern part was like an open wound, with empty bullet-scarred villages and abandoned herds wandering in the parched fields. After an initial orgy of looting, the Turkish army clamped a tight lid on the north. A new Turkish Cypriot administration recruited from among some 40,000 Turks in the north began to make its first uncertain steps in preparing for the arrival of other Turks from the south, who already trickled across the demarcation line in family groups searching for security. Greek Cypriots swarmed around foreign consulates in quest of immigrant visas. While the Turks had hopes of a better tomorrow, the Greeks had little to look forward to. With Makarios still safely in London, Clerides bore the brunt of the boiling anger and frustration of his compatriots, a thankless task he performed with statesmanlike dignity. One of his first acts was to establish a dialogue with Denktash, under U.N. auspices. As a result, several thousand prisoners were exchanged, and many of the missing were located.

Regardless of the efforts of some men of good will, the Cyprus problem plunged the feud between Greece and Turkey to a new low, creating enormous difficulties for the West and particularly for the

United States. Many Greek Cypriots saw Washington's role in the events, simply because the United States had backed the Athens junta and, above all, did not intervene when the Turks stormed ashore. "What's the Sixth Fleet for?" asked angry former cabinet minister and former prominent EOKA fighter, Tassos Papadopoulos.[4] The Greek Cypriots, part of the Third World and vocal at most conferences of the nonaligned countries, basically wanted U.S. intervention against a NATO ally in an effort to save their island. Clever tradesmen and astute businessmen, the Greek Cypriots have rarely been familiar with the basic facts of international politics. Anything that did not directly concern Cyprus mattered little. While important as a strategic outpost and a source of international tension, Cyprus has never been the center of the world stage. This is something few Cypriots understood.

Their wrath turned against the United States. On August 19 screaming crowds besieged the four-story U.S. embassy building, setting cars afire, including that of Ambassador Rodger Paul Davies, who had arrived on the island barely three weeks before the July 15 coup. Banners proclaiming "Kissinger murderer" and "America must pay" were hoisted over the heads of the crowds. As shots rang out from an unfinished building near the embassy, hysterical women shrieked, "Kill them! Kill them!" Davies fell in the corridor outside his office, killed by a high velocity bullet, which had penetrated the wall. Another bullet killed his Maronite Cypriot secretary, Antoinette Varnava. Clerides arrived at the scene shortly afterwards, while crowds still shouted, "Americans must die!" He denounced "this terrible crime against Cyprus" but, mindful of the mood of the crowd, promptly added, "I believe the United States could have exerted more effective pressure to prevent the Turkish invasion."[5]

Much has been written about the U.S. role in the coup and Washington's inactivity during and after the invasion. As most valuable and truthful documents remain classified, this study can shed little additional light on alleged Central Intelligence Agency (CIA) involvement in the effort to topple Makarios. True, the archbishop-president was not an easy partner of the United States, and his courting of Soviet-bloc countries annoyed many U.S. officials. Yet, the idea that the CIA actually gave the green light to the Athens colonels to strike in Cyprus seems hard to believe. Many Greek Cypriots believe that such a strategem was planned to allow the Turks to occupy a portion of Cyprus. In that case, if the United States wanted Turkey to control Cyprus, why not have the Turkish army take the rest of the island as well? After all, Greek Cypriot resistance had crumbled, and recent history shows that any U.N. cease-fire is usually observed when it suits the stronger of the protagonists. Perhaps the most simple answer is that the United States had not anticipated that events would move so quickly beyond control and had no valid contingency plan. The blame rests not so much on U.S. diplomats assigned to Cyprus but on the desk in the U.S. State Department, which appeared to be bored with reports of planned coups and the vicissitudes of a small country. The fact is that many coups had been planned on the island and, if successful, were bound to affect the United States and a number of other countries. At a dinner party in Nicosia in May 1974, Sampson, under some alcoholic influence, said, "Makarios will not live much longer. This time we'll get him." A U.S. diplomat who was present simply shrugged. He had heard similar statements countless times before and knew that Washington was not likely to be interested in yet another rumor report from Cyprus.

To many Greek Cypriots, the United States remained the scapegoat for their island's problems. When, in January 1975, Turkish Cypriots camping at British bases were flown to Turkey to be resettled in the north of Cyprus, crowds set fire to the U.S. embassy in Nicosia. Makarios, who in the meantime had returned from his exile, apologized and promised to pay for the damage.

For several years no one investigated the assassination of Ambassador Davies, and some of those involved bragged about their exploits in tavernas. Eventually, in May 1977, two former policemen and a civilian accomplice were brought before the courts. It was almost a festive occasion; the accused laughed and were cheered by well-wishers, while government witnesses were intimidated and threatened. The defense argued that no one should be accused of killing Davies because he had not been a visible target, being behind a wall inside the embassy building. After a five-week trial, Ioannis Ktimatias, a former police sergeant, was sentenced to seven years in prison "for possessing and using an automatic weapon in the course of a violent demonstration outside the American embassy building" and for "participating in a riot and causing malicious damage to the embassy building." Another man, Neoptolemos Leftis, received a sentence of five years in prison for "possessing an automatic weapon and for participating in the riot." Both men were released in July 1978, a little over a year after the sentencing.

Washington seemed at a loss as to how to cope with the situation created after the coup and invasion. The subsequent congressional arms embargo against Turkey merely reduced U.S. leverage possibilities. The creation of a strong Greek lobby in the United States made U.S. policy appear favorable to the "legal" (meaning Greek) side of the divided island. All accredited diplomats lived on the Greek side, surrounded by Greek friends and a steady flow of Greek Cypriot propaganda. The Turks, inept at public relations in the best of circumstances, dramatically failed to present their case coherently or with credibility. Most resident newsmen in Cyprus were Greek Cypriots, and their dispatches generally reflected the official Greek point of view. Many visiting Western newsmen were easy prey to the intense public relations efforts of the Greek Cypriot Public Information Office. Correspondents have frequently been invited to the island at government expense. The result was a picture of a "raped" island, with little objective search for the causes of the rape. The Turkish side actually helped the Greek propaganda effort by creating numerous difficulties for newsmen who tried to cross the barricade into the Turkish sector to observe for themselves.

In 1982 the Greek Cypriot Press and Information Office (PIO) employed close to 100 persons and published a regular bulletin in six languages. Daily press releases were churned out in staggering profusion, dealing with such items as statements by the chamber of commerce, weather forecasts, and visits to the foreign minister. All articles from the world's presses favorable to the Greek side were mimeographed and distributed.

The Turkish Cypriot PIO had three regular officials rarely able to present their case to visiting reporters. The weekly information bulletin in English was hardly a model of journalism. Press releases were mostly in Turkish and aimed at the local press and correspondents from the Turkish mainland. The Turkish Cypriots were generally oblivious of the coverage of the island in the world press. When, in 1979, *The New York Times* published a full page article entitled "What's doing in Cyprus," in which both sides were treated equally, the Turkish Cypriot representative in New York did not bother to send it to his superiors. This attitude improved somewhat in the early 1980s.

The United States tried to maintain a balanced policy and insisted that a percentage of its aid to Cyprus be given to the Turkish side (18 percent, according to the population ratio). However, the aid was administered by the Greek side, which handed over not the dollars it received but Cyprus pounds. What the Turkish Cypriots needed was foreign hard currency.

The de facto partition of Cyprus was given a formal status by the Turkish side when, on February 11, 1975, the "Turkish Federated State of Cyprus" was established. The first presidential and parliamentary elections were held on June 10, 1976, with Denktash elected as president against three opponents. The first cabinet, which was to last two years, was headed by Nejat Konuk. The north established all the trappings of statehood, including a 40-member parliament and a court system. The whole setup soon became mired in bureaucracy; nonetheless, despite overwhelming reliance on Turkey, the functioning of the northern sector improved steadily. As the term *Cyprus* generally signified the Greek side to the outside world, the Turkish word *Kibris* was substituted; hence, the Turkish Federated State of Kibris (TFSK).

Denktash predictably claimed that everything was on the right track. "The Turks have never had it so good here," he said. "They are making progress in trade, in business, in developing their own security. People have grown to like their freedom. Consequently, in any future settlement one should not expect them to give up any of these things."[6]

There was considerable truth in this statement. What was amazing is that, despite the shortage of trained personnel, things functioned as they did. In May 1982, Denktash said, "Of course, more could have been done. But our achievements should not be belittled. . . . We had to rely on Turkey for our development. If we had had more experienced people, we would not have wasted time on experiments."[7] Considerably hampering those experiments to which Denktash referred was the fact that the TFSK was making its first steps at a time when Turkey was in the throes of major political and economic difficulties.

His reelection as president of the TFSK in June 1981 by a meager 51.7 percent of the vote was a personal blow to Denktash. Both he and his Ankara backers had been confident of at least 70 percent. Denktash campaigned on a platform of a free economy and strong links with the "motherland." Both appeared to have worked against him (despite reports of vote-buying—a time-sanctioned practice in Cyprus). Still, no one doubted the veracity of the outcome. There was understandable concern in Ankara as the first results started coming in; General Haydar Saltik, a man regarded as one of the leading brains behind the National Security Council, personally telephoned throughout the night. The Ankara view was relatively simple: there was, at least in 1981 and early 1982, no viable alternative to Denktash. The Turkish generals, as did their civilian predecessors, deplored the paucity of talent, political and otherwise, in the TFSK. What worried them even more was the emergence of a strong left-wing opposition, particularly represented by Alpay Durduran's Communal Liberation Party (CLP).

The CLP's overall objectives were not dramatically different and were mainly concerned with the question of approach rather than of substance. Thus, while Denktash and his followers recommended a dialogue with the Greek side "only on the highest level," Durduran preached all forms of contact. The CLP also wanted greater state control over the economy instead of Denktash's unfettered free enterprise system. Denktash himself felt that if the opposition managed to get into power, it "would do terrific damage to everything we accomplished here."[8] The question of the relationship with Turkey was a delicate issue, and the links with the "motherland" were taken for granted. Privately, however, CLP members opposed overwhelming reliance on Ankara and its obvious ultimate control over the fate of northern Cyprus. However, neither the CLP nor any other opposition party had an alternative. What the Turkish Cypriots really wanted was a guarantee of protection by the Turkish armed forces, Turkish economic aid, and a minimum of political interference. Such an approach was hardly palatable to the generals in Ankara, who often regarded the north mainly as a valuable bridgehead on a strategic island while professing fatherly love for the Turkish Cypriots.

The debate on the economic system was been going on since the creation of the TFSK in 1975. Denktash and several Turkish Cypriot economists felt that a small strip of land devoid of natural resources could only prosper without stiff controls. The system undoubtedly gave great incentive to businessmen and to some extent stimulated the economic life of the north. At the same time, however, it created two distinct classes of people: the small, affluent free enterprise group and the mass of underpaid workers, civil servants, and subsistence farmers.

While no one in northern Cyprus went hungry and the overall standard of living was higher than that of Turkey, the Turkish Cypriots wanted more. According to columnist Erdal Andiz (writing in the northern Cyprus newspaper *Birlik*), the ruling party was responsible for "smuggling, economic collapse, unemployment and emigration." The opposition claimed that after the Turkish landing nearly 20,000 Turkish Cypriots had left the island in search of opportunities elsewhere and that the influx of 40,000 settlers from Turkey did not represent a viable solution.

The Turkish immigrants, called locally *karasakal* (blackbeards), represented a source of permanent tension, particularly in mixed villages. TFSK officials explained their presence somewhat lamely by describing them as "Turks of Cypriot origin" or badly needed agricultural labor. To the Greek side, the answer was simple: the Turks wanted to increase the population of the north to back their territorial claims in the event of a settlement. Denktash himself claimed that the Turkish Cypriots represented not 18 percent but

24 percent of the total population of Cyprus. It was a well-known fact that immigrants from the mainland received TFSK passports and were inscribed on voting lists. The demographic composition of Cyprus was considerably affected.

The free enterprise class was small but visible—perhaps too visible in a comparatively limited area. It was common knowledge how much a politician or businessman lost or won at the Famagusta or Kyrenia gambling casinos. Cypriots are not given to hiding their wealth; on the contrary, they tend to flaunt it. A gleaming Mercedes-Benz is very much a status symbol. Women show their diamonds and minks in the handful of European restaurants, and men like expensive cigars. In all fairness, it should be stressed that the clientele of such places of entertainment was limited almost entirely to businessmen and visiting or resident foreigners. Most government officials, paid two salaries, did not appear to have amassed wealth from obscure sources. When a wave of economic scandals rocked the north in 1982, including massive smuggling to Turkey, comparatively few respected government officials were implicated. On the whole, eight years after the Turkish landing, the economy of the TFSK lacked a sense of direction or cohesive planning; it simply drifted. Such a situation, compounded by a lack of international recognition, attracted to the north a number of shady foreign entrepreneurs, dabbling in dubious business ventures.

The economic difficulties of the north were compounded by a sustained and well-organized Greek Cypriot effort to block its economic contacts with the outside world. The Greek argument, shared by the entire political spectrum, was that the Turks were illegally using Greek property to foster their economy. A number of Western governments subscribed to this theory, although fewer and fewer as time went by. The British high commission in Nicosia, for example, banned its members from using hotels and restaurants in the north which used to belong to Greeks. (Few diplomats observed the directive.) For some years the international telephone operators in France refused to establish connections with the Turkish-controlled area of Cyprus. The Greek side penalized captains of ships which dropped anchor at the port of Famagusta, threatened charter pilots who flew to the north, and blocked a number of economic agreements. When the Turkish side announced that arrangements were made in 1979 for group tours by Italian tourists, George Tsimon, the so-called mayor of Kyrenia (actually the leader of the Greek refugees from that coastal town), wrote a stiff letter to the Italian ambassador, Giorgio Antonini,

During the last few months my firm purchased from Italy and installed the largest citrus packing plant in Cyprus, worth hundreds of thousands of pounds [Cypriot currency], thus employing many thousands of Italian technicians in making and installing the plant. Now to be confronted with the possibility that some of these technicians will be spending their holidays in our stolen hotels—and perhaps even in my own home—thus spending with the usurpers, the Turks, the money earned from us, the refugees, is beyond anyone's comprehension to accept.[9]

This somewhat curious prose shows one thing: the degree of prosperity of some of the Greek Cypriot refugees, in turn, reflecting the almost miraculous economic recovery of the south.

In many ways, it is a textbook story of success that few foreign observers anticipated. In September 1974, with the wounds of the invasion still raw, Clerides himself predicted a gloomy future for his compatriots. "I believe the people of Cyprus will be called upon to make sacrifices, tighten their belts and even forgo the standard of living to which they have become accustomed," he said.[10] Within a year of the invasion, the economy of the south sprang back to life, despite the loss of nearly 36 percent of the territory, which included (according to the Greek side) the best citrus groves, some of the best agricultural land, and the bulk of the tourist potential.

Early in 1976 more clothing and shoes were being produced in the south than in 1973. Assembly plants for trucks and buses were being built. By 1979, the residential areas of divided Nicosia were a beehive of construction activity. The civil war in Lebanon brought thousands of wealthy Lebanese to the island as well as foreign firms looking for safety. The Greek part of Cyprus, with its excellent telecommunications and efficient postal service, became a major offshore center for foreign firms, although many companies were wary of the potential difficulties.

Inflation, that bane of Western economies, virtually spared Cyprus until 1980. Prosperity was due to two key factors: the flow of foreign aid and the business acumen of the Greek Cypriots. Aid (mainly from the United States, United Kingdom, and Greece) flowed in steadily, and in early 1980 Cyprus, that is the southern side, was perhaps the most heavily subsidized country in the world. It received some $50 million a year in aid for a population of half a million. Nicosia blossomed with brand new shops importing expensive foreign goods. Haute couture clothes came from Paris and Rome; boxes of Havana cigars were stacked in tobacconists' shops. Greek

Cypriot construction firms were active in such distant areas as Saudi Arabia and the United Arab Emirates. With Nicosia airport inactive after the invasion, the Greeks quickly built one at Larnaca on the coast and, in 1981, started construction of another near Paphos. (The Turkish side reactivated an old British airstrip near Tymbou, renamed Ercan; a small modern terminal was completed there in 1977.)

There remained the problem of the refugees from the north (the officially quoted round figure was 200,000). It was printed and distributed throughout the world, shouted at mass rallies, and addressed to international organizations. The Greek Cypriots appeared oblivious of the mass population movements which followed World War II, when millions were displaced or shipped thousands of miles in cattle trains. The plight of their refugees struck them as an enormous international crime, and they persistently appealed to the world for help. There were, of course, other refugees on the island; some 60,000 Turkish Cypriots had left the south and were resettled in the north. This was rarely mentioned, perhaps with some justification: the southern Turks were usually given abandoned Greek Cypriot homes of a considerably higher standard than those they had previously owned. Painters, village shepherds, and forest guards found themselves living in spacious villas, provided with coupons entitling them to washing machines, refrigerators, and other equipment systematically stripped from abandoned Varosha.

Perhaps the more accurate figure of Greek Cypriots who lost their homes in the north is 156,000. At least this figure was used by several Western embassies in Nicosia in early 1976, when the refugee issue was a burning one; some 16,000 persons still lived in tent camps and another 8,400 in shacks, empty garages, or tool sheds. By early 1982, 150,000 refugees had been officially rehoused either through their own initiative or through government-organized programs. A score of new settlements of one-family units have been built throughout the southern sector, mainly with U.S. help. Perhaps not the greatest architectural achievements, the settlements have given solid temporary homes to the peasants from the north. The better educated and well-connected refugees such as "Kyrenia mayor" Tsimon, did much better. Their permanent pain was represented mainly by the sharp outline of the Kyrenia range, beyond which lay their old homes in Turkish hands.

Prince Sadruddin Agha Khan, former U.N. high commissioner for refugees, called them "the only refugees in the world with a parking problem." When this remark appeared in print,[11] an angry government official said, " I can guarantee you that every refugee has adequate space for his car."

Until the death of Makarios in August 1977, the political scene in the south was unquestionably dominated by the "ethnarch." A veteran U.S. diplomat, who spent several years in Cyprus and knew Makarios intimately, claimed the archbishop–president never believed in tackling any issue head-on, unless it challenged his own authority. He described the system between 1960 and 1974 as a "a permissive, benign, inert government." One of the few times when Makarios acted with determination was in July 1974, when he ordered the Greek officers off of the island. The result was the coup and the Turkish intervention.

His successor, Kyprianou, never succeeded in electrifying the Greek Cypriots, although he started with the strong backing of the dominant Democratic party (DIKO). Kyrianou was often supported by the influential Communist party (AKEL), which generally polled between 28 percent and 33 percent of the popular vote. Such a strong communist following in a country living in the shadow of the Greek Orthodox church can be explained by several factors. AKEL claimed to follow in the footsteps of Makarios, still a hero to many Greek Cypriots. Few people questioned its foreign backing or attitude on international issues. What mattered was that AKEL pursued an uncompromising policy toward the Turks and did not preach any sweeping reforms that would affect small shopkeepers or landowners. Above all, its long-time leader, Ezekias Papaioannou, had considerable political charisma. He was regarded as a genuine puritan, indifferent to the temptations of wealth, a man with a vision of an egalitarian society without want.

The strength of Kyprianou's party was steadily eroded by the desertion of members who formed their own groupings. In the 1981 elections, it managed to obtain eight seats in the 35–member parliament, a far cry from the 21 seats won in the previous vote of 1976. AKEL had a strong showing with 12 seats, and another 12 were won by a new force on the Greek Cypriot political scene, the conservative and pro-Western Democratic Rally party (DISI), led by Clerides.

In the late Spring of 1982, as part of his strategy for the presidential elections slated for early 1983, Kyprianou made a formal pact with the Communists. This "marriage of convenience" created a major political controversy on the island.

Before the adoption of a new proportional representation system, DISI, which in 1976 got 29 percent of the popular vote, rated only one parliament member. Its strong showing in 1981 polarized the political scene in the south. It created a tense setting before the presidential elections.

In the early 1980s Clerides was perhaps the only Greek Cypriot politician capable of a working relationship with the Turkish side. As he himself put it, "The Turks know that I am not trying to play tricks or be unreasonable. I have always been very open in my relations with the Turks. Whenever I said that something could be done, I made sure it was done. If I was unable to agree, I said so straight away."[12]

Denktash himself vacillated in his assessment of Clerides, the man he knew as a youth and whom he had faced countless times at the negotiating table before and after the events of 1974. "Yes, I could work with Glafkos," the president of the TFSK said in March 1981.[13] Several months later, perhaps still smarting from his poor showing in the June elections, he angrily described Clerides as "another die-hard enosist."[14]

The result of the presidential contest in the south, in which Kyprianou and Clerides loomed as the main protagonists, was certainly bound to have a strong impact on the development of the situation in Cyprus. On several occasions Clerides expressed the view that, in order to make a breakthrough in the negotiations, "we must discuss something concrete, something which will show how far each side is willing to give in." Above all, Clerides preached increased contact among communities, particularly among those in the younger generations.[15] "Time is not in favor of any community," he said.

Another vocal personality in the south was Vassos Lyssarides, head of the Socialist party (EDEK). The party has strong connections in the Arab world, particularly with the Palestine Liberation Organization (PLO). Its leader traveled frequently to various Third World meetings, at which he was often critical of the West, particularly of the United States. In the 1981 elections, EDEK's strength in parliament dropped from four to three seats. Nonetheless, Lyssarides announced his candidacy in the presidential vote.

All political parties in the south wooed the refugees—an influential bloc but disoriented by the torrent of promises of a return home, which no politician seemed to be able to deliver. As time went by, the refugees took root in the south and increasingly felt themselves mere pawns in the island's political struggles.

The search for a solution went on with ups and downs but few concrete results. Some diplomats saw a major breakthrough in what has become known as the Makarios–Denktash guidelines for a Cyprus solution, adopted on February 12, 1977 (see Appendix B). The document defined the efforts as a search for "an independent, nonaligned, bi-communal federal republic," with each community administering its own area "in the light of economic viability of productivity and land ownership." Questions, such as freedom of movement and return of the refugees, were left for discussion.

Makarios died six months later, and it looked as though the guidelines died with him. Kyprianou, at the time a comparatively unknown politician seriously lacking charisma, was in no position to make any decisive move. Proposals and counterproposals to revive the talks followed, with some halfhearted efforts by outside powers, including the United States. Just about the only concrete act was an agreement in September 1978 to construct a sewage system linking both sides of the divided capital.

The next "breakthrough" took place in May 1979, with U.N. Secretary-General Kurt Waldheim presiding over a meeting between Kyprianou and Denktash. The result was a 10-point protocol in which the two sides agreed to resume negotiations, using the Makarios–Denktash guidelines as their basis as well as the U.N. resolutions relevant to the Cyprus question (see Appendix C). Priority was to be given to the resettlement of Varosha, by then stripped of all movable property, some of which was distributed to the Turkish Cypriot refugees from the south and some of which was inevitably shipped to Turkey by the Turkish army. During the next three years, little movement on the ghost city took place. At one stage Kyprianou described the Turkish offer to allow some 35,000 Greek Cypriots back as "a banana peel thrown by the Turks." The Greek side at first hoped that Varosha would be ceded by the Turkish side, and much newsprint was devoted to the rights of access and other such distant problems. Eventually the Turkish side issued a statement dissipating all illusions: if an agreement on Varosha was reached, the Greek Cypriots would be allowed to return under Turkish Cypriot administration.* Another "glimmer of hope" lost. Varosha continued to be a mournful shell, gently crumbling under the lash of winter rains and the merciless summer sun, the shutters of its houses rattled by the wind, the weeds and rats invading its empty streets.

Clouding any form of dialogue was the question of the so-called missing persons. The Greek side claimed that some 3,000 Greek

---

*This statement was subsequently rectified. The transfer of the Greek Cypriot population to Varosha, according to the new version, would be under U.N. supervision, and the Turkish administration would be temporary, pending an overall solution.

Cypriots had not returned from Turkish prisons, where they were locked up in the invasion's wake. The figure of 2,000 was also occasionally used. As late as 1982 the Greeks insisted they had evidence that some, if not most, of these men were still alive. Committees were formed, and pleas were addressed to the United Nations and other international organizations. As the Ankara government refused to deal with the issue, the Turkish Cypriots bore the brunt of the accusations. Denktash himself felt that "anybody who was missing in 1974 and has not returned must be dead by now. Let them rest in peace."[16]

During the years of arguments and counterarguments, countless theories on the Cyprus problem have been advanced by the protagonists, their backers, and outside observers. They could roughly be divided into two groups: those accusing Turkey of raping an innocent, independent, and small island and those claiming that Turkey acted to protect its suffering ethnic minority. Whenever a foreign government or an international organization suggested that perhaps both sides were to blame, there was the predictable outcry. Such was the case of the former secretary-general of the Strasbourg-based Council of Europe, Franz Karasek, who, in an unusually objective and blunt report, pointed out that much of the blame lay in the conduct of the Greek side. There were howls of protest on the southern side of the Cypriot barricades. To any red-blooded Greek Cypriot, anyone who suggested that Turkey was not at fault was an enemy. The furor over Karasek's report was such that two young soldiers of the U.N. Austrian contingent (Karasek is Austrian) were sexually assaulted and had to be hospitalized.

The verbal skirmishes and propaganda broadsides went on unabated, despite the 1979 agreement between Denktash and Kyprianou. Point six of the summit, which some British newspapers even described as historic, specified that "it was agreed to abstain from any action which might jeopardize the outcome of the talks, and special importance will be given to measures by both sides to promote good will, mutual confidence and the return of normal conditions."[17] Like many other pledges in Cyprus, this one was quickly forgotten. The press was as vituperative as ever and official statements, although more carefully couched, reflected the state of deadlock and incompatibility. After the Turks submitted what they called a comprehensive plan in August 1981, the Kyprianou government took barely two weeks to describe it as "far from satisfactory" and unable to "form the basis of a Cyprus settlement." A typical Turkish comment was by editorialist Arman Ratip: "Once again the Greek Cypriots have torpedoed the talks. Once again the Greek Cypriot leadership has shown that it has no intention of forming an equal partner-ship."[18]

Indeed, there were few signs that the Greek side was willing to accept the Turkish Cypriots as equals, despite sporadic and limited contact by doctors and other professionals, usually outside the coun-try. Most Turks feared that in the event of a settlement (which few believed in 1982) they would again be treated as a cumbersome and second-rate minority.

Such fear apparently obsessed Denktash. "Some of my people would rather die than go back to what we had before the peace operation," he said.[19] "There is only one correct version of the Cyprus events and it is ours." It was fairly obvious that under the pressure of a series of political crises, criticism from the opposition, and murmurs of dissatisfaction from Ankara, the usually cheerful and witty Turkish Cypriot leader was becoming increasingly embit-tered.

Since the proclamation of the TFSK in 1975, Denktash has in-sisted that the best solution was an outright declaration of indepen-dence for the north. He had banked on the support of Islamic countries; Turkish Cypriot officials had courted them without im-pressive results. Once "Kibris" was independent, Denktash argued, it would be recognized by some Arab countries, allowed to establish direct travel and commercial links, and stop being an illegal and ostra-cized entity. In the end, according to this view, "perhaps the Greeks would come around and talk to us differently."

However, following the military coup in Ankara, Turkish offi-cials stopped encouraging any references to the Unilateral Declara-tion of Independence (UDI) by Turkish Cypriots. The reason was obvious: the generals needed U.S. support, and the United States insisted on a negotiated settlement between the Cypriot communities. Early in 1982 Denktash made a volte face, saying that there was no point in any declaration of independence since the two sides were already separated. In this sense he was perfectly correct.

In its approach to the search for a Cyprus solution, the Turkish side inevitably brings up the years of Greek domination and, above all, the atrocities committed during the intercommunal strife. A documentary study of the Turkish position is dedicated to "the memory of our martyrs who made the supreme sacrifice so that the Turkish Cypriot people may survive in their own country and live therein in freedom, security, dignity and in the pursuit of happiness as is the inalienable right of all human beings."[22]

This statement epitomizes the Turkish Cypriot view as well as that of the Ankara government. But the Turkish Cypriots are at heart perfectly aware that more often than not they have been pawns in the perpetual tug of war between Greece and Turkey. Many suspected that Turkey intervened on the island only when the prospect of control by Athens had become a distinct possibility (after the July 15, 1974 coup). According to the view of one embittered Turkish Cypriot politician, Turkey moved "not to save us but when it realized that it would have Greek bases and aircraft on its doorstep."

Significantly, when barricades and gun emplacements divided the two feuding Cypriot sides, clashes and bloodshed stopped. The two communities merely stared at each other through gunsights, as Clerides put it, and communicated on occasion over the telephone. Friction disappeared as if by magic. Thus, the obvious question was, Why search for another solution?

The arguments of the Greek side were based, to a great extent, on international law. The July 15 coup, the Greeks argued, had nothing to do with the Turkish community. At no time during the events which followed the toppling of Makarios and the Turkish landing was the Turkish minority threatened, according to this view.

Seen from the Greek side of the Cypriot barricades, the island's problems were not so much the fault of the Cypriots themselves but of outside powers. According to an analysis by Peter Loizos of the London School of Economics, "There has never been simply one Cyprus problem but several problems, differently defined by different persons. The responsibility for the current situation is shared by a number of major parties including (in no special order) Greek and Turkish Cypriot leaders, Britain, Greece, Turkey, and the United States and the USSR." Loizos seems to single out superpower rivalry in the East Mediterranean as a serious complicating factor on the Cyprus scene. Not without some reason, he concludes that a major responsibility for the continuing problem rests on Greece and Turkey, which "have reacted to Cyprus in terms of their own internal political problems. . . . Both countries' leaders have always been far more concerned with their NATO membership than with the quality of ethnic relations in Cyprus. They appear to have discussed partition as a possible 'solution' as early as September 1956. The question seems to have been where the line would be drawn. . . ."[21]

In 1982 the overriding fact was that Turkey had moved its military force into Cyprus, that it had established a separate Turkish Cypriot ministate, and, short of major upheavals, was unlikely to change its basic attitude. This, however, did not solve the problem of a possible confrontation with Greece on the island. Toward the end of 1981 and at the beginning of 1982 both sides accused each other of building up their respective forces. The Greek press reported Turkish troop reinforcements landing in the north, while the Turkish press exploded in an orgy of colored headlines, which claimed the arrival of Greek men and material after the advent of the Papandreou government.

Impartial confirmation of such allegations was impossible. The Turks ignored a U.N. report denying both the arrival of Greek troops and the Turkish claims of a Greek raid on a U.N. arms depot. But the Turks were still smarting from the fact that before 1974 the United Nations never bothered to report Greek fortifications in the Kyrenia mountain range, which dominates the sea facing Turkey. Consequently, the Turks have always felt that the U.N. peacekeeping force has been pro-Greek. The Turks underlined this conviction by banning U.N. contingents from their territory (but not individual soldiers on weekend passes or food convoys for the enclaved Greek Cypriots in the Karpass peninsula).*

The Turkish reasoning was that the initial objective of the U.N. force—keeping the peace between the communities—had become unnecessary once the friction ceased. In any case, the Turks claimed, there was no need for U.N. intervention in the Turkish zone. As a result, the blue-bereted "soldiers of peace" had become concentrated almost entirely in the Greek south, helping the economy and providing six-month tours of duty in the sun for British, Austrian, Scandinavian, and Canadian soldiers and Australian policemen. The cost-of-living allowances in a comparatively cheap country made the Cyprus assignment a coveted one.

The Turks had been giving lip service to the search for a Cyprus settlement, without too much conviction. Just as the Greeks longed for a return to the status quo antebellum, the Turks basically wanted the maintenance of the status quo established after the 1974 events, with marginal adjustments only.

Faced with the exasperating deadlock and the obvious lack of success of the May 1979, 10-point agreement, Waldheim tried again. The outgoing secretary-general wanted at least some movement on Cyprus that would stop the Greek side from again seeking recourse to the U.N. General Assembly. Waldheim's last effort in the Cyprus imbroglio was a document labeled "Guidelines for the Constitution of the Federal Republic of Cyprus" (see Appendix D). Both sides agreed to accept the guidelines as the basis for discussion, although

---

*Some 2,000 Greek Cypriot farmers still lived there in early 1982.

the Greek side did so with reservations. The reason for the reservations was fairly obvious: the guidelines, prepared by Waldheim's Cyprus envoy, Hugo Gobbi, embodied the basic Turkish demand for physical separation of the two ethnic groups, the well-known concept of bizonality. The Greek side at first contemplated rejecting the document but soon realized that such a move would not enhance its stature in the United Nations. Besides, the guidelines were tabled just before Kyprianou embarked on a trip to several European countries and the United States. This time, the United States was blunt: unless the guidelines were accepted as discussion agenda, there was little point in Kyprianou's seeing President Reagan, the Greek Cypriots were told.

Thus, toward the end of 1981, in the sandbagged former Ledra Palace Hotel in Nicosia's no man's land, festooned with coils of barbed wire, the two sides were faced with long-familiar concepts, which, while to some extent acceptable to the Turks, were hardly palatable to the Greeks.

The guidelines are basically simple and perhaps in another country would have had a chance of success. Their main error is the diplomatic hope that the two communities could cooperate as equals within a Cypriot federal structure. It soon became apparent that, once again, yet another U.N. effort to break the Cyprus stalemate was headed for a series of protracted and futile discussions. It was also clear that the Greek side was unlikely to agree to significant concessions embodied in the guidelines before the presidential elections in the south. Kyprianou, the major candidate, was hardly in a position to risk possible accusations of a sellout, which could cost him votes.

The proposal calls for a federation of the two existing zones, the Greek one consisting of four provinces and the Turkish of two provinces. The crucial territorial question was left open for discussion, with the specification that "for illustrative purposes on the map," the Greek Cypriots would have control over 70 percent of the island, including the present buffer zone along the so-called Attila line, which divides the communities. This 70/30 ratio "might be varied according to the characteristics of the areas. This would be a method of establishing a firm basis for further discussions."[22]

Power in the federation and its effective executive authority would be exercised by a federal council, consisting of six members, four from the Greek and two from the Turkish provinces. The ministerial portfolios would handle all basic tasks, such as foreign affairs, defense, immigration, justice, education, trade and tourism, postal services and telecommunications, finance, labor, and social services.

All members would be appointed for five years. The presidency would rotate between Turkish and Greek Cypriots. The legislature would have two chambers: the chamber of provinces, with 10 members from each community, and the popular chamber, composed of "representatives of the people of Cyprus on a ratio of one member for each 10,000 of the total population," or roughly 65 persons.

The plan went into considerable detail on such comparatively remote issues as public holidays, the official language, and the national anthem. "Each province shall create its own flag using, as far as possible, elements of the federal flag." A fund for the development of the northern (Turkish) province was included in the proposal, with the task of achieving an economic equilibrium between the standard of living of Greek and Turkish Cypriots.

It was clear that what Gobbi intended was, as he himself explained, to give some new impetus to the stymied dialogue. "What we are trying to do with these ideas is to establish a method for discussion," he said in a statement introducing the plan. Ten months after the launching of the proposal no one was nearer progress, despite usual diplomatic utterances of guarded optimism. Gobbi himself insisted that "one of the most important things I have experienced on the island has been the support of the majority of the people of Cyprus. I think that most people, despite the natural skepticism that prevails, believe in the need for negotiations. . . . It is clear that once agreement begins to be reached there will be a better atmosphere within whose context all sorts of things may be possible."[23]

The trouble with Cyprus is that "the natural skepticism" has become part of the national scene, just as have the barbed wire and the gutted buildings along Nicosia's "Green line." The negotiating sessions have become a routine exercise, with few Cypriots believing in any concrete outcome.

To demonstrate some semblance of activity, in the spring of 1982 the cadence of the intercommunal sessions was increased to two a week. A typical press briefing by Gobbi on the subject follows:

> *Question:* When will the next meeting be?
> *Answer:* I do not know exactly, but we are going to have two meetings, one on Tuesday and the other on Friday.
> *Question:* Starting from this week?
> *Answer:* I do not know exactly, but anyway in the very near future, next week.
> *Question:* Have the parties agreed on the acceleration?

> *Answer:* Yes, both parties have agreed on that.
>
> *Question:* Has anything else changed because of this new procedure?
>
> *Answer:* Let's see, everything will change because of this new procedure.[24]

In Gobbi's own words, the protagonists "have become reluctant to give up any of their prerogatives and an ideal solution would be a formula representing a proper balance between their contrary aspirations."[22] No one has found such a formula 22 years after independence from British rule and eight years after the Turkish landing on the rocky northern coast.

Regardless of the thousands of pages of memoranda and tons of paper used by both sides, neither appeared to be rushing toward a reasonable give-and-take. On the contrary, both sides have actually begun to like the separation, apart, obviously, from the refugees uprooted from their homes and promised at rousing rallies that they will return. According to Gobbi, "The Turkish Cypriots have tasted the sweetness of self-determination, unhindered by the Greeks. The Greek Cypriots have tasted the power in their part of the island without the often cumbersome problem of the Turkish minority."[26]

The United States, Turkey, Greece, and the United Kingdom have been perfectly aware of this attitude and of the tremendous obstacles in the path of any reasonable Cyprus solution. Some governments—particularly that of France—hid behind the "illegality" of the Turkish intervention. "France does not recognize the Turkish presence in the island," Ambassador Philippe Oliver told Denktash at a party given in 1981 at the Turkish embassy in the Turkish sector of Nicosia. This diplomatic faux pas took place in front of a number of U.N. officials in full regalia and members of the diplomatic corps.

Many responsible diplomats in Europe and the United States believe that the search for a Cyprus solution is a worthwhile effort simply because the division gives permanent ammunition to the Greek side to clamor for a better deal. This affects a number of international conferences at which the nonaligned Greek Cypriots inevitably get the sympathy of the Third World, with resulting anti-U.S. tirades. Any ambassador in Cyprus worth his salt will admit in private that a solution on Greek terms is virtually impossible, that a separation of the two communities is perhaps the best thing under the difficult circumstances. Yet, in public the same ambassadors, accredited to the legal (meaning Greek) side, participate in the March of Peace, named after the late Makarios; dutifully visit the refugee settlements; and speak of hope for a solution.

Perhaps the most amused are members of the Turkish embassy on the other side of the Attila line, who peruse the Greek newspapers and press releases. "No Greek is going to go home in the North," one diplomat said as far back as 1976.[27] For at least six years this statement has held true.

The crucial question here is, Why bother? Why pay a lot of money for the U.N. peacekeeping force? Why did 24 countries (at the start of 1982) maintain embassies in Nicosia? Why were a succession of U.S. presidents forced to make periodic reports to Congress on the Cyprus situation, which invariably expressed "guarded optimism?"

The answer is relatively simple but as diplomatic as the French ambassador's outcry: no one wanted to antagonize the Greek Cypriots and their Athens backers by spelling out the facts. The facts are that, in 1982 and several years before, no power or group of powers was prepared or wanted to put sufficient pressure on Turkey to give up its Cyprus acquisition. Yes, a compromise was possible—but basically on Turkish terms. Such a compromise would have to recognize the separate but equal existence of the two Cypriot states (or communities), and their federal government would have to be so weak that, in practical terms, it would have little meaning. The policy of open frontiers, about which some politicians speak, is a myth. It does not take much imagination to visualize the stream of Greek Cypriot cars heading toward the Turkish zone once the barrier is lifted. How many of them would be Armenians bent on inflicting death on Turks? How many would be Greek Cypriot relatives of war victims determined to have revenge? Equally, the Greek side was unlikely to allow a similar flow of Turkish Cypriots into its sector for security reasons if nothing else.

Thus, if against heavy odds there is a compromise one day, it will have to be imposed by outside powers, with agreement from Greece and Turkey. Such an arrangement seems a pipe dream but could, by some miracle, happen if enough good will was demonstrated. That commodity appears in short supply as the torrid summer of 1982 envelopes the "Island of Love."

Notes

1. Author's dispatch to the *Washington Star*, February 5, 1967.
2. George Grivas, *Memoirs of General Grivas* (London: Longman's, 1964), p. 2.

3. Author's notes, 1974.

4. In conversation with the author, September 1974.

5. Author's dispatch to the *Washington Star*, August 20, 1974.

6. Conversation with the author, 1980.

7. In an interview with the author for the *Financial Times*, May 4, 1982.

8. Ibid.

9. Text provided by the Cyprus government.

10. In conversation with the author, September 17, 1974.

11. *International Herald Tribune* (Paris) supplement on Cyprus, March 1980.

12. In conversation with the author, 1981.

13. Ibid.

14. Ibid.

15. Ibid.

16. At a press conference, May 1979, in Famagusta.

17. Official text of the 1979 agreement.

18. Editorial by Arman Ratip. *Pan-News Report*, October 1981.

19. In conversation with the author, November 22, 1981.

20. Necatin Munir Ertekun, *In Search of a Negotiated Cyprus Settlement.* (Lefkosa, Cyprus: Ulus Matbaacilik, 1981), p. 5.

21. Minority Rights Group, *Cyprus,* (London: MRG, 1976), p. 22.

22. Text made available to the author, November 15, 1981.

23. In conversation with the author, November 26, 1981.

24. Official transcript, April 24, 1982.

25. Author's notes, November 26, 1981.

26. Ibid.

27. Ibid.

Chapter 6

THE U.S. DILEMMA

We have in recent times been told by some that we are weak; by others that we are strong. Some tell us that we are ineffectual; others say that we are arrogant. Some say we are in retreat; others that we have been running loose. Some say that we are divided and lack purpose; others that we seek to impose our purpose beyond our borders.

Robert McCloskey
U.S. Ambassador to Greece
January 31, 1980

Navigating between the political passions of the East Mediterranean has been one of the more daunting tasks facing U.S. diplomacy. The United States entered the scene at the height of the Cold War to stop what was firmly believed in Washington to be a determined Soviet expansionist policy. During the subsequent 30-odd years, Washington found itself trapped in a web of Byzantine intrigue, national prejudices, and old and new hatreds. The Turks have rioted against visits by warships of the Sixth Fleet. The Greeks have marched countless times on the U.S. embassy in Athens in various protest demonstrations. In Cyprus, that barometer of Greco–Turkish tensions, Ambassador Rodger Paul Davies was shot dead in his embassy, besieged by Greek Cypriot crowds (see Chapter 5). It was perhaps the most poignant and tragic demonstration of the United States' exposed position in the East Mediterranean cross fire.

This study is not an apology for the conduct of U.S. foreign policy toward Greece, Turkey, or Cyprus. That policy has often been high-handed or not assertive enough, particularly in the case of Cyprus. It was hampered by domestic pressures, such as the so-called Greek lobby, and often by excessive concern not to hurt the feelings of the protagonists—to the point of apparent diplomatic weakness. The United States has been the scapegoat of all governments in the area. Successful and unsuccessful plots have been blamed on the Central Intelligence Agency (CIA). Statements by U.S. officials, often taken out of context, have been used for a variety of propaganda purposes. Washington has been accused by Athens of sending too much military aid to Turkey and by Ankara of not giving enough. The Cypriots wanted "peace and friendship" with the USSR and its satellites but clamored for the intervention of the Sixth Fleet when Turkish warships appeared off the northern coast of the island. In short, the U.S. role as an arbiter or protector was an impossible one from the start. What Washington wanted was a strategic consensus against the USSR. That concept was relatively easy in the wake of the Greek civil war, with Turkey worrying about its undermanned frontier with the USSR and Cyprus being reasonably controlled by the United Kingdom. But as time went by and the specter of the Soviet threat became almost routine, the U.S. role became increasingly difficult. With the benefit of hindsight, it could be argued that the United States had a number of options it failed to exercise. But in the heat of political agitation, when decisions have to be made within days if not hours, it is rarely possible to satisfy all those involved. In the case of the East Mediterranean, almost never.

Frequent charges have been made about the poor quality of U.S. diplomats in the area, their insensivity to local problems, and their isolation from the populations of the countries in which they serve. Such criticism is not limited to the East Mediterranean. In fact, it has been leveled—with some reason—against the entire foreign service. It is said that "diplomats are not what they used to be," that they spend too much time on pointless receptions and cocktail parties, particularly in the smaller capitals, where absence can often be regarded as a snub.*

---

*I saw the engagement diary of one of the ambassadors to Cyprus. He had cocktail parties every single working day of the week ahead, sometimes more than once in an evening He expected to see the same people at all of them.

During 15 years of covering the East Mediterranean, I have been in contact with countless diplomats of both Western and Eastern countries. While, inevitably, there have been some second-rate U.S. diplomats assigned to the area, on the whole their performance and preparation for the assignment appeared to be better than that of many of their colleagues. Younger diplomats had frequently undergone language training courses, which provided them with at least a basic knowledge. Many others managed to learn the languages with a considerable degree of fluency, creating favorable impressions in the host countries.

There have obviously been cases of ambassadors taking too much initiative (or not enough) and making the wrong statements at the wrong times, but considerably fewer than those of other countries. The difficulty of being a U.S. diplomat is that one's words and gestures are watched much more carefully than those of other countries.* A U.S. diplomat is expected to monitor the performance of the host government, have high-level and preferably warm personal contacts with officialdom, and at the same time be acutely aware of the activities of the opposition. In countries under military or one-party rule, that is virtually impossible, without causing diplomatic friction. Thus, in October 1971, the U.S. ambassador to Athens, Henry J. Tasca, was the object of a bitter tirade from the military junta for his contacts with Karamanlis, at the time in exile in Paris. A government statement said, "The Greek government regards as inadmissible the practice of foreign envoys, including U.S. ambassador Tasca, of communicating with persons of the old political world who have at present placed themselves outside the lawful framework of the political system."[1] Ironically, Tasca was strongly criticized in Congress for being too favorable to the Greek junta and ignoring the segment of public opinion opposing the regime.

In 1977 the post-junta government in Athens objected to the appointment of William Schaufele as envoy because of statements made by him at a senate hearing. Reported out of context, they gave the impression of an anti-Greek bias. Robert Komer, appointed the

---

*It has been established in most noncommunist capitals that relatively little stature can be expected of Soviet and satellite envoys. More frequently than not they do not speak the local language, and even their knowledge of major international languages is sketchy. In Cyprus, when this study was being written, Soviet Ambassador Sergei Astavin, doyen of the diplomatic corps, never went anywhere without an interpreter.

ambassador to Ankara following his activities in Vietnam, where he supervized the notorious Phoenix program was widely considered by the Turks to be a senior agent of the CIA. Equally, Ambassador Davies, assigned to Cyprus shortly before the 1974 coup and the Turkish intervention, was thought to be "much more than he is" mainly because of his age and wide diplomatic experience.

In Greece, anti-Americanism was rooted mainly in the over-whelming conviction that Washington dominated Greek political life before the military regime, during its seven-year rule, and afterwards. Most Greeks were convinced that the military regime had been imposed on the country as a more secure way of safeguarding U.S. strategic interests. Papandreou's electoral victory in 1981 was certainly helped by the widespread belief that he would stand up to the United States.

There seems to be little doubt that, at least in the East Mediterranean, the United States leans toward strong, right-wing, military rulers. The United States gave its approval to the Turkish generals 15 years after backing the Greek colonels. It is easy to argue that the Turkish takeover was a salutary operation in a country in the throes of chaos. To condone anarchy for the sake of democracy would have shattered whatever was left of North Atlantic Treaty Organization's (NATO) defensive shield in an area bordering on pro-Soviet Syria, expansionist Iraq, and revolutionary Iran—not to mention the USSR. While it is possible for various Western European governments to ignore, approve, or condemn takeovers and political upheavals, a policy statement from Washington automatically has a different dimension.

There have been some dramatic miscalculations of the situation in the Mediterranean by Washington policy makers. Most are easy to explain, particularly years later. But there is no doubt that while the military ruled in Greece, U.S. diplomats assured visiting correspondents of the popular backing of the regime. It was the line imposed by Washington because, privately, many diplomats had different views. In Cyprus, many U.S. officials identified too closely with the Greek establishment, to the point of ignoring the Turkish minority (this was rectified in the late 1970s and early 1980s). In Turkey, some inquisitive U.S. officials found themselves persona non grata—particularly if they spoke Turkish and traveled widely throughout the country.

It is hard to say whether the mistakes in foreign policy were caused by faulty reporting, misjudgement in Washington, or the complexity of the whole situation. A costly example of a combination of such adverse factors was the famous Johnson Letter, sent to Turkey by former president Lyndon B. Johnson in June 1964, when the Turks were readying to rescue their embattled compatriots in Cyprus. Johnson's letter—even now cited by the Turks as a striking example of U.S. high-handedness—told Premier Ismet Inonu that a Turkish military move might involve the USSR. "You will appreciate," the letter continued, "that your NATO allies have not yet had a chance to discuss whether or not they will feel obliged to defend Turkey against a Soviet invasion resulting from an action undertaken by Turkey without their approval."[2]

The U.S. president further warned that the United States would not authorize the use of its military equipment in any operation against Cyprus. The whole thing smacked of *diktat* and aroused Turkish nationalistic feelings. Unfortunately, it was a preview of the subsequent embargo of 1974. However, while the embargo was the work of Congress (against the recommendations of the administration), the Johnson Letter came directly from the highest authority in the United States.

In his *Modern Turkey*, Geoffrey Lewis says, "It may be that if the letter had been less hurriedly drafted its message could have been phrased more tactfully. As it was, the effect on Turkish feelings toward America was disastrous. It seemed that NATO was an organization designed not for mutual aid but simply to advance America's interests; it is from that moment that anti-Americanism in Turkey really dates."[3]

Yet, U.S. objectives in the area covered by NATO's southeastern flank appear mostly straightforward and honorable. Of course, the United States wants a strong defensive shield—in its own and its alliance's interests. It wants to have unhindered access to the various facilities which work for Washington and the rest of NATO. Consequently, it wants friendly governments in the area, preferably democratic. It may seem incongruous that a nation with such a tradition of democracy as the United States has been involved with military regimes in Greece and Turkey. But democracy in the United States is one thing and in the fragmented, passion-wracked East Mediterranean quite another. In the final analysis, it is clear that Washington policy makers would settle for "friendly" if not necessarily democratic governments, if that solution was more expedient.

The cornerstone of U.S. policy in the area is a concept of equal treatment; the idea is that "Greece and Turkey are of equal strategic importance to the United States and to NATO." But the two countries "are also equally resistant to pressure from the United States to make what would be seen as concessions to one another. Indeed, that resistance has sent them both in search of national identities detached and perhaps independent from the United States."[4]

Regardless of the political ups and downs of Greece and Turkey, the United States appears condemned to maintaining its role in the East Mediterranean. Unless, miraculously, a new global strategy is devised, the United States cannot simply walk away from the area or find an effective surrogate for the two allies. U.S. involvement seemed generally welcomed by Turkey as protection against the USSR. In Greece, particularly after the 1981 Socialist victory, it was regarded as a double-edged sword. Yet, by the middle of 1982, the Socialist government of Greece had no viable substitute for NATO membership and its protective and mainly U.S.-supplied umbrella. Despite its vocal criticism of the alliance, Papandreou proceeded cautiously before making any drastic move either in favor of a continuing commitment to NATO or disengagement. But such an uncertain course was of little comfort to the United States. Compounding U.S. difficulties in the area was the accentuation of the Greco–Turkish feud, with the Aegean Sea and Cyprus as the main points of friction.

As mentioned earlier, the United States entered the Greco–Turkish scene in the early post–World War II years, when Greece was racked by civil war and Turkey appeared threatened by Soviet designs. According to President Truman,

> Greece and Turkey were still free countries being challenged by communist threats both from within and without. These free people were now engaged in a valiant struggle to preserve their liberties and independence.
>
> America could not, and should not, let these free countries stand unaided. To do so would carry the clearest implications in the Middle East and in Italy, Germany and France. The ideals and the traditions of our nation demanded that we come to the aid of Greece and Turkey and that we put the world on notice that it would be our policy to support the cause of freedom wherever it was threatened.[5]

Under the Truman Doctrine, there were massive infusions of aid to both Greece and Turkey. The distribution of such aid, particularly military, later became another bone of contention between the protagonists, complicating the U.S.'s Mediterranean tightrope act. Greece firmly believed that a balance of power could only be maintained if the aid ratio was established on a 7–10 basis. U.S. refusal to accept any definite proportion was one of the factors that led to the collapse of the talks on the defense and economic cooperation treaty with Greece in the early summer of 1981. As stated previously, for years the United States adhered to the view that both Greece and Turkey were equally vital to NATO and U.S. strategic interests in the East Mediterranean. Each country has different advantages. Turkey controls the straits leading to the Black Sea and is the site of a string of U.S. intelligence installations, whose value was enhanced after Iran's Islamic revolution. Greece is strategically located both for NATO and for Middle Eastern contingencies; a Balkan country bordering on Bulgaria, Yugoslavia, and Albania as well as Turkey, Greece is also a convenient springboard to the Middle East. It can exercise firm control over air and sea routes in that part of the world. U.S. military installations on the Greek mainland and in Crete provide direct operational support to the U.S. Sixth Fleet and also perform a number of important electronic intelligence tasks.

Thus, it has been virtually impossible for the United States to choose between Greece and Turkey. Of course, the choice could be imposed by sheer political circumstances. However, the loss of one of the defense anchors could hardly be an advantage. On the other hand, the constant squabbling between the protagonists represents an additional strain on U.S. foreign policy, which finds the available options increasingly limited.

Being in a permanent political cross fire is not easy to cope with. The balancing act is inevitably delicate and more often than not misunderstood. In the end, the United States is blamed for most misfortunes by Athens and sometimes but not as often by Ankara. U.S. efforts at evenhandedness were often seen by the Greeks as a pretext for a more pro-Turkish stance. Conversely, for a period, the Turks regarded the United States as entirely manipulated by the Greek lobby

Nothing illustrates the U.S. dilemma more dramatically than the story of the arms embargo against Turkey. Imposed by a self-righteous Congress following the Turkish landing in Cyprus, the embargo became a powerful weapon in the hands of the Greek lobby, which flourished in the United States after 1974, influencing U.S. policy for ethnic reasons, with no consideration for strategic requirements and national interest. Few measures adopted by the United States in recent years have been as counterproductive as the embargo. In Greece the embargo did not dissipate anti-U.S. feelings, stemming mainly from the widespread belief that the United States was responsible for the military rule between 1967 and 1974. Neither did the embargo bring Greece back into NATO's military structure. It did provoke some applause in Cyprus, without, however, any impact on the development of the situation on the island. Above all, the embargo, sapped the strength of the Turkish armed forces, the remaining guardian of NATO defenses in the East Mediterranean. It left Turkish public opinion completely perplexed. It wounded the country's military pride. It is much to the credit of Turkish politicians that the country did not follow Greece's footsteps and pull out of NATO's military wing, too. Nothing could have been easier or more popular in Turkey at the time. The lifting of the embargo in 1978 healed some wounds, but psychological scars remained for years. But while the harm done to U.S.–Turkish relations was not irreparable, the damage to Turkey's defensive posture reached gigantic proportions.

Already obsolete before the embargo, the Turkish armed forces became an international pauper, lacking spare parts and materiel of all types. Following the embargo, barely 50 percent of the Turkish air force was operational. Two years after its lifting, a special report to the Foreign Relations Committee of the U.S. Senate said, "Despite the size of its military forces, it would be extremely difficult for Turkey to perform its NATO missions because of equipment obsolescence and problems with spare parts."[6] The Turks squarely blamed the situation on the embargo—or ultimately on U.S. politicians. The conflict of interests between Congress and successive U.S. administrations was to some extent understood by Turkey's ruling establishment. It was, on the whole, incomprehensible to public opinion or the military cadres, who continued to stand NATO's watch at the head of their equipment-short troops.

The question of the suspension of U.S. military aid to Turkey was first brought up in August 1974, as the Turkish troops were sweeping through the parched Messaoria Plain in the second round of the military operation in Cyprus. The House of Representatives subsequently passed Joint Resolution 1131, putting an embargo on military aid to Turkey "until the president certifies to congress that substantial progress has been made toward agreement on the withdrawal of Turkish forces from Cyprus and that Turkey is in compliance with the foreign assistance act."[7] This was vetoed by President Ford. As a result of the veto, Congress passed a resolution (approved by both houses) that postponed the ban on military aid to Turkey until December 10, 1974. Ford signed the resolution, representing a compromise between the administration and Congress.

On December 1, 1974, Senator Kennedy charged that the United States had increased its arms shipments to Turkey, presumably in an effort to build up stocks before the embargo went into effect. The State Department replied that such increases were within the law. On December 10, Congress ratified the embargo, with a provision that the actual ban on arms shipments take effect on February 5, 1975. In vain, Secretary of State Henry Kissinger argued that such a measure would be catastrophic for the defense of the Western world. Congress was ostensibly motivated by the outcry that U.S. weapons were used by Turkey in invading without pretext a small and defenseless island. The Greek lobby had scored its most important victory.

The importance of the Greek lobby stemmed directly from the Turkish intervention in Cyprus. Virtually overnight, Greek–American organizations became a vocal element, shaping U.S. foreign policy to a degree matched perhaps only by the so-called Jewish lobby in the Arab–Israeli conflict. The Cyprus events unified the 3 million Greek-Americans, in the past divided over such issues as U.S. support to the Athens junta and military aid to Turkey. Although difficulties between Greece and Turkey over the Aegean were often potentially more explosive, the issue was too distant and too complex to galvanize the average Greek–American. Cyprus, with its tremendous emotional impact, had become a catalyst and watchword. The imposition of the arms embargo on Turkey was a spectacular coup by the lobby, which became a multipronged operation, manipulating congressional votes and, to some extent, the media. For example, in assessing the strength of the Turkish troops in Cyprus, the number of refugees, and the extent of war damage, the U.S. media almost exclusively used Greek-supplied figures. As late as May 1982 an Associated Press dispatch spoke of 40,000 Turkish occupation troops in Cyprus, a figure frequently quoted by the Greek government. The most reliable Western estimates at that time put the number at 19,000.

In 1975 the lobby had such effective legislators as Senator Thomas Eagleton of Missouri and Congressmen John Brademas of Indiana, Paul Sarbanes of Maryland, and Benjamin Rosenthal of New York. Other congressmen of Greek origin at the height of the "embargo battle" were Louis Bafalis of Florida, Paul Tsongas of Massachusetts, and Gus Yatron of Pennsylvania. All denied any lobby connection. Their views were perhaps best described by Sarbanes: "We have simply sought to enforce a provision of the existing law. We do not feel the U.S. should sanction aggression."[8]

The Greek voice on the U.S. scene was effectively propagated by such organizations as the American Hellenic Institute and the American Hellenic Educational Progressive Association (AHEPA). Although the activities of these Greek–American groups received less attention as time went by, they continued bombarding politicians with statements and issuing declarations mainly on the Turkish military presence in Cyprus. In fact the activities of the lobby became a source of some embarrassment to the government in Athens. "Don't call it the Greek lobby, call it the Cyprus lobby," a foreign ministry official snapped.[9]

At the end of 1975, AHEPA had about 400 chapters, grouping some 50,000 members, and an additional 700 chapters of auxiliary organizations. Backing its intense lobbying effort was a New York public relations firm. There were then about 70 different Greek–American organizations, some one-third of them created following the Cyprus events. The lobby benefited from the advice and funds of such prominent Greek–Americans as Andrew Athens (at the time president of the Chicago-based Metron Steel Corporation), shipowners George Livanos and Pericles Calimanopoulos, former San Francisco Mayor George Christopher, and a number of others. Even as late as January 1982 AHEPA's supreme president, Gustav Coffinas, appealed to President Reagan to use U.S. influence to encourage Turkey to make conciliatory proposals in order to reestablish the status quo on the island. "It is our considered judgement that no progress is being made in Cyprus and that it cannot be made until the Turkish army of occupation withdraws and the leaders of the Turkish-Cypriot community begin to offer substantive proposals for the return of the 200,000 refugees to their homes and land," Coffinas wrote.[10] Most red-blooded Greek–Americans firmly believed that the Turkish occupation of northern Cyprus was paid for, either directly or indirectly, by funds from the United States.

Such a view was not limited to Greek–Americans. When, in April 1978, he was shown a U.S.-financed hospital in the Turkish sector of Cyprus, A. I. Rosenthal, executive editor of *The New York Times*, exclaimed, "Why are we building hospitals here? After all, it's under Turkish occupation." The fact that the hospital was built for the Turkish Cypriots and not for the army appeared of little relevance.

To such Greek–Americans as Eugene Telemachos Rossides, head of the American Hellenic Institute, the Turkish intervention in Cyprus was "equal if not worse than the Soviet aggression against Czechoslovakia and Hungary and Hitler's aggression against Czechoslovakia and the Balkan nations."[11] Such a strong feeling is understandable on the part of the son of a Greek Cypriot father and a Greek mother. What is less comprehensible was the fact that as the Greek lobby gathered momentum in 1975 and 1976, vital U.S. interests in the

East Mediterranean were sacrificed because of a pro-Hellenic fervor in Washington.

The lobby had a powerful ally in the Greek Orthodox church in the United States, which, within a year of the Turkish intervention in Cyprus, set up some 50 fund-raising committees and had direct access to a number of congressmen and other politicians. The U.S. State Department itself was hardly immune to Hellenic pressures. Ambassadors to Greece, Cyprus, and Turkey had to be careful in their assessments of the situation and its ramifications. One striking example was that of Ambassador William R. Crawford, who represented the United States in Cyprus between August 1974 and March 1978. When an AHEPA delegation visited Cyprus in 1977, its members told Greek Cypriot officials that "Crawford was not pro-Greek enough and would soon be replaced."[12] Crawford left the island in the spring of 1978 after what seemed a sufficiently long tour of duty. Nonetheless, in numerous conversations with the author he expressed considerable concern at the pervasive influence of the lobby, which rarely took overall U.S. interests into consideration in its anti-Turkish campaign.

Rossides himself told various Greek Cypriots in August 1977 that "we will not rest until we get the Turks out of Cyprus and out of NATO." Rossides happened to be on the island when Archbishop Makarios died. He used the U.S. embassy telephone to freely communicate with supporters in the United States and organized an official flight for the funeral. Riding in the motorcade to the burial site at the Kykko monastery in the Troodos Mountains, Greek–American officials, including Congressmen Brademas and Sarbanes; waved at the tearful Greek Cypriot crowds; and shouted promises of "long struggle" and "we will push the Turks into the sea."

Much activity in the United States was carried out by the Greek Cypriots themselves through well-oiled public relations apparatus as well as the Cypriot embassy in Washington. Particular attention was paid to the media, with an avalanche of letters to the editor following any mention of the Turkish presence in Cyprus, which the Greek Cypriots regarded as not critical enough. When the author of this study wrote a travel article on Cyprus for *The New York Times* (June 17, 1979) describing both parts of the divided island, there was a barrage of angry letters from Greek–Americans. The consul-general of Cyprus in New York, Charalampous Christoforou, himself charged that the article was "a partisan policy message, . . . one that has been official Turkish policy toward the Cyprus question and to which the republic of Cyprus is irrevocably opposed—namely, division of the island into two separate states."[13] *The New York Times* editors replied that the article was merely "advising travelers that if they go to Cyprus this year they must accommodate themselves to the present division of the island."[14]

One particularly busy person in the United States, writing to such newspapers as *The New York Times, The Washington Post,* and *The Baltimore Sun,* seemed to know every intricacy of the complex Cyprus problem and reacted instantly to any article that did not follow the Greek line of thinking. The letters were meticulously accompanied by quotations from the pertaining treaties and articles of the United Nations Charter (with which few reporters covering the area are familiar) and were usually distributed in toto by the Greek Cypriot Public Information Office in Nicosia, although the newspapers to which the writer wrote usually only printed excerpts, if that.

This systematic—and obviously fruitful—campaign caused a predictable chorus of opposition from the Turks, both in Cyprus and in Turkey. According to Denktash, "One could only see that this effort has not as an aim a fair solution in Cyprus but a solution to the liking of the pressure-making body, the Greek lobby in the United States."* Ankara officialdom was less vocal; the Turks seemed to be resigned to bad press in the West and regarded the Greek lobby as one of the inevitable consequences of their Cyprus involvement. However, with considerable foresight, officials in Turkey kept predicting that "eventually the lobby will run out of steam." It did, indeed, under relentless pressure from the Carter administration, which watched the alarming erosion of NATO's strength on the southeastern flank. However, Papandreou's electoral victory in Greece in 1981 appears to have spurred Greek–Americans to a greater effort.

Congressional hearings on the lifting of the embargo gathered momentum in 1978. The trend was unmistakable: one by one senior State Department and Defense Department officials issued warnings about implications of the embargo's continuation. On June 28, 1978, General Alexander Haig, in his capacity as commander-in-chief of the U.S. European command, described Turkey at a Senate hearing as a "staunch and loyal ally," a country whose "strategic geographic position affords the United States irreplaceable sites for observing Soviet strategic and naval activity. . . . We should also recognise that

---

*Denktash to the author, 1978.

Turkey's contribution to the defense of Greek and Turkish Thrace is irreplaceable. As long as Turkey remains fully within the alliance, any Warsaw Pact attack on Greece would be a highly risky adventure.[15] Haig concluded his testimony by saying, "The full and active participation of this proudly democratic nation in the affairs of the alliance is thus indispensable. . . . In this context prompt action designed to normalize an increasingly estranged military relationship and assure for the West the full contribution of this valued ally is essential."[16]

Earlier that year, on May 31, Parker T. Hart, a former U.S. ambassador to Turkey and former Assistant Secretary of State for Near Eastern Affairs, warned at a news conference that unless Congress lifted the embargo, the Turkish government "cannot avoid final closure, in retaliation, of all American military installations in the country."

The State Department itself cleared the deck for the repeal of the punitive measure at a press briefing on April 21, 1978, in answer to the question, "Is Turkey violating American law by virtue of its presence in Cyprus?" The official spokesman replied:

> The laws of the United States do not, of themselves, create obligations for foreign countries to do or refrain from doing anything. They may, of course, impose duties upon the executive branch. The question is, therefore, whether the Turkish presence on Cyprus or Turkish activities there now oblige the administration to take particular actions to discharge its duties under U.S. law.
>
> The 1974 Turkish intervention in Cyprus prompted the enactment by congress of special legislation specifically applicable to Turkey. That legislation required the suspension of military assistance, sales and licensing with respect to Turkey, although the president was subsequently authorized to permit some sales to Turkey.
>
> There are many other provisions of law of general application which affect the administration's conduct of foreign policy. These include provisions relating to human rights, expropriation of U.S. property, seizure of U.S. fishing vessels, and many other subjects. WE DO NOT BELIEVE THAT THE TURKISH PRESENCE IN CYPRUS REQUIRES THE ADMINISTRATION TO TAKE ANY ACTION UNDER ANY OF THESE PROVISIONS. [Emphasis mine][17]

The partisans of the embargo continued opposing its lifting on a variety of moral and legal grounds. A typical approach was demonstrated by Senator Claiborne Pell at one of the Senate Foreign Relations Committee hearings. "Would it be feasible for Turkey to at least make a move toward withdrawing American weapons from Cyprus?" Pell asked. "If they want to engage in this occupation let them do it with French weapons, Soviet weapons, any other kind of weapons, but should there not be an effort made to remove the American weapons that are used in the occupation?"[18]

On July 25, 1978, the Senate voted 57 to 42 in favor of lifting the embargo. The House of Representatives followed suit on August 1, 1978, by a vote of 208 to 200. The decisions were in the form of amendments to the Foreign Assistance Act of 1961, different in the House and Senate. A compromise formula was subsequently drafted, approved by the Senate on September 11 by voice vote, without dissent, and by the House on September 12 by a roll call vote of 225–126. On September 27 President Carter issued a certification to Congress that the resumption of "full military cooperation with Turkey is in the national interest of the United States." Carter also certified that "Turkey is acting in good faith to achieve a just and peaceful solution of the Cyprus problem." Despite considerable domestic pressure, the United States showed that it was capable of acting in its own strategic interests. The lifting of the embargo vindicated Turkey after three-and-a-half years, during which time Ankara bore the penalty with amazing stoicism.

During various congressional discussions, Turkey drew considerable comfort from the relentless effort by the Carter administration to have the embargo scrapped. On July 26, 1978, Ecevit, at the time Turkey's premier, said in a statement, "The efforts recently made by President Carter, by some members of the congress and many influential personalities, are no doubt indicators of the importance attached in the U.S.A. to friendship with Turkey."[19] When Carter finally signed the document lifting the embargo, Ecevit hailed it as a new era in U.S.–Turkish relations. The road was paved to a new agreement on the status of U.S. bases in Turkey, an act which eventually took place two years later.

As expected, the lifting was hardly palatable to the Greek Cypriots. Bitterly, President Kyprianou said that "only those who are not concerned about justice, freedom, human rights and democracy in Cyprus are rejoicing over this decision."[20] There was no way the United States could please the nonaligned Greek Cypriots, except by punishing Turkey, a NATO ally. The Greek lobby suffered a setback from which it was unable to recover, at least during the subsequent four years. The cause of Greek Cyprus was periodically revived in Congress, without, however, much impact on U.S. policy in the East Mediterranean. One typical congressional gesture was the celebration marking the seventh anniversary of the Turkish invasion on July 20, 1981, during which 34 congressmen went on record asking for the withdrawal of Turkish troops and the need for a "just, peaceful and lasting solution" of the Cyprus problem. But the solution was not something the United States could deliver easily, although it certainly would help to defuse part of the Greco–Turkish conflict and, thus, strengthen NATO's posture in a highly vulnerable area.

U.S. involvement in Cyprus, ostensibly peripheral, has nonetheless been a deep one. Cyprus is not only a devisive issue between the traditional East Mediterranean protagonists but also the home of British sovereign bases, which, in the late 1970s and early 1980s, were partly financed with U.S. funds. There has been considerable speculation about the degree of U.S. financing or use of the base areas and facilities. Periodically the Cypriot Communist Party (AKEL) raised the issue of U.S. activities in Cyprus. These activities have been described as "a two-tier presence: highly visible and the discreet."[21]

The visible activities were represented, among others, by the U.S. radio monitoring station, known as the Foreign Broadcasting Information Service (FBIS), generally thought to be a benign adjunct of the CIA. Located before 1974 in Karavas on the northern coast, the FBIS later moved its activities (albeit on a limited scale) to the legal side of the island.* Other forms of the U.S. presence included the U–2 spy planes stationed at the British Akrotiri air field since 1970, first to monitor the Suez Canal ceasefire and, later, the activities in the Sinai.

The discreet U.S. presence involved U.S. participation in various British electronic intelligence installations deployed on the island. The British bases have been used on occasion by small units of U.S. marines and other Sixth Fleet personnel. Such presence was inevitably decried by the Greek Cypriot press, always ready to expose any sign of U.S. military involvement in the area. Under steady pressure, mainly by the Greek Cypriot media, the British government clarified to some extent the issue of the bases in March 1982. Jerry Wiggin, parliamentary secretary of state (armed forces) at the Ministry of Defense, explained that the cost of maintaining the bases was 72 million pounds sterling a year (129 million dollars at the prevailing rate of exchange) and that the United States was paying part of the bill.

---

*Its detailed transcripts of radio broadcasts from several Arab countries and parts of the USSR could be purchased by subscription in the United States.

"The United States government pays for all the facilities that it uses at RAF [Royal Air Force] Akrotiri in support of the U-2 flights monitoring the Middle East Peace-Keeping arrangements," Wiggin said.[22] He added that "we have no intention of giving up our rights to the sovereign bases."

Of considerable concern to the United States was the militant pro-Third World stance adopted by the Greek Cypriot government. Such a policy was already very much evident before 1974, under the leadership of Archbishop Makarios. It intensified following the Turkish intervention simply because the Greek Cypriots believed the U.S. pendulum was swinging toward Turkey and that, consequently, any form of pressure was useful. They intensified relations with the USSR and its allies, virtually all of whom maintained strong embassies or missions on the island, including military attachés of colonel's rank. A number of commercial and cultural exchange treaties have been signed between Cyprus and Soviet bloc countries. The Cyprus government refused to condemn the Soviet intervention in Afghanistan in 1979 because of what was officially described as "international inactivity" in the face of the continuing Turkish military presence.

On several occasions the United States attempted to use its good offices to heal the island's rift, starting with Secretary of State Dean Acheson's efforts in 1964. It was Cyrus Vance who prevented a Turkish landing on Cyprus in 1967. After the events of 1974, Clark Clifford attempted to foster a dialogue based on the Makarios–Denktash guidelines, with no success. In 1978 State Department Councellor Matthew Nimetz visited Cyprus and submitted recommendations for expanding the negotiations, subsequently described as the "American plan." This was eventually superseded by the Kyprianou–Denktash agreement of 1979 and modified by the Waldheim guidelines, reducing the U.S. role (see Appendix F).

The field in which the United States was highly active was aid to the island in the invasion's wake, particularly to the refugee fund. Between 1974 and 1982, a total of 131 million dollars was spent on refugee rehabilitation. The neat refugee settlements of one-family units built in the southern portion of the island were largely financed by the United States. Yet, there was comparatively little acknowledgement of this effort on the Greek side of the Cypriot barricades. On several occasions Ambassador Crawford pointed out his frustration at the silence of the Greek Cypriot press on the issue of U.S. aid, while considerable space was given to Greek aid and various comparatively insignificant gestures by the Soviet bloc.

In February 1982 the U.S. General Accounting Office (GAO) made a formal report, which states that "although the United States has been the only major contributor to the Cyprus recovery program since 1976, public recognition in Cyprus is rarely given."[23] The report further said that despite the efforts of the U.S. embassy and the Agency for International Development (AID) to obtain wider recognition, "government of Cyprus officials, when dedicating completed housing projects, had not always acknowledged this assistance."

The U.S. government pursued the policy of dividing its aid between the two ethnic groups of the island, according to the established population ratio. Thus, of the 111 million dollars used for specific projects, 90 million went to the Greek south and 20 million to the Turkish zone. Between 1975 and 1982, a total of 232 U.S.-financed projects were undertaken in Cyprus, 123 in the south and 109 in the north. Early in 1982 the U.S. government recommended elimination of much of the aid in view of the island's "significant economic recovery." However, in May a congressional foreign affairs subcommittee voted to continue the funding.

There was little the United States could do to win the sympathy of the Greek Cypriots short of putting strong political or perhaps even military pressure on Turkey. Since the Greek lobby had lost much of its initial strength in Washington, such a course was highly unlikely. Besides, Turkey was increasingly emerging as the more solid ally. Gradually, various U.S. officials were becoming convinced that a return to the status quo in Cyprus was impossible and that, perhaps, a physical separation of the island's feuding communities was the best feasible solution under extremely difficult circumstances. Such a view, if publicly expressed, would not make the United States popular in the Greek-speaking part of the island, and would automatically reduce Washington's leverage possibilities. Consequently, given the circumstances, the United States decided to adopt the policy of offering its good offices whenever possible, but, on the whole, relying on United Nations efforts in Cyprus.

This was reiterated by Secretary of State Haig during his visit to Ankara in May 1982; he also said that the United States had "no interest in mediating between Greece and Turkey." Thus, while the two countries squabbled over the Aegean, with Papandreou thundering about a Hellenic crusade and Cypriot negotiators basically just going through the motions, there were few hopeful signals in mid-1982. Perhaps the most alarming factor was the low-key U.S. approach to the problem and its apparent desire to stay clear of the Mediterranean passions. Such an approach could, at best, be a delaying tactic, unlikely to attenuate the feud. Some could even see it as tantamount to abdicating U.S. responsibilities in the East Mediterranean at a particularly difficult juncture.

Notes

1. Author's notes, October 26, 1971.

2. Official text of President Johnson's letter, June 1964.

3. Geoffrey Lewis, *Modern Turkey* (London: Ernest Benn 1974), p. 205.

4. U.S., Congress, Senate, Committee on Foreign Relations, "Turkey, Greece and NATO: The Strained Alliance," a staff report (Washington D.C.: Government Printing Office, 1980), p. 62.

5. Harry S. Truman, *Years of Trial and Hope* (New York: Doubleday, 1956), p. 52.

6. U.S., Senate, Committee on Foreign Relations, "Turkey, Greece and NATO," p. 16.

7. Official text of Joint Resolution 1131, August 1974.

8. "New Lobby in Town: The Greeks," *Time*, July 14, 1975, pp. 25–28.

9. In conversation with the author, 1980.

10. *Hellenic Chronicle*, January 7, 1982.

11. Author's notes, 1976.

12. Ibid.

13. *New York Times*, July 15, 1979.

14. Ibid.

15. Official U.S. government text of a hearing on June 28, 1978.

16. Ibid.

17. Text provided by the Department of State, April 21, 1978.

18. Text of hearing, May 4, 1978.

19. Official text of a speech given by Ecevit in Ankara, July 26, 1978.

20. Cyprus government press release.

21. Jesse W. Lewis, *The Strategic Balance in the Mediterranean* (Washington D.C.: American Enterprise Institute for Public Policy Research, 1977), p. 77.

22. Official text of a speech given by Jerry Wiggin in London in March 1982.

23. GAO Statement, February 1982.

Chapter 7

IN SEARCH OF A SOLUTION

NATO still has the vigor and honesty to face current problems and challenges squarely. . . . This fact, coupled with past performance, augurs well for success in overcoming them.

Joseph Luns
NATO Secretary General
June 1982

Abdi Ipekci was fatally shot on a rainswept Istanbul street in February 1979, one of the many victims of terrorism bleeding Turkey at that time. As editor of the respected daily *Milliyet,* he was not only one of the country's most influential journalists, he was also one of the men and women devoted to a better understanding between Greeks and Turks and a tireless organizer of conferences bringing together writers, artists, and scientists of both countries. His aim was to break down the historic and atavistic barriers. At the time of his death he was involved in organizing a visit by a group of prominent Greek journalists to Turkey. His avowed killer, Mehmet Ali Agca, subsequently had an additional claim to international notoriety: the shooting of Pope John Paul II in May 1981.

One can only hope that the effort of breaking down Greco-Turkish prejudices has not died with Ipekci. In the turmoil sweeping Turkey following his death, little attention was paid to external problems. The establishment of military rule in 1980 was not likely to inspire confidence and promote international exchanges; eventually, however, Turkey had become more peaceful, if not democratic, than in many preceding turbulent years. There was still plenty of desire among men and women of good will in Greece and Turkey to renew the dialogue, despite the helmeted image of martial law.

In Turkey things appeared to be moving in the right direction when the ruling military National Security Council facilitated Greece's reentry into the North Atlantic Treaty Organization (NATO) military structure. That, however, could have been interpreted as an act of political expediency rather than a gesture of pure good will. After all, Turkey could only benefit from Greek participation in Western defenses of the Mediterranean. Nonetheless, what mattered was that the Turkish generals did make that first step in the direction of Greece. The subsequent arrival to power of the Socialist government in Athens certainly made further dialogue difficult, at least during Papandreou's first nine months in office. His appeal for a Hellenic crusade in Cyprus, threats to suspend the intercommunal dialogue, demands for the evacuation of Turkish troops, and frequent references to the Aegean were not exactly measures aimed at improving the political climate in the East Mediterranean. It was obvious that such a stance by Papandreou had to be answered by Turkey sooner or later, further exacerbating the issue and clouding the political atmosphere.

Perhaps even more ominous was the suspension—apparently on orders from Papandreou himself—of contacts between professional groups in Greece and Turkey. Such contacts are perhaps the best existing avenue toward a better understanding. In August, 1982, there were some indications that the previous dialogue between senior Greek and Turkish foreign ministry officials might be revived.

Such meetings produced few historic results but did provide a badly needed safety valve. As long as the two sides communicated on a regular basis, the danger of escalation was automatically lessened. A periodic meeting, scheduled well in advance, is much better than a frantic, last-minute effort to try to defuse a crisis (often when it is too late). There is no doubt that a system of regular high-level contacts—perhaps on the highest level—would immeasurably help to improve the strained relations between Ankara and Athens. One striking example is the practice of Franco–German summit meetings. Although not necessarily newsworthy, the summits keep a permanent channel of communications open, help establish personal rapport, and pave the way to solutions to many seemingly insoluble problems. A number of Turkish and Greek diplomats agree that it would be an excellent system in the context of their countries' relationship as well.

There is no doubt that a dialogue is needed on a permanent basis. The stakes are simply too high; passions can easily get out of control; the Mediterranean is too small for a Greco–Turkish explosion. Above all, such a clash would produce no winner; it could result in a short-term victory—occupation of an island or two or of a strip of land, the destruction of an industrial complex or a naval task force, and another flight of a group of hapless refugees. These are, on the whole, ephemeral triumphs, in the final analysis benefiting no one but merely causing trauma to both sides. Given the strategic considerations in the early 1980s, including the military possibilities and foreign alliances of the protagonists, neither Greece nor Turkey was capable of a decisive victory. Moreover, such a conflict would be highly inflammable in a broader sense, inevitably involving NATO and possibly the USSR, which is always ready to exploit any sign of tension within the Western camp.

Assuming that a Greco–Turkish explosion does not spread beyond the East Mediterranean, it would still have an enormous impact on the West as a whole and on NATO in particular. No alliance can exist as a vibrant force with two wounded enemies in its midst. A ceasefire in the event of a Greco–Turkish conflict, whether imposed by NATO itself or by the United Nations, could hardly repair the damage. There could be no victory except a Pyrrhic one if Greeks and Turks clash again. The time of sweeping conquests has passed. The Turks were expelled from Greece a century and a half ago, and the Greeks were routed in Western Anatolia in the early 1920s. In today's Mediterranean geopolitical context, such dramatic upheavals are impractical. The last sizable population movement took place in the wake of the Turkish landing in Cyprus, when Greek Cypriots fled the north of the island; the Turkish Cypriots eventually abandoned their homes in the south for the security of the Turkish Federated State. Although the return of Greek Cypriot refugees remained a major political slogan in the Greek south and a serious obstacle in negotiations, few Cypriots or foreign observers believed in the feasibility of another mass uprooting of people.

Consequently, if there was to be a package solution or any piecemeal process, it would have to be found within the context of political realities. This would require a lot of good will and sacrifice on the part of both Greece and Turkey. It would also necessitate considerable diplomatic persuasion and the cooling of passions in Cyprus. In this respect, the cooperation of Greece and Turkey would be essential as well as creating a possible role for the United Kingdom, the former colonial power, and the United States, the leader of the Western camp (as such, vitally interested in securing harmony in the East Mediterranean on a permanent basis).

The three main stumbling blocks in the path of Greco–Turkish reconciliation are the Aegean Sea, the problem of ethnic minorities in both countries, and Cyprus. Underlying them is a web of ancient fears, animosity, and battle scars. None of the problems are insoluble, provided there is a will on both sides to solve them. On the basis of countless conversations in all three countries of the East Mediterranean triangle and official documents and briefings by United Nations officials and foreign diplomats, I feel able to suggest a series of steps that could, in time, lead to more constructive and permanent gestures.

As outlined in previous chapters, the problem of the Aegean is a complex one, and in the early 1980s neither of the protagonists was willing to modify their well-known views. What was essential was an effort to reduce the tension to a level which would eliminate the Aegean as a permanent flashpoint. This could be accomplished by a number of significant gestures. As Turkey is the larger of the two quarreling powers, it would seem reasonable for it to take the first step, such as a formal policy statement (perhaps in the form of a charter) stating that it had no claims to any of the Greek. islands sprinkling the Aegean. An announcement along these lines would undoubtedly be a historic gesture. It would assuage the fears of those Greeks who see Turkey as an expansionist power. It could put the whole relationship on a different footing.

A further step, requiring perhaps more daring statesmanship, would be to reduce the Turkish army in the Aegean along with its flotilla of landing craft, which inevitably symbolizes to the Greeks a Turkish intention of invading some of the islands. Strictly from a military point of view, it would hardly be an act of national suicide. The Turks could still maintain an effective defense of their coastline, moving in reinforcements if need be. But a reduction in deployment (certified by NATO observers) should, in principle, encourage Greece to respond in kind. Once the troop concentrations are reduced and once the islands and the Turkish coastline stop being a string of permanently manned bunkers and lookouts, the difficulties over the Aegean seabed could be discussed in a much calmer atmosphere. Who knows, such discussions could even lead to joint seismic exploration of the area, although at this writing the concept appears to be in the realm of fantasy.

No one in 1982 underestimated the explosiveness of the Aegean. The crisis between Argentina and the United Kingdom over the Falkland Islands illustrated dramatically enough the degree of international havoc that could be caused by a claim to a group of islands and one rash act. As far as Greece and Turkey were concerned, Cyprus was a highly emotional problem but remained basically a sideshow to the entire Aegean issue. Still, the more skeptical (or perhaps realistic) among diplomats in the area argued that Turkey had, in effect, made enough gestures, without reciprocity from Greece. According to such arguments, it was Greece's turn to show good will and diplomatic flexibility. At this writing, there were no such indications.

Yet, historic feuds do not necessarily have to linger on forever. No one dismisses the strength of nationalism—one of the most galvanizing yet most destructive of forces. Considerable progress in this respect has been made in Western Europe, where, despite the scars of World War II, most former enemies have managed not only to coexist in peace but to cooperate economically, politically, and militarily. There is absolutely no reason why Greece and Turkey, both countries with a Western vocation and committed to a Western political system, should not follow the example of their Western allies.

In this respect, a major reeducation campaign in both countries would have to be undertaken. The idea had already been discussed at various meetings of journalists, such as the one Ipekci tried to organize when he was killed. A number of responsible editors in Greece and Turkey have expressed a willingness to tone down the nationalistic fervor. But these promises were largely ignored following Papandreou's electoral victory.

The creation of a joint cultural commission would be of essence. Such a commission could propose ways of reducing tension by revising some of the shrill references in textbooks and reducing the level of intense propaganda to which the young in both countries are exposed. After all, similar measures have been taken in France, Belgium, and the Federal Republic of Germany. They do not have to amount to a rewriting of history but merely put it into a more reasonable perspective. No claims to national fame should be ignored— but they should not be used to fuel nationalistic passions. It is a monumental task, but not without precedent.*

---

*The latest such effort took place in Japan in 1982.

Above all, an example should be set by the leaders in Athens and Ankara. It is assumed that the governments are pledged to the well-being of their countries. It is clear that the continuation of the feud is not likely to serve the best interests of either Greece or Turkey and certainly not of NATO.

It is not sufficient merely to declare that an olive branch has been offered, as politicians in Greece and Turkey have said on occasion. No olive branch is valid unless it is backed by concrete gestures, some of which have been suggested here. Once an atmosphere of calm is reestablished between Ankara and Athens and once a permanent political dialogue is resumed and nationalistic statements are discarded, a new era will be possible. One can hardly expect visits by folklore ensembles and symposiums by scholars when a Turkish ferry boat causes riots, such as those in Rhodes in the summer of 1980.

The problem of minorities need not be. Virtually all the Turks living in western Thrace hold Greek passports. At a time when the Papandreou government is promulgating laws on the separation of church and state (a step of enormous impact and consequences) there is no reason for differentiating between citizens. Being Greek does not have to be tantamount to being Orthodox. If the Muslim inhabitants of Thrace are treated like the other citizens of Greece, their grievances will gradually disappear. Of course, time will be needed to accomplish this.* (See Appendix E.)

The Greek government will have to face the fact that these citizens are perfectly entitled to have their own cultural heritage as well as links with the Turkish "motherland." There are several examples not too far away, mainly in Yugoslavia. Granted there is considerable ethnic unrest among Kosovo Albanians, and relations between Orthodox Serbs and Catholic Croats are not always smooth; but there are a number of minorities perfectly content in the Yugoslavian federal structure, while maintaining links across the borders. One such example is the Hungarian minority in the autonomous province of Voyvodina, a residue of the Austro–Hungarian Empire. There are over half a million Hungarians in Yugoslavia. In 1977 they had a

---

*Answering Turkish charges of property expropriation in Thrace, the Greek embassy in Washington in April 1982 distributed a lengthy statement in which it said that what occurred in Thrace "was action to evict illegal squatters on public land. The action applied, without the slightest discrimination, to all the illegal squatters, both Christian and Moslem."[1] The same statement accused Turkey of various repressive measures against Greek citizens living there.

IN SEARCH OF A SOLUTION / 147

total of 195 elementary schools, a daily newspaper, and a radio station. A number of Hungarians have reached positions of responsibility in Yugoslavia.[2] Surely, it would be a worthwhile effort to include the Turks in Thrace—a maximum of 200,000 people—in the mainstream of Greek national life.

Equally the secular state of Turkey would do well to stop distinguishing between Turk and Greek. Once an inhabitant obtains the citizenship of an adopted country, one should not be singled out as a foreigner, prone to becoming a scapegoat in times of tension. And, as pointed out earlier in this study, when things go wrong in Greco–Turkish relations, Turkish wrath often turns on the remnants of Istanbul's Greek colony. This has led to the flight of those Greeks who held Turkish passports. The mobs were not interested in passports, and the authorities, all too frequently, continued to regard these Turkish citizens as Greeks.

Of considerable importance in efforts to improve the climate between Greece and Turkey is the economic stability of the two countries. In this respect, Greece is in a somewhat better position, having become a member of the European Economic Community (EEC), although that membership has certain drawbacks. Following the military takeover in 1980, Turkey demonstrated an ability to pull itself together and made impressive headway in some fields, such as construction contracts in the Middle East and food exports to the Arab world. On the whole, however, Turkey in 1982 could hardly be considered economically healthy, despite an unquestionable improvement over the chaotic late 1970s. An economically weak Turkey, with a dissatisfied population, can hardly fulfill its NATO role, which appears to be growing rather than diminishing. This is the area in which the United States could play a positive role. Indeed, there were indications that the Reagan administration was favorably inclined to increase U.S. assistance to Turkey, although serious congressional objections remained. Thus, despite the statement quoted earlier that both Greece and Turkey are "equally resistant to pressure from the United States," increased U.S. economic and military assistance could be used as leverage. There is little point in aid with no strings attached, and such an attitude appears changing. Most countries realize by now that there are always some strings, that the United States cannot be expected to provide funds without at least some effort on the part of the beneficiary to fit in with the grand design of U.S. foreign policy. That policy in the East Mediterranean most certainly calls for the attenuation of the Greco–Turkish dispute. If it has not yet included more ambitious goals, such as the reconciliation of two old foes, it is simply because the political climate has not been right. Increased U.S. aid to Turkey could, perhaps, persuade that power to make some reassuring gestures toward Greece, obviously not to the detriment of its national interests.

There is no question that Cyprus is one of the worst points of friction; as long as no satisfactory solution is arrived at, no other issues can be successfully tackled. Although it can be argued that Cyprus as such does not directly affect the interests of Greece and Turkey, the emotional aspect of the problem cannot be stressed enough. History has shown all too frequently the impact of Cyprus on relations between Athens and Ankara.

An island outside NATO and, moreover, linked to the Third World, Cyprus has become very much a NATO problem simply because of its impact on Greece and Turkey. It has been said that both Ankara and Athens have considerable influence on their respective ethnic groups on the island. But there are limits to this influence, particularly on the Greek side of the demarcation line (when suggestions from Athens do not suit Cypriot politicians). Stubborn, individualistic, and self-centered, the Cypriots are difficult political partners for any country. The stalemate that followed Turkish intervention in 1974 accentuated those difficult national traits shared by both communities. Above all, eight years after the Turkish landing, politicians in both portions of the island had become trapped in categorical attitudes, futile promises, and fears, many of which they helped to create. It is their task to start dismantling some of the psychological barriers they erected—the Greek Cypriots in search of a return to the status quo, and the Turkish Cypriots in an effort to safeguard their own separate entity and identity.

A person familiar with Cyprus can well understand the sensitivities of the islanders—their problems, emotions, and fears. More frequently than not, outsiders have considerable difficulty in grasping local intricacies. There is a tendency, particularly in Western Europe, to regard the Turkish fear of the Greeks as exaggerated. Western opinion frequently tends to favor the Greek side in the Cyprus dispute, simply because the West has always been more familiar with things Christian and Greek. Also, the Turkish side in Cyprus has systematically mishandled its public relations effort; it can be said without much doubt that the Turkish Cypriots have failed to present their case to the world in a coherent and convincing manner. They have often resorted to rhetoric and slogans that sound odd to the Western ear. They have chosen to capitalize on Greek atrocities, something which is of tremendous importance to them but which has little impact on the outside world. In Cyprus the victims of atrocities could be counted in hundreds or a few thousand at most. It is little compared to the carnage of Africa, Southeast Asia, Central America, or Lebanon.

The so-called interlocutors at the intercommunal talks managed to make progress on a number of issues, and this was often cited as a sign that the problem is not insoluble. But they found it more expedient to skirt the essence of the Cyprus problem. This includes the sharing of power within the proposed federal structure, territorial concessions by the Turkish side, and the delicate question of the freedom of movement between the zones. The Turks were adamant that they should control such movement for fear that they might be overrun by the Greeks. The Greeks claimed that the island should be considered one country.

Despite some progress in the talks, serious attempts at solution of the main issues were not expected until well into 1983, if not later. In 1982 the Greek side was preoccupied with the forthcoming presidential elections in which President Kyprianou was a candidate. Kyprianou was unlikely to make any concessions that could cost him votes. Further hampering an understanding in Cyprus was the personal antagonism between Kyprianou and Denktash. A number of diplomats on the island believed that as long as Kyprianou remained president, Denktash—whose term is due to expire in 1986—was hardly likely to be flexible. Thus, Kyprianou's reelection in 1983 would not be a happy development for the intercommunal talks, already strained by Papandreou's nationalistic stance, which rankled the Turkish side.

Above all, what hampered the progress of the talks was the lack of national cohesion. The two sides talked to each other not as members of a Cypriot nation but as Turks and Hellenes. Denktash himself subscribed to this view. "If there ever was a Cypriot nation, history must have passed it by," he told me. "There are only Greeks and Turks living on Cyprus."*

While true to a great extent, such a view can be regarded as an enormous obstacle. One can ask Greeks and Turks to coexist in their respective countries, but one cannot forge a federated state in Cyprus unless the islanders decide that they are Cypriots (with different relitions and ethnic origins) and not Greeks and Turks. Unless this is unequivocally accepted by both sides, there is little point in trying to

---

*Denktash modified this view somewhat in May 1982, when he told me, "At this stage the creation of a Cypriot nation is not likely but if a Cypriot culture were created, a nation could grow out of it later."

find a federal solution. Any concept of a Greco–Turkish federation in Cyprus is doomed to failure. It can only work as a federation of Cypriots.

In order to achieve this, a serious effort has to be made by both sides to build some sense of Cypriot nationhood—at the expense of Hellenism and Turkishness. Fueling Greek and Turkish patriotism oriented toward the respective "motherlands" in Cyprus is not going to help it become one state. The Turkish Cypriots should stop flying the flag of Turkey and the Greeks that of Greece. Such symbols merely exacerbate the issue. In this respect, it would perhaps help if the flag of Cyprus (rarely flown anyway) were redesigned to include the colors of the ethnic origins of the Cypriots: the red of the Turks and the blue of the Greeks. It would be a step toward acknowledging different origins in a people hoping to become one nation. It might help break some barriers.

One of the most glaring examples of the stubborn attitude of two Cypriot leaderships is the case of Nicosia International Airport. Equipped with a modern terminal, the airport has been inactive since the 1974 invasion, surrounded by a U.N. cordon. Each side has constructed its own airport rather than agree on a system of sharing the facilities of the existing one, within easy reach of both communities. The Turks have demanded a 50–50 ratio on immigration and customs control, still smarting from the period when Turkish Cypriot passengers were subjected to inordinately tedious checks and an often cavalier attitude by the Greek Cypriot airport personnel. To the Greek side, granting equal status on the airport issue would be tantamount to a dangerous precedent.

Both Greece and Turkey share the blame for delaying a Cyprus solution by insisting on strong links with their Cypriot brethren. Papandreou's Hellenic crusade has been sufficiently mentioned in this study; Turkey has already changed the demographic structure of the north by implanting some 40,000 immigrants from the mainland in the villages abandoned by Greek Cypriots. These mainlanders have become citizens of the north but remain distant from Turkish Cypriots and vice versa. If both Greece and Turkey agreed, a strong effort could be undertaken in Cyprus to start rebuilding the bonds shattered by intercommunal strife and separation. The Turkish side could make a gesture by allowing small groups of Greek Cypriots to visit their former towns and villages. The Greeks could do likewise.

Perhaps here the floor should be given to Clerides, one of the few politicians on the Greek side who has shown considerable pragmatism.

It is pointless to talk about vague concepts such as the "bicommunal," "bizonal," or "biregional" nature of the future federation. Let us discuss something concrete, something which will show how far each side is willing to give in. . . . Of course, the U.N. is not strong enough to exert pressure on either side. But with good will, constitutional experts could easily work out an acceptable formula. With the backing of the major powers, it could be imposed on the island. I know the Turks worry about their security. We do as well, with the Turkish military presence. But once we have freedom of movement the "secure boundaries" would not play such a role.[3]

Above all, Clerides feels that the establishment of a joint institution of higher learning is essential. It would help bring together the younger Cypriots who have grown up "without contact with each other, except through gunsights. It is our duty to work for a different kind of contact."

The Cypriots have acquired a tremendous asset during the 80-odd years of British colonial rule: familiarity with the English language, which became a strong factor in forming the new republic in 1960. As a minority, surrounded by Greek-speaking Cypriots, the Turkish Cypriots frequently spoke Greek. Quite a few Greek Cypriots, particularly in the villages, had some knowledge of Turkish. But English was the working language, a link between the two communities. All legal documents were in English, and most government decrees were published in the three languages of the island. Cabinet sessions and many court hearings were held in English. While the knowledge of English continued to be cultivated on the Greek side after 1974, it was neglected among the Turks. In their initial euphoria of liberation, the Turkish Cypriots wanted to become more Turkish. The accent in schools was on perfecting a knowledge of Turkish rather than that of English. This in itself has removed the younger generation from the other side. After a few years, mainly because of their contacts with the United Kingdom, the Turkish Cypriots realized that this attitude was counterproductive. But precious time has been lost.

There is plenty of scope for a different kind of contact (as suggested by Clerides) on an island where some friendships have survived the separation of the communities. Cypriots of both confessions have met at various international meetings outside the island and frequently expressed the desire to improve and intensify such encounters. There have been efforts by Greek Cypriot doctors to include their Turkish Cypriot colleagues in a joint professional association. But the Turkish Cypriots, perhaps justifiably obsessed by years of Greek domination, felt they were being used.

Here again, the two motherlands could play a more active role. They should not only encourage such relations but facilitate and organize them if need be. Of course it is rather difficult if professional contacts between Greece and Turkey are suspended. But all this should be part of a generalized effort to struggle for a solution. There are no solutions without compromise.

In Cyprus an unquestionable step forward would be Varosha's resettlement by Greek Cypriots, before the modern part of Famagusta crumbles. Such details as the roads of access and territorial adjustments around the port could be worked out in due course. The key problem is to have an actual movement of Greek Cypriots back to their Varosha homes or whatever is left of them. The Turks themselves suggested U.N. supervision of such an operation. This proposal, rejected by Kyprianou, had subsequently been overtaken by Waldheim's guidelines. Many foreign observers regret that Varosha has not been made the key item of the negotiations, ahead of other more complex problems. The Turkish Cypriots could easily facilitate territorial adjustment by starting to evacuate those border villages they are prepared to cede. The Greek side would hardly be justified in any intransigence in the face of such proof of Turkish good will. Unfortunately, at this writing both good will and statesmanship appear to be lacking on both sides. The Greeks could easily relax some of their efforts at blocking economic contacts for the north with the outside world. Actions, such as the sentencing of the captain of a Dutch ship to three months in jail for loading citrus fruit in Turkish-controlled Famagusta, are hardly likely to ease the climate of suspicion.

Given the stakes involved, the United States can hardly sit back and watch the problem from a distance. Washington is principally interested in helping to solve the Cyprus dispute not so much because of the 650,000 quarreling islanders but as a way of removing the main stumbling block between Greece and Turkey and, consequently, of strengthening NATO. Without its impact on the Greco-Turkish feud, a Cyprus settlement in itself would be a worthwhile humanitarian operation, but hardly more. However, with the exception of some low-key contacts and diplomatic feelers, the United States has not demonstrated much clout in Cyprus. Yet, its leverage on the island is hardly insignificant: money. With the economy of the south losing steam and the north in permanent difficulties, the United States could be an important source of outside help. As far as Washington is concerned, the sums are comparatively small: an annual grant of 50 million dollars would do marvels for the island. It would make only a small dent in U.S. foreign aid spending, but it might help in a Cyprus settlement—particularly if the United States insisted on joint ventures in which the two sides would be forced to work together.

To reiterate, it is pointless to give aid without conditions. In the case of Cyprus, conditions should be made in the interests of the Cypriots. Joint water development projects and agricultural schemes, perhaps shipping, could be organized—the field is vast. U.S. diplomats should stop massaging the ego of the Greek Cypriots as the legal government of the island. Of course, legality should be observed, but not the futile repetition of stale slogans. The establishment of a separate Turkish entity is a fact. The existence of the two zones is not likely to be dramatically changed. But closer ties can only be brought about by pressure; so far persuasion has failed. One can compliment Washington on its careful diplomacy in Cyprus, but frequently diplomacy should give way to statesmanship. It does not have to be brutal or highhanded, but it has to be decisive and firm. The issue is not Greco–Turkish harmony on the "Island of Aphrodite" but the future of Western defenses and, consequently, Western values in the Mediterranean theater. Surely it deserves more effort than a few diplomatic platitudes.

Notes

1. Official text of a statement, April 1982.
2. Minority Rights Group, "World Minorities" (London: MRG, 1977), p. 160.
3. In an interview with the author, March 1981.

Appendix A
LIST OF RESTRICTED ITEMS

The government has stated that the import of items listed below into Turkish Cypriot areas are considered to be restricted with effect March 1, 1965. This list may be changed at any time the government wishes to do so. This list supercedes all previous lists issued.

1. Iron poles (angle-iron, pickets)
2. Iron rods and thick steel plates
3. Timber
4. Crushed metal, stone, sand, gravel
5. Barbed wire
6. Wire
7. Camouflage netting
8. Cables
9. Wire cutters
10. Mine detectors
11. Power exploders
12. Wireless sets (police or military pattern)—domestic radios excluded
13. Telephones
14. Cartridges for shotguns
15. Explosives (TNT, gelatine dynamite, etc.)
16. Detonators
17. Sulphur
18. Ammonium nitrate
19. Steel wool
20. Fuel in large quantities
21. Automobile spare parts
22. Tires
23. Accumulators and dry batteries
24. Circuit testers
25. Firefighting equipment
26. Bags (sacks, canvas, jute, or linen types)

27. Boots, boot studs, leather laces
28. Rubber soles
29. Khaki cloth
30. Leather jackets
31. Gloves
32. Socks (woolen and/or cotton and/or any mixture thereof)—excluding ankle socks
33. Mackintoshes (including plastic raincoats)
34. Woolen materials (including knitting wool)
35. Imported coal (type used in a blacksmith's forge)
36. Thermos flasks
37. Plastic pipes

Source: Government Press and Information Office, Nicosia, Cyprus.

Appendix B
THE MAKARIOS–DENKTAS GUIDELINES

The guidelines agreed upon between President Denktas and the late Archbishop Makarios on February 12, 1977.

1. We are seeking an independent, nonaligned, bicommunal, federal republic.

2. The territory under the administration of each community should be discussed in the light of economic viability or productivity and land ownership.

3. Questions of principles like freedom of movement, freedom of settlement, the right of property, and other specific matters are open for discussion, taking into consideration the fundamental basis of a bicommunal federal system and certain practical difficulties that may arise for the Turkish Cypriot community.

4. The powers and functions of the central federal government will be such as to safeguard the unity of the country, having regard to the bicommunal character of the state.

Source: Government Press and Information Office, Nicosia, Cyprus.

Appendix C

THE KYPRIANOU–DENKTAS AGREEMENT

The agreement between President Spyros Kyprianou of Cyprus and Raouf Denktas of the Turkish Federated State of Kibris, with the participation of U.N. Secretary General Kurt Waldheim, on May 19, 1979.

1. It was agreed to resume the intercommunal talks on June 15, 1979.

2. The basis for the talks will be the Makarios-Denktas guidelines of February 12, 1977 and the U.N. resolutions relevant to the Cyprus question.

3. There should be respect for human rights and fundamental freedoms of all citizens of the republic.

4. The talks will deal with all territorial and constitutional aspects.

5. Priority will be given to reaching agreement on the resettlement of Varosha under U.N. auspices, simultaneously with the beginning of the consideration by the interlocutors of the constitutional and territorial aspects of a comprehensive settlement. After agreement on Varosha has been reached, it will be implemented without awaiting the outcome of the discussion on other aspects of the Cyprus problem.

6. It was agreed to abstain from any action that might jeopardize the outcome of the talks, and special importance will be given to initial practical measures by both sides to promote good will, mutual confidence, and the return to normal conditions.

7. The demilitarization of the Republic of Cyprus is envisaged, and matters relating thereto will be discussed.

8. The independence, sovereignty, territorial integrity, and nonalignment of the republic should be adequately guaranteed against union, in whole or in part, with any other country and against any form of partition or secession.

9. The intercommunal talks will be carried out in a continuing and sustained manner, avoiding any delay.

10. The intercommunal talks will take place in Nicosia.

Source: United Nations Office, Nicosia, Cyprus.

Appendix D
GUIDELINES FOR THE CONSTITUTION OF THE FEDERAL REPUBLIC OF CYPRUS (1981)

Introduction

1.   This evaluation of the intercommunal talks is in no way final, but on the contrary it is only an analysis, which emphasizes the points of coincidence and those of equidistance, which have as a goal to find middle ways or to establish bridges in order to close the existing gaps. Obviously, these preliminary considerations do not exhaust the subject in which some vacuums should be filled, through thorough negotiations.

2.   For instance, the executive will be exercised in accordance with Article 13. Regarding the method of election of the members of the council, the president and vice president, this will be the object of discussions during the intercommunal talks. Regarding the safeguards for the Northern Province and other aspects of the executive, I will make the evaluation at a more advanced stage of the talks.

3.   If the negotiations are successful, the implementation of the re-settlement of Varosha should be a priority issue.

4.   In fact, what we are trying to do with these ideas is to establish a method for discussion, following a comparative study of the constitutional proposals.

5.   Finally, we did not tackle some points of divergence, such as taxation, amendments to the constitution, and international guarantees. We believe that the first two items are technical and can be solved by working groups of specialists. The last item is a political question that should be discussed at the appropriate level after agreement on all other aspects has been reached.

PART I — General Provisions

1.   The Federal Republic of Cyprus shall be an independent, sovereign, and nonaligned republic.

2.   The territory of the Republic of Cyprus shall comprise the Northern and Southern Provinces and the Federal District.

(i)   The Federal District shall be the seat of the federal government.

(ii)   The Northern Province shall be divided into two administrative districts.

(iii)   The Southern Province shall be divided into four administrative districts.

3.   Secession, integration, or union of the republic in whole or in part with any other state shall be forbidden, and any act aiming at such union shall be considered a criminal offense punishable by law.

4.   The republic shall have international personality; the federal government shall exercise sovereignty in respect of all of the territory.

5.   The people of the federal republic shall comprise the people of the provinces and the Federal District. There shall be a single citizenship of the Republic of Cyprus, regulated by federal law.

6.   The Republic of Cyprus shall be demilitarized with the exception of the police forces necessary to maintain law and order in the provinces and the Federal District.

7.   The official languages of the republic shall be Greek and Turkish. The official working language in federal matters may be English.

8.   Each province shall appoint one representative to agree on a neutral federal flag and a national anthem for the republic. Each province shall create its own flag, using, as far as possible, elements of the federal flag. The federal flag shall be flown on federal buildings and federal locations, to the exclusion of any other flag.

9.   The federal government shall observe the holidays of the Republic of Cyprus. Each province shall observe the federal holidays as well as those established locally.

PART II — Fundamental Rights and Liberties

10.   Subject to the reinforcement of specific principles in accordance with the Greek Cypriot and Turkish Cypriot proposals (e.g., nondiscrimination and equality before the law) and minor drafting changes. Articles 6 to 35 of the 1960 Constitution shall apply.

11.   Matters relating to education and marriage shall be regulated by the provinces in accordance with the fundamental rights and liberties of the federal constitution. Higher education shall be a federal matter.

12.   As a transitory provision, two commissions or working groups under the chairmanship of the interlocutors and consisting of six members, three from

each province, shall be established to overcome the practical difficulties for the implementation of:

(i) the rights established under Article 13 (i) of the 1960 Constitution; and

(ii) the rights established under Article 23 of the 1960 Constitution.

PART III — The Organs of the Federal Government

13. The executive authority of the republic shall be exercised by a federal council, composed of six members, one for each administrative district (2 from the Northern Province and 4 from the Southern Province).

14. The federal government shall have the following ministerial portfolios:

(i) Foreign Affairs;

(ii) Defense, Citizenship, Immigration, Emigration, Extradition, and Federal Police;

(iii) Justice and Higher Education;

(iv) Coordination of International Trade and Tourism, Postal and Telecommunication Services, International Navigation (including authority over ports and airports in connection with international matters);

(v) Federal Finance, Central Bank, Currency, Customs, Weights, Measures, and Patents; and

(vi) Coordination of Environmental Matters, Natural Resources and Health, Labor and Social Services.

15. Members of the federal council shall be appointed for five years.

16. The president of the federal council shall represent the Republic of Cyprus at home and abroad.

17. The federal council of the republic shall:

(i) Promulgate federal statutes and decisions and promulgate laws passed by both chambers;

(ii) Appoint and recall ambassadors and envoys;

(iii) Address Letters of Credence and Letters of Recall from foreign diplomatic representatives and issue instruments of ratification and international treaties;

(iv) Confer decorations of the republic;

(v) Take the necessary measures in the event of an emergency;

(vi) Lay down general principles concerning the internal organization of federal administrative agencies;

(vii) Allocate the federal budget;

(viii) Set the policies of the federal government.

18.   The Federal Council shall appoint the Federal Attorney general and his deputy, the Federal Auditor General and his deputy, the Governor of the Federal Reserve Board and his deputy, and the Federal Accountant General and his deputy. The deputies shall not be from the same province as their superiors.

19.   There shall be an independent Federal Public Service Commission, which shall consist of six members, one for each administrative district, to be nominated by the Federal Council. The same ratio of representation, four to two, shall apply in the Council of Ministers and in the Federal Public Service. The federal functions shall be carried out by federal public officers in the Federal District. In other districts, federal public officers shall act with the approval of the member of the respective administrative district in the Federal Public Service Commission.

20.   The federal legislative power shall comprise two chambers:

(i)   The Chambers of Provinces, which shall represent the provinces on an equal basis of 10 members each (the provinces shall assure the proper participation of the administrative districts); and

(ii)   The Popular Chamber, which shall be composed of representatives of the people of Cyprus on a ratio of one member for each 10,000 of the total population.

21.   Elections shall be direct and universal. All Cypriot citizens, residents of either province, upon attaining the age of 18, shall be qualified to elect.

22.   The Federal Supreme Court shall be composed of five members, designated by the Federal Council, two from each province, and a fifth member, who may be a non-Cypriot. The Federal Supreme Court shall have original jurisdiction to hear disputes between the provinces and shall operate in accordance with the basic provisions of the 1960 Constitution, Articles 133 and 164.

PART IV – Provincial Government

23.   The Provinces shall draft their own constitution in conformity with the federal constitution.

24.   Each province shall elect by universal suffrage, without any kind of discrimination, a provincial chamber, whose responsibilities shall include approval of the necessary provincial legislation.

25.   Each province shall have no jurisdiction in federal matters. The area of its competence comprehends matters other than those set out in Paragraph 14.

26.   Each province shall establish its own administration of justice and will control the provincial police.

PART V — Transitional Provisions

27.   The provinces shall establish a Joint Board of Claims to deal with compensation claims arising from the establishment of the republic. The Federal Supreme Court shall act as a Court of Appeal for the decisions of the Board. The Federal Supreme Court shall establish a summary proceeding to deal expeditiously with these claims.

28.   A fund for development of the Northern Province shall be established, with a view to achieving an economic equilibrium between the two provinces. The federal government shall contribute to this fund. Foreign governments and international organizations shall be invited to contribute to the fund.

29.   A Federal Real Estate Bank shall be established to provide credit and economic assistance to displaced persons for the purpose of their permanent settlement.

Territorial Guidelines

When assessing the positions taken by the Greek Cypriot and Turkish Cypriot sides on the question of territory, it appears that the terms of reference provided by the interlocutors during the intercommunal talks cannot easily be reconciled.

Furthermore, qualitative and quantitative divergencies of views have also emerged with regard to the search for objective criteria. The two sides' estimates of natural resources, land ownership, infrastructure, percentage of land under each side's control, and number of displaced persons differ. This, of course, has led both sides to suggest territorial arrangements that are hardly compatible, and consequently there is no easy basis for an objective suggestion. Nevertheless, during discussions at the intercommunal talks, two major concerns have emerged, which should evidently be taken into account when searching for a territorial solution: resettlement of a large number of Greek Cypriot refugees in the territory comprising the Greek Cypriot province and economic viability and security of the Turkish Cypriot community. Therefore, the analysis of housing resources, mining, timber, irrigation, and reservoirs should be considered within the territorial framework.

Within the same framework a fund for development of the north could be established. This fund would deal with the socioeconomic consequences of the territorial adjustment and, at the same time, would represent an important element of the basis for a vigorous economy and ensure a balanced development in the republic.

The lack of concurrent information on criteria makes it very difficult at this stage to envisage concrete percentages of territorial areas. Yet, the real socioeconomic impact of any adjustment can only be properly measured once factors have been quantified. In addition, the need for security of both communities should be taken into account.

Therefore, to facilitate a result-oriented negotiation in the question of territory, it may, for practical reasons, be useful to attempt to quantify these factors section by section in the areas for demarcation. A first step, which would be only for illustrative purposes on the map, would be to work on the basis of a line drawn so that the area under Greek Cypriot jurisdiction was at least 70 percent, including the buffer zone, which is the minimum for the resettlement of a substantial number of refugees. This 70/30 ratio might be varied according to the characteristics of the areas. This would be a method of establishing a firm basis for further discussions.

Source: United Nations Office, Nicosia, Cyprus.

Appendix E
PRESS RELEASE
FROM THE EMBASSY OF GREECE
(April 1982)

The Moslem and Greek Christian Minorities

In March 1982, a statement by a Turkish Foreign Office spokesman implied that the authorities in Greece were threatening to expropriate property belonging to members of the Moslem population of western Thrace. Such action against the Moslem element of Greece would, said the spokesman, lead to reprisals (presumably against the few Greek Orthodox Christians who still live in Turkey).

The allegation, as it turned out, was totally false. What had occurred in western Thrace, as an official Greek government statement pointed out, was action to evict illegal squatters on public land. The action applied, without the slightest discrimination, to all the illegal squatters, both Christian and Moslem.

The incident, not major in itself, was typical of the tendency of Turkish governments, at times of friction in relations with Greece, to use the Moslem minority of western Thrace as a weapon in the propaganda war, suggesting that the Moslem minority of western Thrace is being ill-treated and denied its legal rights.

As the following brief summary of the facts proves, the truth is quite the opposite: while the Moslem minority of Greece flourishes in an atmosphere of nondiscriminating tolerance, protected not only by international treaties but also by the Greek constitution and the Greek laws, the once large and historically rooted Greek Christian population of Turkey has all but vanished entirely as a result of sustained official oppression of its ecclesiastical, educational and civil institutions—in direct violation of solemn treaty obligations.

Without going into historical detail, it is important to point out that the minorities in question are the remnants of much larger populations which existed earlier in this century. In all, during the period 1912–1924, some 1.3 million Greeks abandoned their homes in Asia Minor and eastern Thrace; while 400,000 Turks left Greece to settle in Turkey. A major share of this migration occurred as a result of a large-scale population exchange which followed the Greek–Turkish armed conflict in 1922. The 1923 Treaty of Lausanne, which ended the conflict, made provision, however, for "non-exchangeable" populations on both sides to remain as minorities within Greece and Turkey, and laid down strict conditions (Part III — Articles 38–45 of the Treaty) for the protection of the rights of those minorities to life and liberty and to freedom from all discrimination on the basis of nationality, religion, language or race.

The extent to which those guarantees have been implemented by Greece toward the Moslem minority of western Thrace, and flouted by Turkey in its treatment of the Greek Orthodox minority of that country, is indicated by the following simple figures:

The original Moslem minority in western Thrace at the time of the Treaty of Lausanne (1923) numbered 100,000 and has now increased to 110,000 (1981 data). Two members of this community represent their constituents in the Greek Parliament. That Moslem population of western Thrace has the use of 205 mosques and 90 smaller places of worship, all supported by Greek state funds.

There are 261 Moslem grade schools in western Thrace, attended by 12,760 pupils. The two Moslem high schools have a total of 641 students. And there are also two religious seminaries.

By contrast, the 1923 total Greek Orthodox population of Turkey was 200,000. It was almost halved by the time of the 1934 census by the Lausanne Commission; down to less than 80,000 following the violent mob attacks on Greek property in Istanbul in September 1955; and is currently reduced to a bare remnant of some 5,000.

There are now only some 15 Greek elementary schools in Turkey, attended by 433 pupils; and 6 high schools with 378 students. That is all that remains of a once flourishing Greek educational system.

The dramatic decline of the Greek minority in Turkey which these stark figures indicate has been the consequence of a long sequence of official discriminatory policies and practices which, in violation of Turkey's treaty obligations, has made conditions intolerable for the Greek minority as the following brief examples show. This discrimination permeates every aspect of the life of the Greek minority.

Measures to restrict the influence of the Greek Orthodox Church, of which Istanbul is the centuries-old center under the Patriarch, have included intervention in the elections of the Patriarch; the closure in 1971 of the historic Orthodox seminary of Halkis; the expropriation of church buildings and church property; the imposition of heavy real estate taxes; explusion of some Orthodox priests from the country; travel restrictions on others; refusal of permission for essential repairs to church structures; prohibition of Greek Orthodox prayers in schools and group church attendances by Greek school pupils; closure of Patriarchy's printing press, etc.

Greek education has suffered similarly as a result of measures which include: intervention in the composition of school governing bodies; the substitution of Turkish deputy-headmasters in the unfilled posts formerly occupied by Greek principals; severe restrictions on repairs to school buildings; crippling taxation; a requirement to teach all so-called "optional" lessons in the Turkish language, etc.

In commerce, Greeks of Istanbul have been forced out of business over the years by harsh discriminatory taxation. Under a measure introduced in November 1942, a real estate tax levied disproportionately on "non-Moslem minorities" resulted in the Greek population of Turkey, which was 0.55 percent of the total, being loaded with some 20 percent of the total tax burden. Those unable to pay, numbering 1,400, were sent to concentration camps. Another measure—the unilateral renunciation by Turkey, on March 16, 1964, of the 1930 Greek–Turkish Treaty of Residency, Trade and Navigation, was followed by the deportation in the period 1964–66, of 11,000 Greeks carrying on trades and professions. Those remaining were expelled in 1972 and 1973. The value of the property belonging to the deported Greeks, seized or "frozen" by the Turkish authorities, was reliably estimated at £80 million.

The Islands of Imvros and Tenedos

It is in these two islands of the Thracian Sporades that Turkey has been responsible for some of the most glaring violations of the Lausanne Treaty.

These two Greek islands of the Aegean, formally incorporated within the Greek state in 1920, were placed by the 1923 Treaty of Lausanne under Turkish sovereignty in deference to Turkey's claim that they could not remain under foreign control for strategic reasons. Aware, however, of the injustice being inflicted on the Greek inhabitants of the two islands, the drafters of the Lausanne Treaty made special provision for their protection: in addition to all the safeguards noted above for the rights of the Greek minority remaining in Turkey, a special provision of the Treaty (Article 14) gave a complete range of self-governing institutions to these Greek-populated islands—including their own local police force.

All these safeguards have been systematically violated by Turkey in subsequent years: the teaching of the Greek language has been abolished; Greek schools and communal institutions have been closed down and expropriated; and some 6,800 acres of the cultivable land on Imvros (out of a total of 8,500 acres) has been nationalized by Turkey—most of it for the creation of a prison farm for criminals from the mainland.

The demographic changes caused by such actions, supplemented by the importation of Turkish populations, have been dramatic: at the latest count, the 7,500 Greek population of Imvros at the time of the Lausanne Treaty had shrunk to 1,564; in Tenedos, only 232 were left of the once-flourishing Greek community of 1,200 in 1923.

Source: Embassy of Greece, Washington, D.C.

Appendix F

PRESIDENT REAGAN'S PERIODIC REPORT TO CONGRESS ON CYPRUS

Following is the text of President Reagan's periodic report on Cyprus, which was transmitted to the Congress on May 25, 1982.

In accordance with the provisions of Public Law 95–384, I am submitting the following report on progress made during the past 60 days toward reaching a negotiated settlement of the Cyprus problem.

In the course of continuing discussion of the United Nations "evaluation" of the intercommunal negotiations, the Greek Cypriot and Turkish Cypriot negotiators met on April 14, 21, and 30, and May 4, 6, 11, 13, and 18. The negotiators have continued to focus their discussion on elements of the United Nations "evaluation" of the intercommunal negotiations. Having completed their initial review of many of the "points of coincidence," the communities are now beginning examination of "points of equidistance" including such issues as the freedoms of movement, settlement and property ownership in any future agreement. The negotiating sessions continue to be useful and constructive discussions with good relations between the participants.

United Nations Secretary General Perez de Cuellar met in Rome on April 4 with Cypriot President Kyprianou and in Geneva on April 9 with Turkish Cypriot leader Denktas. These meetings provided a thorough review of the status of the negotiations and both sides agreed to accelerate the pace of the talks and hold two meetings per week. The negotiating parties also agreed to meet again with the Secretary General in New York in June for a further review of the negotiating process.

We believe that the intercommunal negotiations are firmly established as a strong and effective tool to promote progress toward resolving the Cyprus problem. I wish to congratulate both the United Nations Secretary General and his Special Representative on Cyprus, Ambassador Hugo Gobbi, for their commitment to bringing the Cyprus problem to a just and lasting settlement. They have my full support for their efforts. We hope that the negotiators will seize the opportunities offered by the United Nations "evaluation" to make progress toward resolving outstanding differences between the communities.

Source: U.S. Embassy, Nicosia, Cyprus.

NOTES REGARDING
THE APPENDIX SECTION

These appendixes have been edited for house style and may differ slightly from the original documents.

BIBLIOGRAPHY

Books

Allen, Henry R. *Turkish Transformation*. London: Greenwood, 1968.

Balfour, Patrick. *The Orphaned Realm*. London: Percival Marshall, 1951.

Carey, Jane Perry and Andrew Galbraith Carey. *The Web of Modern Greek Politics*. New York: Columbia University Press, 1968.

Churchill, Winston. *The Second World War*. London: Cassell, 1952.

Durrel, Lawrence. *Bitter Lemons*. London: Dutton, 1957.

Ertekun, Necati Munir. *In Search of a Negotiated Cyprus Settlement*. Lefkosa, Cyprus: Ulus Matbaacilik, 1981.

Grivas, George. *Memoirs of General Grivas*. London: Longman's, 1964.

Heyd, Uriel. *Foundations of Turkish Nationalism*. Connecticut: Hyperion, 1979.

Hotham, David. *The Turks*. London: John Murray, 1978.

Kinross, Lord. *Ataturk*. New York: William Morrow, 1965.

——. *Within the Taurus*. London: John Murray, 1954.

Koumoulides, John T.A. *Greece in Transition*. London: Zeno Publishers, 1977.

Lewis, Bernard. *The Emergence of Modern Turkey*. London: Oxford University Press, 1968.

Lewis, Geoffrey. *Modern Turkey*. London: Ernest Benn, 1974.

Lewis, Jesse W. *The Strategic Balance in the Mediterranean*. Washington, D.C.: American Enterprise Institute for Public Policy Research, 1977.

Luke, Harry. *Cyprus*. London: George G. Harrap, 1957.

McNeil, William H. *The Metamorphosis of Greece since World War II*. Chicago: University of Chicago Press, 1978.

Papacosma, Victor S. *The Military in Greek Politics*. Kent, Ohio: Kent State University Press, 1977.

Sciaky, Leon. *Farewell to Salonika*. London: 1946.

St. Clair, William. *That Greece Might Still Be Free*. London: Oxford University Press, 1972.

Stephens, Robert. *Cyprus, A Place of Arms*. London: Pall Mall, 1966.

Truman, Harry S. *Years of Trial and Hope*. New York: Doubleday, 1956.

Vali, Ferenc A. *Bridge Across the Bosporus*. Johns Hopkins University, 1971.

——. *The Turkish Straits and NATO*. Hoover Institute, 1972.

Official Publications

Research and Publicity Centerm. *Greece: A Portrait*. Athens, 1979.

State Information Organization of Turkey. *Facts about Turkey*. Ankara, 1971.

Turkish Federated State of Kibris. *The Cyprus Problem*. Lefkosa, 1979.

U.S., Public Information Office. *Congressional Concern for Cyprus*. Nicosia, 1981.

——. *Cyprus Intercommunal Talks*. Nicosia, July 1981.

U.S., Department of State. *Administration Policy for the Eastern Mediterranean*. May 1978.

North Atlantic Treaty Organization. *NATO and the Warsaw Pact.* Brussels: NATO, 1982.

Turkey Greece and NATO: The Strained Alliance. A Staff Report to the Committee on Foreign Relations, United States Senate, March 1980. U.S. Government Printing Office, Washington 1980.

Journals and Periodicals

Baytok, Taner. "Recent Developments in the Middle East and Southwest Asia." *NATO Review,* August 1981, pp. 10–13.

Borowiec, Andrew. "Evren Cleanses Turkey." *8 Days,* May 23, 1981, pp. 22–23.

——. "Turkey's Obsolete Army." *8 Days,* December 6, 1980, pp. 30–31.

Caligaris, Paola. "Under a Nuclear Storm Cloud." *The Middle East,* November 1981, pp. 20–23.

——. "NATO's Soft Spot." *The Middle East,* September 1981, p. 31.

Coats, George. "Four Sides of a Defense Square." *8 Days,* July 11, 1981, pp. 30–34.

"The Gods Smile at Last." *Economist,* September 20, 1975, Survey 3–34.

"The East–West Struggle," *Economist,* December 26, 1981.

Glakas, Thomas Peter. "Instability in the Gulf Region." *NATO Review,* February 1981, pp. 21–24.

Kutchera, Chris. "The Price of Security." *The Middle East,* September 1981, p. 20.

Ratip, Arman. Editorial. *Pan-News Report,* October 1981, p. 2.

Unsigned. "New Hobby in Town: The Greeks." *Time,* July 14, 1975, pp. 25–28.

Wright, Claudia. "The Ugly Ally of the West." *MacLean's,* August 4, 1980, pp. 20–23.

Newspapers Mentioned in the Text

Atlanta Constitution (Atlanta, Georgia)

Baltimore Sun (Baltimore, Maryland)

Birlik (Nicosia, Cyprus)

Cyprus Mail (Nicosia, Cyprus)

Cyprus Weekly (Nicosia, Cyprus)

Financial Times (London)

Hellenic Chronicle (U.S.)

Hurriyet (Istanbul, Turkey)

International Herald Tribune (Paris)

Kathimerini (Athens, Greece)

Milliyet (Istanbul, Turkey)

New York Times

Observer (London)

Son Havadis (Istanbul, Turkey)

Tachydromos (Athens, Greece)

Times (London)

Washington Post

Washington Star

Pamphlets

Minority Rights Group. "CYPRUS." London: MRG, 1976.

Minority Rights Group. "WORLD MINORITIES." London: MRG, 1977.

INDEX

Crete, 10, 11, 80, 129
Croats, 146
Crowe, Admiral William, 4
Cypriot National Guard, 90, 96, 98, 100
Cyprus, x, xi, 12, 22, 24, 30, 31, 65, 69, 82, 83, 90, 91, 98, 111, 112, 115, 116, 119, 121, 124, 125, 127, 128, 132, 133, 138, 142, 144, 145, 148-53;
  and anti-Americanism, 103-4;
  area of, 90;
  atrocities in, 24, 97-98, 102, 175;
  British bases in, 90, 95, 96-97, 102, 104, 137;
  British rule of, 90-91, 93, 94, 151;
  constitution of, 96
  coup of 1974 and, 25, 77, 98-99, 116;
  description of, 90-91;
  economy of, 107-10;
  enosis and, 73, 83, 89, 93, 94, 97, 98;
  EOKA and, 72, 93, 94;
  EOKA "B" and, 98
  Hellenism in, 77, 83, 89, 93, 94;
  history of, 91, 93, 94;
  independence of, 93, 95;
  intercommunal strife in, 24, 89-90; 97;
  intercommunal talks and, 25, 98, 149;
  Orthodox church in, 92, 111;
  Ottoman rule of, 92, 93;
  politics of, in the north 106-7;
  politics of, in the south 111-12, 149;
  propaganda in, 105, 133, 134;
  refugees in, 108, 109, 110, 111, 112;
  strategic importance of, 89;

  Turkish enclaves in, 24, 97, 98;
  Turkish invasion of, 10, 11, 16, 25, 47, 66, 77, 84, 90, 99-101, 111, 131, 135;
  Turkish minority in, 89, 90, 92, 93, 95, 96, 97, 102, 104, 106, 110, 113, 114, 115, 126, 132;
  Turkish troops in, 132;
  U.S. involvement in, 95, 99, 103-4, 109, 113, 118, 126, 132-33, 137-39;
  Waldheim guidelines and, 117-19;
  Zurich Agreement and, 95
Czechoslovakia, 132

Dabagyan, Levon Panos, 55
Dardanelles, the, 5, 7
Davies, Rodger Paul, 103, 104, 123, 126
Davos, Ioannis, 11
Demirel, Suleyman, 35
Democratic party in Cyprus (DIKO), 82, 111
Democratic rally party in Cyprus (DISI), 111
Democratic Union (EDA), 73 (*see also* Greece)
Denktash, Rauf Raif (Turkish spelling Denktas), xi, 96, 98, 102, 105, 106, 107, 108, 112, 113, 114, 115, 134, 149
Denmark, 16
Der Spiegel, 43
Dev Sol (Revolutionary Left), 35, 39, 41
Dhekelia, 90 (*see also* Cyprus)
DIKO (*see* Democratic Party in Cyprus)
DISI (*see* Democratic Rally Party in Cyprus)
DISK labor union, 62
Disraeli, Benjamin (Lord Beacons-

field), 92
Diyarbakir, 46, 54
Dodecanese, 27
Durduran, Alpay, 106-7

Eagleton, Thomas, 131
Eastern Europe, 76
East Mediterranean, xii, 3, 30, 71,
      100, 116, 123, 124, 125, 126,
      129, 130, 137, 142, 143;
   U.S. role in the, 127, 128, 132,
      136, 139, 144, 147;
   (see also Mediterranean)
Ecevit, Bülent, 16, 34, 42, 45, 51,
      99, 136;
   accusations against, 42-43;
   and martial law, 53, 57
Economist, The, 69, 77, 81
EDA (see "Democratic Union")
EDEK (Socialist party in Cyprus),
      112
European Economic Community
      (EEC), 42, 43, 50, 69;
   and Greece, 50, 65, 69, 72, 79
Egypt, 2, 6, 8
Elâziğ, 56
Embargo, arms, U.S., on Turkey, xi,
      1, 15 (see also United States,
      Turkey)
enosis, 73, 83, 89, 93, 94, 99 (see also
      Cyprus)
EOKA, 72, 93, 95, 99, 103 (see also
      Cyprus)
EOKA "B," 98 (see also Cyprus)
Erbankan, Necmettin, 40
Ercan, 110
ERE (see National Radical Union)
Ersin, General Nurettin, 33
Ersoy, Bülent, 41
Erzurum, 40
Esenboga, 46
Eskieşhir, 45

Europe, x, 4, 36, 37, 50, 52, 68,
      70, 76, 79, 120;
   criticism of Turkey by, 44, 51;
   and the European Economic Com-
      munity (EEC), 42
   (see also Western Europe, and
      Eastern Europe)
Evren, Kenan, 33, 35, 38, 39, 42, 43,
      44, 51, 82;
   attitude of, 45-46;
   on islamic cooperation, 52;
   on Kurds, 54

Falkland Islands, 145
Famagusta, 91, 98, 102, 108, 152,
      154
Financial Times, The, 29
flight information regions (FIR), 10,
      28
Ford, Gerald, 130
Foreign Broadcasting Information
      Service (FBIS), 137
France, 22, 30, 68, 120, 128, 145
French forces, 23

Gallipoli, 47, 48
Gazi (Atatürk's title) 39, 46
Gaziantep, 57
gecekondu (shanty towns), 58-60
Genc, Alper Faik, 101
Geneva:
   convention on the Continental
      shelf, 27;
   conference on Cyprus, 1974, 101-2
Georgalas, George, 76
George II, king of Greece, 70
Germans, in Greece, 71
Germany, West, 16, 48, 49, 72, 128,
      145
Gibraltar, Strait of, 3
Girne (see Kyrenia)
Giziks, Phaidon, 78

183

Kuchuk, Dr. Fazil, 96, 97
Kurdistan, 54
Kurds, 35, 41, 53–54
Kykko, 98, 133
Kyprianou, Spyros, 82–83, 84, 111,
    112, 113, 115, 118, 136, 149,
    152
Kyrenia:
    town of, 91, 98, 100, 108, 110;
    mountain range, 90, 100, 110,
    117 (*see also* Girhe)

Lambrakis, Demetrius, 73
Larisa, 11, 12
Larnaca, 101, 110
Latakia, 6, 7
Latife, 46
Lausanne, Treaty of, 55
Lawton, John, 100
Lebanon, 2, 6, 89, 109
Ledra Palace Hotel, 118
Leftis, Neoptolemos, 104
Leninsk, 47
Levant (*see* Middle East)
Lewis, Flora, 13
Lewis, Geoffrey, 127
Libya, 6, 7, 8, 83
Limassol, 91
Limnos, 17
Livanos, George, 132
Loizos, Peter, 116
London, 99, 101, 102
Luns, Joseph, ix, 5, 141
Lusignans, 91
Luther, Martin, 34
Lyssarides, Vassos, 112

Macedonia, 19
Mahmoud, Sultan, 22
Makarezos, Colonel Nicolaos, 74, 76
Makarios, Archbishop, 77, 94, 95, 96,
    98, 99, 101, 102, 103, 104, 111,

113, 120, 133, 138
Makarios–Denktash Agreement (or
    Guidelines), 112, 113, 138
Malatya, 56
Marmara, Sea of, 24, 46
Marxism, 76
Mediterranean Sea, 3–5, 18, 70, 92,
    142, 143;
    area of, 4;
    description of, 4;
    Soviet fleet in the, 5, 6;
    U. S. interests in the, 126, 153
megali, idea, 23, 31
Mersin, 50, 98, 100
Messaoria, 90, 130
Metaxas, General Iannis, 70,
Metrol Steel Corporation, 132
Mevlana cult, 35
Middle East, xi, 4, 7, 14, 19, 46, 50,
    52, 60, 92, 128, 129, 137–38;
    Greek trade in the, 83–84;
    Turkish trade with the, 53, 83,
    147
Milliyet, 141
Minnesota, University of, 66
Mitsotakis, Constantine, 11, 85
Montreux, Convention of, 7
Morocco, 6, 8
Moscow (*see* the Union of Soviet
    Socialist Republics)
Muhammad, Prophet, 53
Munir, Metin, 35
Muslim Brotherhood, 2
Mussolini, Benito, 75
McCloskey, Robert, 80, 123

Naples, 2, 3, 10
National Action party (NAP) in
    Turkey, 57
National Liberation Front (EAM), in
    Greece, 71
National Radical Union party (ERE),

Pell, Claiborne, 135
Peloponnese, 21
Persian Gulf, x, 2, 13, 52, 53, 83
Phoenicians, 91
Palestine Liberation Organization
(PLO), 51, 83, 112
Poland, 30, 45, 84
Popular Liberation Army (ELAS) in
Greece, 71
Portugal, 51
Prinkipo Island, 24
Prometheus, 74
Prote, 78
Ptolemies, 91

Royal Air Force (RAF), 86
Rallis, Dimitrios, 72
Rallis, George, 12, 65, 79, 80
Ratip, Arman, 115
rapid deployment force (RDF), x, 13,
52
Reagan, Ronald, 132;
administration of, 3, 15, 16, 147
Republican People's party (RPP),
in Turkey, 42
Rhodes, 31, 146
Rice, Anne M. 134
Rogers, General Bernard, 1, 10, 14–
15
Romania, 69;
army divisions of, 8
Romans, 91
Romios, 92
Rosenthal, A. I., 132
Rosenthal, Benjamin, 131
Rossides, Eugene, 132, 133

Sahinbas, Farouk, 15
Sahinkaya, General Tahsin, 33
Salonika, 23, 24, 30, 38, 67
Saltik, General Haydar, 106
Samos, 27

Sampson, Nikos, 99, 102, 104
San Francisco, 80
Sarbanes, Paul, 131, 133
Saudi Arabia, 53, 83, 110
Schaufele, William, 125
Semipalatinsk, 47
Seraphim, Archbishop, 86
Serbia, 19, 146
Sèvres, Treaty of, 23, 54
Seychelles, 95
Shamanism, 56
Shites (*see* Alevis)
Sinai, 133
Sinop, 46
Siros, 84
Sisco, Joseph, 99
Sismik I, 27
Sixth Fleet, U. S. 2, 4, 9, 46, 80, 103,
123, 124, 137 (*see also* United
States)
Smith, Colin, 96
Smyrna, 22, 23, 46 (*see also* Izmir)
Sobieski, Jan, 20
Socialist party (EDEK), 112
Sokolov, Sergei, 6
Son Havadis, 55
Souda Bay, 80
South Yemen, 7
Southeast Asia, 52, 149
Southwest Asia, ix, 16
sovereign base areas (SBA), (*see*
Cyprus)
Soviet bloc, 71, 103, 138
Soysal, Mumtaz, 25
Spain, 51
Spain, James, 44
Spiegel, Der, 43
Stalios, George, 72
Stefanopoulos, Stefanos, 74
Strasbourg, 42
Suez Canal, 137
Sunnis, 53, 56–57 (*see also* Turkey,

135, 136;

U. S. installations in, 5, 46, 129, 135;

war of independence in, 23, 37, 47

Turkish Cypriots, 89, 93, 100-1, 102, 105, 106, 113, 132, 143, 148, 150, 152 (see also Cyprus)

Turkish Federated State of Kibris (TFSK), 96, 105, 106, 107, 108, 115, 143

Turkmen, 56

Turkmen, Ilter, 20

Turks, 18, 34, 36;

and religion, 30-31;

in Thrace, 25, 26, 29;

as workers in Europe, 51

Tuzlam, 45

Tymbou, 110

Tzemlik, 31

ul-Haq, Zia, 52

Ulusu, Bülent, 25, 29, 35, 62, 83

Ummayyad, 18

Union of Soviet Socialist Republics (USSR), 83, 99, 116, 124, 127, 128, 132, 134, 138, 143;

and the Armenians, 55;

and the border with Turkey, 3, 48;

electronic surveillance of the, 46-47;

infiltration of Iran by the, 2;

Mediterranean squadron of the, 6-8, 80;

naval expansion of the, 1, 4, 5;

naval maneuvers of the, 6;

penetration of the Middle East by the, 7, 8

United Arab Emirates (UAE), 110

United Nations, 34, 51, 113, 114, 117, 118, 134, 139, 143, 151, 152;

Commission on Human Rights, 26;

General Assembly, 117;

peace-keeping in Cyprus, 24, 90, 95, 97, 117, 121, 150;

Security Council, 27

United Press International (UPI), 100

United States, x, 13, 28, 48, 52, 66, 68, 84, 89, 99, 115, 118, 120, 121, 124, 126, 127, 129, 147;

Agency for International Development, 139;

aid to Greece, 76, 128;

aid to Turkey, 48, 49, 128;

arms embargo on Turkey, xii, 1, 15, 48, 51, 90, 104, 130, 131, 134, 135, 136;

bases in Greece, 64, 65, 69, 80-81, 129;

bases in Turkey, xi, 46, 129, 135;

Congress, 81, 121, 130-31, 134, 135, 136, 137;

action in Cyprus: 99, 102-4, 105, 109, 113, 116, 133, 137, 138-139, 144, 152, 153;

Department of State, 80, 87, 104, 131, 133;

diplomacy, 124-26;

foreign policy, 123, 124, 129, 147;

Mediterranean strategy, 4, 123;

rapid deployment force, x, 13, 52;

Sixth Fleet, 2, 4, 9, 46, 80, 103, 123, 124, 129, 137

USSR (see Soviet Union)

Van province, 16

Vance, Cyrus, 25, 98, 138

Varnava, Antoinette, 103

Varosha, 102, 110, 113, 152 (see also Famagusta)

Venetians, 92

Venizelos, Eleftherios, 72

Vienna, 18, 20

Vietnam, 126
Voyvodina, 146
Vranopoulos, Dimitrios, 67
VOLKAN, 95

Waldheim, Kurt, 113, 117–18
Warsaw Pact, 9, 11, 16, 82, 135
Washington (*see* United States)
Washington Post, The, 43, 68, 134
Weinberger, Caspar W., 14, 43, 78
Western Europe, 51, 52, 53, 60, 79,
    126, 145, 148
Wiggin, Jerry, 137–38
World Bank, 62
World Court, 28

World War I, 47, 48, 55, 68, 93
World War II, 23, 66, 70, 85, 93,
    110, 128, 145

Xánthi, 26

Yanoulopoulos, Yanis, 73, 74
Yatron, Gus, 131
Yorukselim, 56
Yugoslavia, 7, 8, 10, 69, 129, 147;
    in the Greek civil war, 71;
Young Turks, 39, 47

Zurich, Agreement of, 95

ABOUT THE AUTHOR

ANDREW BOROWIEC has written on international affairs since he became a foreign correspondent in 1956. For 10 years he reported for the Associated Press from Europe, Africa, and Vietnam. He was subsequently a roving correspondent for *The Washington Star* in Africa, the Middle East, and Europe. Currently he writes on Middle Eastern and East Mediterranean affairs for *The Chicago Sun-Times.*

Mr. Borowiec received the 1963 Overseas Press Club of America award for Best Reporting from Abroad and a citation in the same category in 1965. In 1971 he was given the Washington–Baltimore *Guild* Front Page Award for international reporting. Mr. Borowiec holds an M.S. from the Columbia School of Journalism. He is the author of *Yugoslavia after Tito*, published by Praeger in 1977.